The Unremembered Inn

Four hundred years of social history

Max Harris

BREWIN BOOKS

BREWIN BOOKS
56 Alcester Road,
Studley,
Warwickshire,
B80 7LG
www.brewinbooks.com

Published by Brewin Books 2015

A CIP catalogue record for this book is available from the British Library.

ISBN: 978-1-85858-512-3

Printed and bound in Great Britain by 4edge Ltd.

The Unremembered Inn

2015

To Roger
Happy birthday, from now on
you will never view "The Spar &
'Boots' in quite the same light
when buying that bottle of ted
& picking up your pills.
            Best Wishes
                love Jan xx

Contents

For

Toby, Emilia and Ingrid,

– a new generation

Thomas Kitchin's Map of Worcestershire, c. 1786.

Acknowledgements

FIRST and foremost I must thank John Talbot Cooper for presenting me with a black box containing the old title deeds without which this book would never have been conceived, and for his assistance with information concerning John Gibbs.

I owe a great debt of gratitude to Roger Whitworth of Whitworth Genealogical Research for many successful hours of research at the National Archives, the British Library, and several local record offices, his knowledge and expertise have saved me hours of research and a great deal of footwork. I must also thank the staff of the National Archives and the British Library who spent a considerable time answering his queries.

I want to express my sincere thanks to Shirley Bellwood for her wonderful and most evocative drawings, and Basil Sellwood for his research for her drawings and the plan of Upton-upon-Severn. I am grateful to Daniel Cummings for recommending such a talented artist. I would also like to thank Richard Harris for giving up his valuable time to produce the 1622 site plan and layout of the rooms.

I would like to thank Worcestershire Archive and Archaeology Service for permission to reproduce copies of documents in their custody, to the staff for their assistance and in particular John France for producing such fine digital images of their records and my documents; the History Department of Trinity College Dublin for permission to use material from the Bisse Depositions and Dr. Micheál Ó Siochrú for supplying further information concerning Robert Best in Kinsale.

I am grateful to Reverend Frances Wookey for her kind permission to use material from the Upton-upon-Severn parish registers; Gloucestershire Archives for their permission to use the material concerning African people in Gloucestershire; the Bodleian Library for permission to use their cartoon: 'Fatal Facility; or, Poisons for the Asking' (*Punch*, 1849) and the Hanley Swan website for the material concerning P.G. Wodehouse and '*Buck-U-Uppo*'.

I would also like to thank all those people who kindly allowed me to quote from their publications; Professor Chris Dyer '*Making a Living in the Middle Ages, The people of Britain 850-1520*'; Professor Peter Clark for several extracts from the '*English Alehouse*'. Pearson Education Publishing for quotes from '*An Autobiography* and Other Essays' and 'English Social History' by G. M. Trevelyan. Bloomsbury Publishing plc for extracts from the 'Rural Economy of England' by Joan Thirsk, Susan Moore to quote from her publication 'Family Feuds' and Joe Hillaby 'Ledbury – A Medieval Borough'.

I am very grateful to those people who provided historical information: Hal Dalwood of Worcestershire Historic Environment and Archaeological Service for his comments on the early settlement of Upton-upon-Severn, its burgage plots and medieval inns; Simon Wilkinson for answering numerous queries about Upton and its inhabitants; Allan Sibley, editor of the Great Northern News and Dave Sutton of the Great Northern Railway Society for information concerning Elisha Wright Oldham, and Allan Orme for research in his local library. It must be added that a considerable amount of information in this book would not have readily come to light without the use of Internet search engines and 'on-line' indexes from the National Archives, local record offices, the British Newspaper Archive, the London Gazette and many other sources.

I must thank the staff at the Museum of the Royal Pharmaceutical Society for their assistance with the identification of several obscure items in John Day's inventory; Brendan Lawler for clarifying some of the finer points of the law and supplying a copy of the 1553 Statute; Linda Watson from Transcription Services Ltd., for correcting my efforts at document transcription (any remaining errors will be mine) and Kristina Bedford for her transcription of the manorial record.

I would also like to thank all those people who supplied genealogical information thereby saving me many hours of research: Sue Ballard for information concerning William Alfred Bradley; Jackie Tench and Deborah Fernando for the extensive genealogy of the Bounds of Upton-upon-Severn; Mike Musgrove for information about John Willoughby; Graham Thacker for supplying copious amounts of notes and documents concerning Thomas Thacker and Samuel Croft Thacker; Michael Scaife from the Scaife Study Group for details of Arthur Scaife, and Cathy Soughton for her research on John Green.

My thanks to Alan and Alistair Brewin for patiently waiting for the manuscript and all my family and friends for their encouragement over the years and finally, last but definitely not least, I must thank my long-suffering wife for performing grammatical surgery on the manuscript.

I very much regret that several people are not alive to see the publication of this account, particularly Lavender Beard who gave her enthusiastic encouragement for this project and who kindly loaned John Gibbs' pharmacy certificate, and also Peter Price who anticipated this book nearly twenty years ago.

Foreword

If, like me, you have stood in front of an old building and wondered at its history and how you would love to peel back its layers and learn about its past and the people who lived there, then this is the book for you.

A large building in the High Street of the Worcestershire town of Upton upon Severn divided into two shops – a Spar supermarket and a chemists – it could surely have little history. But with the fortunate preservation of title deeds and an enormous amount of research, Max Harris has shown us a property that came to life from the early sixteenth century when it was an inn. It tells the story of the many fascinating people who lived and worked in the building. Some were successful and some were not, ending up in prison for debt or involvement in illegal enterprises, troubled by the excise men, divorce laws or sewage problems.

As the newspapers of my youth used to put it "All human life is here" and in present day usage "Enjoy".

Henry Sandon.

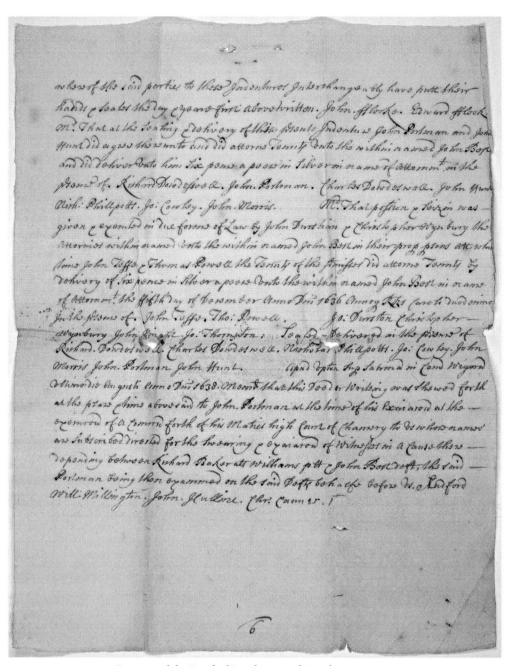

Page six of the Deed of Purchase, 2nd October 1636,
Flook to Best – The beginning of this adventure.

Preface

O N the fifth day of December 1636 a small group of people gathered outside the King's Arms, an inn of some antiquity situated in the High Street in Upton-upon-Severn near Worcester. They had assembled to take part in the ancient ritual of 'seizin' – a process in law dating back to time immemorial whereby freehold property was conveyed from vendor to purchaser. The party included John Durston, an innkeeper, and Christopher Wynbury, a mercer, who had been appointed attorneys acting on behalf of the vendors, John and Edward Flook.[1] Also present were, John Best, who was purchasing the inn, John Teffe, tenant and innkeeper of the King's Arms, Thomas Powell, tenant of another building being conveyed, together with John Portman and John Hunt who had also been appointed attorneys.

This 'livery of seizin' was described in a memorandum on the last page of a title deed concerning this ancient inn. The deed, dated 2nd October 1636, was the earliest in a bundle of documents contained in a rather old black metal box given to me by my predecessor in business; the collection included about thirty title deeds and other papers covering the period from 1636 to 1862, relating to the property I purchased in 1993. This was not the original document but a later transcript, almost certainly made when the property next changed ownership in 1710. The original document had been written two months before the ritual of seizin and the memorandum confirmed that seizin had been duly performed. The document covered six pages and also on the last page was a second memorandum, appended at the later date of 31st August 1638, which gave a brief mention of a 'Cause in Chancery' – an intriguing reference to an earlier history of the building:

> **Appended** Upton super Sabrina in Comitatus Wigornia ultimo die Augusti Anno Domini 1638.
>
> Memorandum that this Deed or Writeing was shewed forth at the place & time abovesaid to John Portman at the time of his Examinacion at the execucion

---

1   An attorney in this instance was not a lawyer but an individual appointed to act on behalf of another person.

of a Commission forth[2] of his Majestie's high Court of Chancery to us whose names are subscribed directed for the swearing & examinacion of Witnesses in a Cause[3] there depending between Richard Baker alias Williams plaintiff & John Best defendant, the said Portman being then examined on the said Defendant's behalfe before us.

[Anthony] Ludford, William Millington, John Hollins, Christopher Canner.

An Internet search of the The National Archives (TNA) files produced details of the relevant Chancery Court case dated 1637. Copies of the documents were obtained from TNA and although the original documents had suffered terribly from the ravages of time, damp and rats sufficient text was legible to reveal the existence of another, earlier, case in Chancery dated 1623. The 1637 Chancery case also revealed the existence of a further case in the Court of Common Pleas dated 1626. The name of one of the occupants, John Hall alias Oliver, led to the discovery of even earlier documents within TNA. These documents revealed that in the sixteenth and early seventeenth centuries the building had been known by the name of the 'Crown Inne'. The sign was later changed to the 'King's Arms' and at the beginning of the eighteenth century it became the 'Queen's Arms'. As time progressed the research became more extensive and led to the discovery of numerous wills, inventories, manorial records and several more cases in the Court of Chancery which concerned the inhabitants of the building. Whilst the reading and transcribing of many of these ancient documents can be rather tedious there is a certain fascination to them and some wonderful phrases appear. There is a certain expectancy with *'and to the heires of his body lawfully begotten or to be begotten'*, whilst *'Interrogatories to be administered to witnesses'* sounds rather unpalatable, and, at the end of inventories of the seventeenth century is sometimes written, *'Item: Things unremembered ~1 shilling'*.

It has taken nearly twenty years to research the history of this building and the lives of its occupants to produce a manuscript ready for publication, although for many years the time available was very much limited by other commitments. Occasionally the narrative wanders to distant towns and counties, foreign countries and even a far off continent. I hope the reader will find these detours worthwhile. Before commencing this project I knew little about the Courts of Chancery and Common Pleas, ancient inns, the bankruptcy and insolvency laws as well as other diverse subjects such as tobacco growing in England and the 'Plantations' of Ireland. The research has been very time consuming but immensely interesting and having been led down countless byways, the time has come to put this fascinating story into print.

---

2 forth = 'out'.

3 suit.

Introduction

The poetry of history lies in the quasi-miraculous fact that once, on this earth, once, on this familiar spot of ground walked other men and women, as actual as we are to-day, thinking their own thoughts, swayed by their own passions, but now all gone, one generation vanishing after another, gone as utterly as we ourselves shall shortly be gone like ghosts at cock-crow.

G.M. Trevelyan: *Autobiography of an Historian.*

THESE oft quoted words of the historian George Macaulay Trevelyan are particularly apt for these 'present writings' which concern a small plot of English soil and the buildings built thereon and, in particular, the inhabitants and people whose common thread is an association with this property for nearly five hundred years. Unlike the more famous, or even infamous, personalities of English history the thoughts and deeds of ordinary mortals from centuries past are rarely recorded. Often, the only glimpse we have into the minds of our predecessors is from the words of their last will and testament and for many others the only record of their passage through life is but a few entries within the parish register.

This account follows the history of a building situated in the High Street in the small town of Upton-upon-Severn. Nikolaus Pevsner, in his volume '*The Buildings of England: Worcestershire*', gives the property a very brief mention: '... a nice mid-Georgian house of only one bay with a Venetian window and quoins'. This description gives little indication of the history concealed behind the quiet Georgian facade of a high street retail premises which for several centuries has borne silent witness to the vagaries of human nature. For over four hundred and fifty years this building was not only a place of commerce where past generations made their living but it was also their home, a place where their children were born and raised, where they made their wills and prepared their souls to meet their maker and redeemer. This was a time when there was a narrow margin between life and death and the slightest breath of pestilence could change the course of lives irrevocably. Of the new generations, a few would remain and follow the trade of their forebears, most would leave and tread another path through life and some would raise their position in society from 'trade' and become 'gentlemen'. In the early period of its history the occupants lived out their lives in the building and it is not until the middle of the eighteenth century that we have any suggestion of them retiring from business to the relative comfort of the 'country estate'. This narrative also encounters those worlds that Charles Dickens knew so well and wrote so much about – the two worlds of the insolvent debtor and the Court of Chancery.

Upton-upon-Severn lies on the west bank of the river Severn south of Worcester; there was a settlement here before the Norman Conquest and in 1086 Upton was mentioned in the Domesday Book. However, as it shared its Domesday entry with the village of Ripple on the opposite bank of the Severn it is not possible to come to any definite conclusion regarding its size. The population of the two communities comprised two priests, forty villeins, sixteen bordars, eight serfs and a bondwoman. A mill was also mentioned but not its location. The earliest description of the settlement was by John Leland in his 'Itinerary' in 1549: 'Upton standith in ripa dextra Sabrinae apon a Cluster 4 Miles above Theokesbyri, and here is a Bridge of Wood on Sabrine, and here is a greate Stable of the Kinges a late occupied for great Horses, and a nother at Theokesbyry'.[4] Leland made a further comment about Upton and its bridge: 'There is noe Bridge on Severne beneath Gloucester. Neither is there any Bridge on Severne above Gloucester, 'till the Townelett of Upton at 11 or 12 Miles from Gloucester, whither at high Tydes Severne Sea doth flowe.'[5] There can be little doubt that the town's development was a consequence of its location at a crossing point of the Severn where the road from Pershore in the east, running towards Ledbury, Hereford and the Welsh Borders met the road running south along the west bank from Worcester into Gloucestershire.

In the late fourteenth century Edward le Despencer and his wife Elizabeth had acquired the manor of Upton. It has been suggested that the Despencer family were responsible for founding a borough but no record of a charter for Upton-upon-Severn has been traced, although there are frequent references to a borough in the fifteenth century and it was still referred to as a borough in 1703. By the early fifteenth century burgage or tenement plots had been laid out along Old Street[6]; the arrangement of the settlement prior to the fifteenth century is conjectural. The burgage plots were let out to the tenants (burgesses) at a fixed money rent, often one shilling, without the obligation of providing labour service and other duties to the manor. This gave the burgesses greater property rights than other manorial tenants; they were able to sell, sub-let or mortgage their properties. They also had the advantage of not being restricted to selling their wares on market days and were allowed to conduct their business in the local market without paying a toll to the

---

4   The Itinerary of John Leland, Vol. 6, (2nd Edn. 1744), p.71.

5   The Itinerary of John Leland, Vol. 4, (1711), p.64.

6   Hal Dalwood, *Archaeological assessment of Upton upon Severn*. p.9.

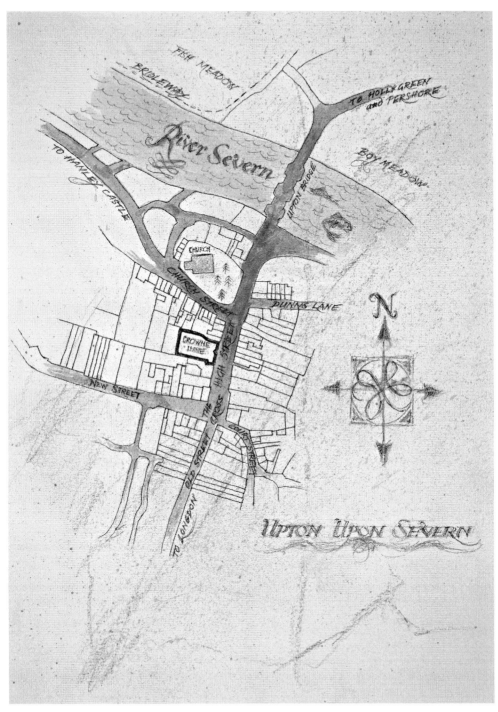

Site of the Crown Inn in the High Street, Upton-upon-Severn. Based on an 1886 estate map in connection with charity lands (WAAS BA4453/9).

manor.[7] The size of the burgage plots varied from place to place but was based on a measure of 'perches'; the statute perch measured 16½ feet (5.03 metres). When John de Coutances, Bishop of Worcester, laid out the new borough of Stratford-upon-Avon in 1196 on a site near the 'strete ford', where the road from Banbury crossed the River Avon, the burgage plots were approximately a quarter of an acre in area with 3.5 perch frontages (17.5 metres) and approximately 12 perches deep (60 metres). The burgesses paid one shilling per year in rent to the bishop. Medieval burgage plots were frequently subdivided into smaller and narrower units, especially those close to the market place as demand for town centre sites increased, each plot providing valuable frontage onto the high street. Within fifty years of its foundation many of the plots in Stratford-upon-Avon had been subdivided. Conversely, whole or part burgages were amalgamated to give a wider street frontage and this can be seen in the building of large inns in the Tudor period, two examples of which are to be found in Ledbury – the Feathers and the Talbot.[8] The Crown Inn situated in the High Street in Upton-upon-Severn occupied a site of approximately one whole burgage plot (the site measured about 20 metres in width by 37 metres deep). The width of the plot was consistent with the character of late medieval or post medieval inns and its location was close to where the earliest parts of the settlement of Upton were to be expected – around the church and the road leading to the river crossing.

The crossing point of the river at Upton-upon-Severn had in all probability existed for many centuries; the earliest reference to a bridge is in about 1480, which was the probable date of its construction. The original wooden structure replaced a ferry that had been in use since at least 1307-8 when it was first mentioned. There were two quays on the waterfront which must have been in existence long before the river bridge was constructed. The river trade made a considerable contribution to the development of Upton-upon-Severn which was one of several inland ports found along the lower Severn valley. Upton had links with the port of Bristol dating back many centuries and wine was one important commodity conveyed up-river. It has been said that Upton, and Tewkesbury a few miles downstream, were places where cargoes were trans-shipped between smaller vessels with sufficient draft to voyage up-river, and larger trows that travelled downstream towards the Bristol Channel.[9] The trows could only travel a certain distance each day depending upon the conditions on the river, and Upton, with its quays and accommodation, would have been a regular halting place. Many people used the riverboats as a convenient means of transport, perhaps more comfortable than horseback and certainly safer than the roads of the fifteenth and sixteenth centuries. By the sixteenth century Upton-upon-Severn had expanded into a 'townlett' whose inhabitants still depended on agriculture to some degree, although by the end of that century it

---

7   See Dyer, *Making a Living in the Middle Ages*, p.145.

8   Joe Hillaby, *Ledbury a Medieval Borough*, p.21.

9   Colin Green, *Severn Traders*, p.93 and p.102.

A View of Upton-upon-Severn from Ryall Hill.

was described in the Quarter Sessions as a 'market town'. In the eighteenth century Upton-upon-Severn was one of the ten market towns mentioned in Nash's *History of Worcestershire*.

Other authors have written about this small riverside town, notably Mrs Emily Lawson in the nineteenth century who wrote '*The Nation in the Parish*' and more recently Pamela Hurle with '*Upton: Portrait of a Severnside Town*' (1988). Both of these authors covered the history of the town, the parish and its environs, mentioning various characters associated with Upton-upon-Severn. This book looks into the lives of those individuals who were directly or indirectly associated with one particular building from the middle of the sixteenth century until the early years of the twentieth century. Upton-upon-Severn always lay within the shadow of the city of Worcester to the north and the abbey town of Tewkesbury, in Gloucestershire, to the south and making a living in the town was never without its difficulties. Some merchants succeeded in their trade whilst others faltered and we discover a constant undercurrent of debt, insolvency and litigation throughout the history of this building. Where we find debt we also find default and its inevitable sequels – bankruptcy or debtors' prison. Yet, remarkably, some of these debtors rose like 'phoenix from the ashes' and prospered once more. Disputes over ownership and the title deeds of the building were the cause of at least three cases in the Court of Chancery. Some occupants became involved in Chancery cases concerning other property and inheritance and this provides an absorbing insight into the workings of Chancery and its effect upon the lives of the plaintiffs and the defendants. This account perhaps focuses a little more on the sixteenth and seventeenth centuries, the beginning of modern England when the English way of life was still clinging to its medieval roots, a time in history when, as Christopher Dyer related, 'indeed there is a particular fascination in revealing the thoughts and actions of people living in an age unlike our own, when most people worked on the land, were dominated by an aristocracy and an all-embracing church'.[10] There is indeed a certain fascination in attempting to re-enact the lives of these individuals from the evidence in long forgotten Chancery cases and from their wills and inventories. For the first two hundred years of its recorded history the occupants were the sons or descendants of yeomen or husbandmen who had acquired sufficient wealth to purchase the property and establish themselves in 'trade'. It is ironic that those inhabitants who kept to the 'straight and narrow' generally left few records when they 'shuffled off this mortal coil' but the rogues and villains had their lives well documented through the courts of law.

This is a tale of two parts. Until the beginning of the eighteenth century the building was a small rural inn with a succession of innkeepers and their families in possession. At some time towards the end of the seventeenth century a 'sales shop' was established in the building and whilst the first one hundred and fifty years of this record concerns the history of a small English inn, the following three hundred years follows the lives and problems of the various retailers, artisans and their families who occupied the premises. In the earlier years there came a series of owner-occupiers but the beginning of the nineteenth century saw a period with landlords; established trades-people who used the building as an investment with tenant shopkeepers. Remarkably, through various taxes and excise duties, this property has been a source of revenue for central government for the greater part of the last four hundred and fifty years. These 'taxes' included the wine licences of 1571, excise duty on soap, candles and hops in 1710, taxes on medicines, purchase tax and finally the insidious and all pervading VAT.

Although this property in Upton-upon-Severn has undergone structural changes over the years some indication of its size and arrangement can be obtained from seventeenth century inventories. It is fortunate that the names of the owners within the title deeds and other documents have led to the discovery of three inventories in the period from 1591 to 1645. Two of these inventories referred to the various rooms in the inn and from these a probable layout of the building could be drawn. The property that was purchased in 1993 was approximately one half of the much larger premises which was divided around the beginning of the eighteenth century. Up to that date this history concerns the whole building and afterwards concentrates on the portion acquired in 1993, which, at some time before 1700, had become a separate 'sales shop', a role that has continued to the present day.

---

10   Christopher Dyer, *Making a Living in the Middle Ages, The People of Britain 850-1520* (Yale University Press, 2002), p.1.

Notes

The use of an 'alias' in surnames

The research into this building was complicated by the fact that several families associated with it during the sixteenth and seventeenth centuries were in the habit of using an alias and it is important to establish the concept of 'alias' in connection with surnames. There were several reasons why an alias was adopted. It was most usually used in connection with the inheritance of property and in particular copyhold tenure. Copyhold was a form of customary tenure which was recorded in the rolls of manorial Court Baron. The tenant's title deed to the property was a copy of the entry in the court rolls. A difficulty with customary tenure could arise following the death of a child's natural father and the remarriage of the mother. To protect any title to such copyhold land it was necessary to maintain the connection with the natural father and the child would adopt both surnames by the use of an alias. It could also occur in cases of illegitimacy where paternal and maternal names were both given.

One particular family in Upton-upon-Severn who used an alias was the Halls, who were also known as Hall alias Oliver or simply went under the name of Oliver which can cause some considerable confusion. For instance, in the Indexes to Wills at Worcester Record Office a will of 'Edward Oliver' and an inventory for 'Edward Hall' were found to be for the same person. Unless the researcher is aware of the use of an alias it can be extremely difficult to locate and identify relevant documents. The order and usage of the two surnames can be variable so different documents or even the same document can refer to: *John Hall, John Hall alias Oliver, John Oliver and John Oliver alias Hall*, all of whom could be the same person. The difficulty is finding sufficient corroborative evidence to establish the identity of a particular individual. In the sixteenth and early seventeenth centuries this particular alias occurred almost exclusively in the parish of Upton-upon-Severn but occasionally it was found in other parishes; two examples being in 1587 when a William Hall alias Oliver married Thomazen Sneade in Staunton and then in 1598 a John Oliver alias Hall of Chatley was named in a marriage bond.

The earliest use of the alias so far discovered appears in the Upton registers in 1580 when a William Hall alias Oliver married Jane Smithe. The reason behind the use of this particular alias remains a mystery for there is no apparent connection between the name Hall and Oliver, and as many pages in the early Upton parish registers have been damaged further investigation is difficult. The origin of the alias could even pre-date the earliest register.

Calendar and Dates

England originally used the Julian calendar established by Julius Caesar in Classical Rome. By this system of reckoning the New Year began on the 1st January. However, during the Middle Ages as a result of Christian influence, other dates were introduced for the beginning of the New Year including the 25th of December. Towards the end of the twelfth century England adopted a system of reckoning which had started in certain European countries with the New Year commencing on the Feast of the Annunciation (Lady Day), the 25th March. Until the reforms of 1751 this was the official mode of reckoning in England. As a consequence of this, great care has to be taken in the dating of events. For example, taking events that occurred in the year 1622, the 4th of January 1622 is a later date than the 15th of December 1622.

Monetary system

For the period covered by this history the currency in use was the old pre-decimal style of pounds, shillings and pence which was abbreviated £ s d from the Latin words libra, solidus and denarius. The inventories from the sixteenth and seventeenth centuries were usually priced using roman numerals with the superscripts '*li*' (or '*l*') '*s*' and '*d*'. The terminal '*i*' was usually written '*j*' i.e. '*iij*' = 3. For those not familiar with this system there were twelve pence in one shilling, twenty shillings in one pound and two hundred and forty pence to the pound. The penny was further subdivided into the halfpenny and farthing (a quarter). One shilling was worth five new pence and one old penny about 0.4 new pence. All references to 'pence' in the text are for the old pence of twelve to the shilling. 'Shilling' is often abbreviated, i.e. three shillings is written: 3/-. There are occasional references to other coinage: the groat was a coin worth four pence, a noble was a gold coin worth six shillings and eight pence whereas a mark was a 'money of account' of thirteen shillings and four pence in value but did not exist as a coin.

Monetary Conversion

Monetary values have been converted to present day (2015) values using the MeasuringWorth.com's calculator (www.measuringworth.com). The '**real price**' figure has been used which is based on the percentage increase in RPI. Other methods of comparison such as '**labour values**' produce very much higher figures.

Textual reconstructions in transcriptions

Square brackets [ ] have been used in transcriptions where an attempt has been made to insert missing text for a better interpretation of the documents. Abbreviated words in the original text have been extended using italics – as in 'Ten*emente*', 'yeoma*n*' *or* 'Domin*i*'.

Abbreviations

CCED: Clergy of the Church of England Database.
BRO: Bristol Record Office.
GA: Gloucestershire Archives.
TNA: The National Archives.
WAAS: Worcestershire Archive and Archaeology Service.
VCH: Victoria County History of Worcestershire.

1.

The Halls of Upton-upon-Severn

THE Chancery Court case mentioned in the title deeds revealed that in the sixteenth and seventeenth centuries the High Street property was in the ownership of three generations of the Hall family. During this period the building was an inn and was in their possession from sometime prior to 1565 until 1626. Before the Hall's tenure it was owned by Francis Baker alias Williams, of whom very little is known, one of those many individuals of the Tudor period whose origins pre-date the parish registers. The earliest intimation of the existence of an inn in Upton-upon-Severn is from documents within series E176 of the Exchequer Records at The National Archives. These documents relate to infringements of a Statute of Edward VI dated 1553 *'The Act to avoid the excessive Prices of Wine'*, the preamble of which commenced:

> '**For** the Avoiding of many Inconveniences, much evil Rule and common Resort of misruled Persons used and frequented in many Taverns of late newly set up in very great Number in Back-lanes, Corners and suspicious Places within the City of London, and in divers other Towns and Villages within this Realm......'

Whilst this Act sought to control the numbers of taverns or 'wine-sellers' in various towns and cities it also raised revenue for the Crown. It proceeded, in an attempt to control the illicit sales of wine, to deal with 'who may have wine in his house, and who not' etc., and restricted who could keep 'any of the said Wines of *Gascoign, Guyen, French* or *Rochel* Wines, containing above the Quantity of ten Gallons to the Intent to spend or drink the same in his or their House...'. The Act also laid down the maximum prices that could be charged for various wines. For Gascoign, Guyen or French the maximum rate was eight pence per gallon; for Rochel wines the rate was four pence per gallon; any other wines being subject to a maximum of twelve pence per gallon. Offenders were to be fined 'upon Pain that every Person doing the contrary shall forfeit for every such Offence five pounds of lawful Money of England'.

In 1570 Sir Edward Horsey received Letters Patent from the Crown authorising him to grant licences to keep taverns and sell wine in various towns and cities in England. The records within series E176 are mainly tripartite indentures made between Richard Ellis (deputy to Horsey); the vintners or retailers of wine; and a third party, the justices of the peace or other corporate officials. Within this series are a number of prosecutions under the statute in the form of 'informations', many of which arose from the activities of Hugh Bonell, a professional informer, of the parish of St. Clements in London. Of the fines imposed under the statute one half went to the Sovereign, and her agent, Horsey, retained the other half. In 1576 the patent was extended to allow further taverns in London, Westminster, Chester and Oxford, together with new ones in 'every thoroughfare, clothing town, haven town and fisher town'. It was later alleged that there had been abuses of Horsey's patent and in 1583 Sir Walter Raleigh was granted new Letters Patent to collect fines from vintners. In addition to the income from the fines Raleigh was also granted an annual fee from each licensee.

Two indentures within series E176 refer to a John Hall or Halle, a vintner, of Upton-upon-Severn. This title signifies that he was a merchant trading in wine and possibly that he also kept a tavern or an inn. Later evidence would confirm that John Hall was indeed an innkeeper in Upton-upon-Severn. Each indenture was dated 28th September 1571 and related to offences committed by John Hall dating back to 26th September 1565.[11] These dates suggest that John Hall had acquired the inn sometime prior to 1565 and that after he had been in business as an innkeeper for some few years had found himself in difficulties with the Tudor licensing authorities. The indentures recited:

> '**Witnesseth** that where the said John Hall hathe sythence the xxvjth daye of September in theigth year of the Reign of our sayde Soveraigne Lady [1565] untyll the daye of delivery hereof used hade & kepte one Tavern or wyne Cellar within the sayde Towne without Lawfull warrante or authoritye and hathe bought solde and uttered[12] there in grosse and uttered by lesse and greater measure the number and quantitye of two tonns and a half of all kynde of wynes at greater & higher price than be lymited or appoynted by the Statute made in the Seventh yeare of the Reign of our late Soveraign Lorde Kinge Edward the

---

11   TNA E 176/7/20 and E 176/13/22. These are virtually identical documents with some slight variations within the text. One refers to John Hall and the other to John Halle.

12   Utter: To offer goods or wares for sale, to vend or sell. A word frequently used in this sense from c. 1540 to c. 1655.

sixth & other Lawes & statutes of this Realm contrary to the true intent and
expresse words and meaninge of the said Lawes and statutes.......'

('Two tonns and a half' was approximately 630 imperial gallons or the equivalent
of about 3,800 of our modern bottles of wine.)

For a period of at least six years John Hall had not only been overcharging his
customers but had also been selling wine without a licence. These misdeeds could
have led to his 'utter undoing':

> **'By Reason** whereof the sayde John Hall hathe witnessed the danger of the
> paynes & penalties & forfeitures contayned in the same lawes & statutes &
> thereby forfeited to our sayde Soveraigne Ladye dyverse and great Sums of
> money which beinge demanded by thextremitye & severitye of the same Lawes
> & statutes might & would tourne to the utter undoing of the sayd John Hall ...'

Fortunately for John Hall her sovereign majesty Queen Elizabeth was prepared
to show some mercy towards her wayward subject, but with a financial penalty:

> **'Nevertheless** our sayd Soveraigne Lady meaninge to forbeare towards all men
> offendinge herein who knowing their offence and desserved punishment for the
> same shall humbly and thankfully submitte & conforme themselves to agree
> and paye suche reasonable fynes or somes of money for theire discharge as by
> her trusty & welbeloved servant Edward Horsey or his deputie or deputies,
> assigne or assignes shalbe compounded concluded and agreed upon in manner
> & forme in her Majesties lettres patente mencioned ....'
>
> **'And Therefore** for and in consideration of the Somme of Twentie Shillings
> of Lawfull money of England payde by the sayde John Hall to the sayde Rychard
> Ellis for and in the name of a fyne their moytie[13] thereof to be reasonable
> by the sayde Edward Horsey his executors deputies or assignes to our sayde
> Soveraigne lady into her sayde Courte of Excheqer & thother moytie the sayde
> Edward Horsey his executors or assignes shall & maye gave enjoye to his &
> theire owne onely use according to the purporte & meaning of the sayde
> Lettres patente ....'

John Hall escaped relatively lightly as he was not fined the full five pounds as
stipulated in the Act, and for the payment of twenty shillings he was acquitted of
the offence and pardoned by her majesty's deputy:

---

13   moytie = moiety: a half.

'And In respecte regarde & consideracion of the sayde Lettres patente & by virtue of the deputacions[14] afoure sayde for the Somme above sayde the sayde Rychard Ellis dothe by these presents release acquitte pardon & discharge the sayde John Hall ....'

In the sixteenth century the description 'vintner' referred to a merchant trading in wine but many vintners, notably in London and in provincial towns and cities, also owned taverns. The Vintners Company of London dates from before 1363 when it was granted a charter giving it a monopoly of the wine trade with Gascony; it also had an ancient right within the capital to open taverns at will. In Stratford-upon-Avon one vintner of note was Thomas Quiney who owned a tavern in that town and was married to Judith Shakespeare, daughter of the bard, William Shakespeare. Vintners in the larger towns would have supplied wine by wholesale to taverns, inns and the households of the lesser gentry. The larger households of the more affluent landed gentlemen, nobility and clergy would more often deal directly with the wine shippers. Prior William More of Worcester and the notable Talbot family of Bromsgrove obtained much of their wine directly from the Bristol merchants.[15] The journal of Prior William, which covers the period from 1518 to about 1535, shows that he received over one hundred and eighty hogsheads of red wine and claret (about 11,000 gallons) from Bristol. His supplies of wine were carried up-river by the Severn trows, one entry for 1528 reads:

> Item for carage of ij tonne of wyne with hallyng to ye trowe . . . . . . 5s. 0d.
> ij tonnes of wyne. Item payd for ij tonne of gaston Wyne
> viz. vj hoggsheeds of claret & ij of redd price ye tonne 8li. 6s. 8d. Summa 16li.
> 13s. 4d.

A tonne or tun could be a cask of 252 old wine gallons capacity but in this instance it was a measure of volume used in reckoning. Wine appears to have been ordered in quantities of 'tuns' but supplied in hogsheads of 63 wine-gallons.[16] The Prior supplemented these deliveries from Bristol with regular orders for smaller quantities of various wines, often sweet wines, which were probably purchased from the Worcester vintners and taverners.

It has been suggested that the authorities were more concerned with the collection of the fines than with controlling the vintners. Central government

---

14 'Deputacion' was a document conveying an appointment, commission or warrant.

15 Alan D. Dyer, *The City of Worcester in the Sixteenth Century*, p.91.

16 The hogshead was a cask of variable measure depending upon its contents. A London hogshead of beer held 54 gallons whilst casks of ale held 48 gallons. The volume of casks for wine was regulated by Assize. This was confirmed by an Act of Henry VI, (*Vessels of Wine, Oyl and Honey, shall be gauged.* 18 Henry VI, c.17. (1439)).

was always anxious to secure sources of revenue and the number of fines was not insignificant (Series E176 contains over six hundred indentures, some involving several individuals). Many vintners in Worcestershire were fined by Horsey; one in Broadway, three in Bromsgrove, two in Droitwich, two in Kidderminster, one in Shipston-upon-Stour and five within the city of Worcester. Innkeepers as well as vintners were fined; one was Thomas Leeke, an innholder of Worcester. Even in the Middle Ages innkeepers and hostellers had acquired a reputation for overcharging their clientele. In the fourteenth century Parliament was petitioned with complaints concerning excessive prices and in 1349 Edward III promulgated a statute that obliged hostellers and herbergers to sell food at reasonable prices. This statute had a limited effect and four years later a second statute was enacted in an attempt to control 'the great and outrageous cost of victuals kept up in all the realm by inn-keepers and other retailers of victuals, to the great detriment of people travelling throughout the realm'.[17]

John Hall was able to obtain supplies of a variety of wines from the port of Bristol. From the twelfth century the main imports were the 'Gascon' wines from southwest France together with smaller quantities of Rhenish wines. By the end of the fourteenth century wines from other regions were being imported into Bristol and by the fifteenth century sweet wines were arriving from Mediterranean countries including malmsey from Crete and romeney from the Ionian Islands. Bristol, in the sixteenth century, depended upon the wine trade for nearly half of its imports – an important contribution to its economy. In the sixteenth century, wine carried up-river was distributed inland by the Worcester vintners over a large area which included towns such as Coventry and Stratford-upon-Avon in Warwickshire.

The surname Hall occurs frequently in the sixteenth century records for Upton-upon-Severn; perhaps the earliest is for an Oliver Hall who appears in taxation lists for 1524 and 1525.[18] The name regularly appears in the earliest parish registers which start in 1546 and one person of note was Edward Hall who is remembered to this day with the Edward Hall Charity that is still extant and his name is also perpetuated in Edward Hall House situated in School Lane, Upton-upon-Severn. As previously mentioned the name 'Hall alias Oliver' first appears in the Upton registers in 1580. If the deduced genealogy is correct then the alias name occurs almost exclusively with Edward Hall and his descendants; one explanation of its origin could be that Edward's mother, Joanne Hall, had re-married. Whilst there is no mention of the alias name in the will of his brother, Thomas Hall, who died in 1571 it does occur in the will of Thomas' wife, Jane, who died in 1587. The burial entry for Jane reads 'Johane Hall alias Oliver'. It is possible that some event, perhaps

17   See J.J. Jusserand, *English Wayfaring Life*, (1970), p.61 and Statutes 23 Edward III, ch. 6 and 27 Edward III, ch. 3.

18   Great Subsidy, Oswaldslow Hundred: Exchequer, Kings Remembrancer, Subsidy Rolls (132) 3 Jun 1524 & (456) 1 Feb 1524/5.

a dispute over land occurring between 1571 and 1580, had caused the adoption of the alias 'Oliver'.[19]

In the sixteenth century there were several families by the name of Hall or Oliver living within the parishes of Upton-upon-Severn and Ripple with connections to the gentry and armigerous families of Worcestershire. Mrs Lawson, writing in the nineteenth century about life in Upton-upon-Severn, reflected that those 'more ancient well-to-do families have quite disappeared, ... our boatmen and fishermen are the people of really ancient lineage. There were Bricks, Farleys, Biddles and Halls in Upton in the reign of Henry VIII, and, it is likely, for many centuries previously'. The Halls may not have been involved in the river trade; many were yeoman farmers and husbandmen and several of their wills and inventories are to be found in record offices. The Halls owned land and property in this area of south Worcestershire; in 1599 Nicholas Hall held land in Upton, and also a 'capital messuage' in Newent, Gloucestershire, the rental income of the latter (five nobles or thirty three shillings and four pence per year) was left in trust for a period of sixteen years to provide an annuity for his youngest son, Francis, until he became of full age.[20]

John Hall, the innkeeper, was born about 1536, and was the son of Edward Hall alias Oliver, yeoman, of Upton-upon-Severn. The 'presumptive evidence' leads to the conclusion that Edward was the brother of John Halle, of Ripple, who was perhaps the most prominent member of a family whose occupations ranged from shoemaker to lord of the manor.

John Halle of Ripple

John Halle of Ripple was born about the beginning of the sixteenth century and held property, land and manors in both Worcestershire and Gloucestershire; he was possibly one of the 'nouveau riche' of Tudor England who owed their wealth to the wool trade. This was a time when movement from one social class to another was freely accepted as circumstances changed, fortunes were made and land and property acquired.

John Halle was connected to several land-owning families in this area and had married Alice Pynnock, sister to William Pynnock who held the manor of Tiltridge near Upton-upon-Severn. In 1545 John Halle together with Henry Sheldon of Abberton was granted 'in fee' the manor of Hill Court in Worcestershire and in the following year they also acquired Archers Manor in Stoke Orchard. (Stoke

---

19 There is earlier but obscure mention of a John Oliver in connection with Upton-upon-Severn in 1538 when John Oliver LLD and Edmund Conysbe were patrons to the appointment of William Leyson as priest to the parish church – presumably they held the advowson. (Nash, *History of Worcestershire*, Vol. II, p.448).

20 This was probably the same property, situated in New Street, Newent, sold in 1631 for £42 by another Edward Hall alias Oliver, of Upton-upon-Severn, to Thomas Hawkins of Newent, a butcher, and Susanne his wife. (GA D2957/212/40).

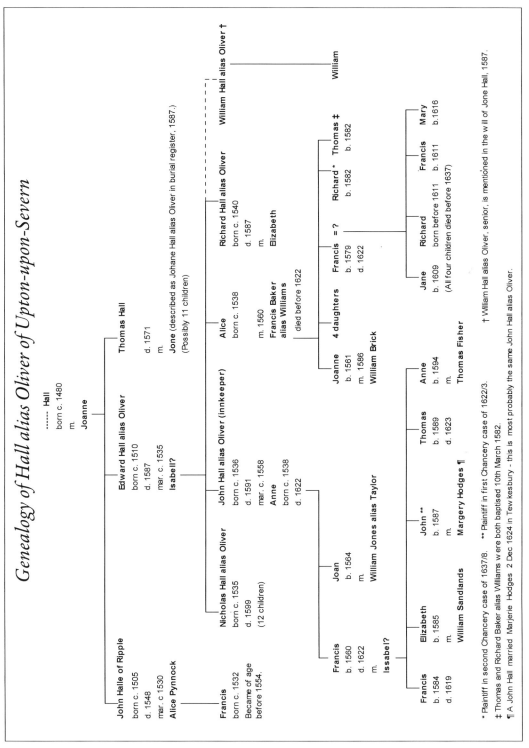

Genealogy of the Halls of Upton-upon-Severn.

Orchard was a small hamlet within the parish of Bishop's Cleeve, Gloucestershire, situated some six miles northwest of Cheltenham).[21]

In the sixteenth century the Sheldons were some of the largest landowners in Worcestershire and Henry Sheldon was a younger son of Ralph Sheldon who held the manors of Abberton and Beoley, and land in Upton-upon-Severn which was bequeathed to Henry's brother Thomas Sheldon. Henry Sheldon's grandfather was Baldwin Heath who, in 1519, was granted the office of the Keeper of the King's Stables at Upton-upon-Severn.[22] The connection between John Halle and the families of Sheldon and Pynnock implies that he was not from the lower levels of Tudor society but of the landed gentry. Whilst the above manorial acquisitions could suggest a family link between John Halle and Henry Sheldon this may have been purely a financial arrangement between them, with Halle providing the capital for the purchase.

John Halle of Ripple did not live long enough to enjoy the benefit of his manorial estates for he died two years later in 1548. There was one particularly significant bequest in his will: 'I give and bequeath to Edward my brother my farme with the appurtenances set lying and being in Upton upon Seaverne', but the bequest came with the stipulation that Edward had to provide for their mother Joane: 'for the which farme I will the said Edwarde to give yerely to Joane my Mother during the terme of her naturall lyffe xx⁵ sterling'. Regrettably the will does not give any indication as to the location of the farm. There were two other notable bequests in John Halle's will, one to William Bradstocke and the other to John Pynnock, both of whom were his brothers-in-law. A William Bradstock of Queenhill and a John Pynnock of Burlingham, Worcestershire were both named as trustees in the Edward Hall Charity document of 1575. With this corroborative evidence and with the absence of any other suitable Edward Hall, yeoman farmer, it is assumed that the Edward Hall named in the will and Edward Hall alias Oliver, husbandman or yeoman, of Upton-upon-Severn who died in 1587, and who is associated with this charity were one and the same person.

The Archers Manor was held 'in fee' from the Crown. Consequently, following the demise of John Halle an Inquisition Post Mortem was held to establish the tenure of the property that he held. His son, Francis Halle, heir to all his lands and the manor, was a minor and his uncle, William Pynnock, acquired the wardship. The value of the estate cannot have been insignificant as William Pynnock paid forty pounds for the wardship (for this payment Pynnock had the benefit of the profits of the manor until his ward became of full age). Francis Halle came of age in

---

21 Although the grant was to both Halle and Sheldon the purchase price of £372 18s 4d was paid by John Halle. Henry Sheldon later relinquished his moiety of the Archers Manor to John Halle. The manor of Hill Court evidently passed to Henry Sheldon as he died seised of it in 1558. (See GA D269A/T50).

22 VCH Worcs., p.213 and Letters and Papers Henry VIII, iii, g.581 (12).

1553/4 and livery of the manor in Stoke Orchard was then granted to him, but he subsequently sold the manor to a John Baker in 1560/1.[23] In common with many people of this period John Halle left a bequest to the poor of the parish: 'I give and bequeath to every poore bodye within the parish of Rypple two bushells of barley' (about fifty-five kilos by weight). It was quite common for wills to contain charitable bequests to the poor and to the church. Testators regularly made charitable bequests for the upkeep of bridges and for the repair of roads and there are several instances of bequests towards the upkeep of the bridge over the river Severn at Upton. These bequests were usually quite small, often more in the interest of piety than secular concerns. In 1543 Robert Holle of Ledbury bequeathed two bushels of wheat 'to the repairing of Upton bridge' and in 1571 a Thomas Hall of Upton left 6s 8d 'for mendynge of Upton bridge'.

The river bridge and highways were vital to the small town of Upton with its weekly market and fairs. The yeoman farmers, husbandmen and tradesmen all relied upon the roads and the river Severn for commerce. Prior to the Highways Acts of 1555 and 1562, which placed the responsibility for maintenance of the highways onto the parish, the duty lay with the landowners through whose land the roads passed. These highways were also important for the trade of other towns, both locally and further afield. The author of '*Ledbury A Medieval Borough*' comments that 'the land passage between the town and Upton was essential to the growing grain trade. It was Ledbury's lifeline.'[24] Other important commodities were transported out of Herefordshire, notably wool and cloth. Upton-upon-Severn was both a crossing point of the River Severn and a small river port from where goods were unloaded or loaded for onward carriage and the alehouse-keepers and more particularly the innkeepers would depend upon travelling merchants, carriers, waggoners and hauliers for much of their livelihood.

The maintenance of the roads and the river bridge would have been of constant concern to the townspeople and one notable local benefactor was John Halle's brother-in-law, William Pynnock of Hanley, who lived through one of those turbulent periods in English history. The matrimonial difficulties of Henry VIII had caused a schism with the Church of Rome and in 1534, by the Act of Supremacy, Henry was declared Supreme Head of the Church of England. The Suppression Acts of 1536 and 1539 authorised the dissolution of the monasteries and the acquisition of their estates. Much of the property appropriated was sold to raise revenue for the Crown and Pynnock purchased some of the estates belonging to Malvern Priory. He held extensive lands and property in Worcestershire (within Hanley Castle, Little Malvern, Powick and Welland) and in Gloucestershire. William Pynnock died in 1555 and his will referred to the wardship of his nephew 'I geve and bequeath unto Francis Haull ... his hole mariage money which I paid for his wardship ... that is to

23   See Gloucestershire Archives, on-line notes to D269/A.

24   Joe Hillaby, *Ledbury A Medieval Borough*, p.104.

say fourtie poundes'. Presumably Pynnock had recouped the outlay on his original investment. He was a person of considerable wealth and within the many bequests in his will was one for the construction of a causeway and the upkeep of the roads leading into Upton-upon-Severn: 'I give and bequeath to make the highwayes from Upton Bridge to Holly Greneward Twentie pounds And to make A Causeway from polehouse [Poolhouse] land unto Courte Orchard Style another Twentie pounds to be bestowed as by such one as myn executors shall thinke convenient. And he to have of my bequest further for his paynes fyve marks......'. These bequests referred to the roads leading out of Upton towards Pershore to the east and Powick and Worcester to the north. Twenty pounds was a large sum of money, sufficient to have paid the wages of three labourers for one year. William Pynnock also made substantial charitable bequests for the 'poor people dwelling in Upton fourtie shillings, Wenland [Welland] ten shillings, Hanley fourtie shillings, Crome fourtie shillings, Ripple fourtie shillings, Quenehill fourtie shillings, Malvern fourtie shillings And Tewkesbury one hundred shillings'. The total of these bequests to the poor amounted to £17 10s 0d – again a large sum of money at this time. His bequests also included an income of twenty shillings during the year following his decease for all his servants who included one named Edward Haull.

Following the death of William Pynnock in 1555 the manor of Tiltridge passed to his brother John, who died later in that same year. John Pynnock made a similar bequest for the upkeep of the highways: 'Also I bequeath unto the mending of ij hyeways in Upton upon Severne the one called small Brygge Coseway and the other called Colynghurst Coseway unto every of theym fyve poundes...'. Again these bequests referred to other roads leading out of Upton, south to Newent and Gloucestershire and west towards Ledbury and into Herefordshire. The causeways raised the roads above the level of the flood plain ensuring that the highways were always passable even during the periodic overflowing of the river Severn. These philanthropic bequests from William and John Pynnock would have been of significant benefit to this small riverside community.

John Hall alias Oliver, the elder, innkeeper of Upton-upon-Severn

We can only surmise what effect John Halle's bequest of the farm in Upton-upon-Severn had on Edward Hall's household, but without doubt it must have had a significant influence on the family's financial situation. Within a few years, sometime before 1565, Edward's son, John Hall, had access to sufficient capital to be able to purchase the Crowne Inne, situated in the High Street, from Francis Baker alias Williams (Francis Baker had married John Hall's sister, Alice, in 1560). By estimation the purchase price was in the region of one hundred pounds (it was later sold in 1626 for £130). Prior to 1565 no record of this inn has come to light and the only suggestion of its origins is found in a 'Bill of Complaint' dated 1623 where it was described as being 'situate in Upton aforesaid in the said County of

Worcs nowe and of ancient tyme heretofore allwayes used occupied enjoyed as a comon Inne and comonly called and knowne by the name of the Crowne in Upton aforesaid'. [25]

It is important to differentiate between the various sixteenth and seventeenth century drinking places, the 'alehouse', the 'tavern' and the 'inn'. A tavern was not an inn but originally was a 'public house' where wine was retailed as opposed to an 'alehouse' which retailed only beer or ale and as one observer has remarked: 'The difference between the inn and the tavern is therefore obvious. The one was instituted for the weary traveller, the other for the native; the one furnished food that the traveller might continue his journey, the other furnished drink for the mere pleasure of neighbours; the one was open to the traveller for protection at night, the other turned its guest out at the very moment when he most needed protection, and left him to find it, if his remaining senses permitted him to do so, in his own home. It is unnecessary, therefore, to point out the fact that a tavern is not an inn, and that the innkeeper's duties do not extend to the tavern-keeper'.[26]

Prior to the establishment of the inns in Upton in the sixteenth and early seventeenth centuries the only accommodation available for many travellers was the alehouse. Whereas in the larger towns these could be quite substantial premises with comfortable furnishings, the majority were small with limited facilities and accommodation.[27] Many of these alehouses were kept by the poorer elements of society supplementing their livelihood by selling ale, an activity that was often undertaken by their wives hence the term 'ale-wife'. Alehouses and inns were the focus of village life, providing drink, nourishment, accommodation and entertainment for both villagers and travellers. Inns provided for the more refined types, and if the writings of contemporary observers are to be believed, the conditions in the early English alehouse were best not contemplated and would suggest that the facilities suited the more robust sort of guest:

> The vile obscene talk, noise, nonsense and ribaldry discourses together with the fumes of tobacco, belchings and other foul breakings of wind, that are generally found in an ale-room ... are enough to make any rational creature amongst them almost ashamed of his being. But all this rude rabble esteem the highest degree of happiness and run themselves into the greatest straits imaginable to attain it. [28]

---

25 The name of the inn the 'Crown' is said to be one of the oldest English inn signs with the earliest recorded being in 1467. It is also the commonest with over one thousand houses under this sign in England. The sign of the Crown does not always signify that the inn was once Crown property. See Larwood and Hotten, *English Inn Signs*, p.64.

26 Joseph Henry Beale, *The Law of Innkeeping and Hotels etc.*, p.4.

27 Peter Clark, *The English Alehouse – A Social History 1200-1830*, p.72.

28 *A Dissertation on Drunkenness* 1727 – (from Peter Clark, *The English Alehouse – A Social History 1200-1830*, p.341.)

Some of these 'houses' brewed their own ale or beer whilst others were supplied by brewers found in the larger towns. In Worcester the brewers were among the wealthiest tradesmen in the city.[29] One Worcester brewer, Hugh Robinson, whose inventory was appraised in 1607 had moveable goods to the value of £260 19s 6d and the list of his effects showed that he lived very comfortably in substantial premises.[30] The inventory of John Turner from Upton-upon-Severn, who died in 1691, suggests that he had been actively involved in brewing and had made a good living. The total of his goods and chattels amounted to £177 17s 1⅓d and of this figure his stock of malt and barley was valued at £77.

The lines of distinction between the three types of victualling house were not always precise, and to quote Clark: 'Yet despite these problems, for much of our period we can distinguish with reasonable confidence between inns, usually large, fashionable establishments offering wine, ale and beer, together with quite elaborate food and lodging to well-heeled travellers; taverns, selling wine to the more prosperous, but without the extensive accommodation of inns; and alehouses, normally smaller premises serving the ale or beer (and later spirits) and providing rather basic food and accommodation for the lower orders'.[31] Many writers ignore these distinctions and in today's world the three have become synonymous. This was not so in the seventeenth century when the parish constables, in their presentments[32] to the Worcester Quarter Sessions, always made a distinction between the three 'houses'. There were specific enquiries that the constables had to make regarding innkeepers including: 'What rates are charged at inns for men and servants?' and: 'What price is charged by innkeepers for horses and their food?'.[33] The constables also appeared to differentiate between 'alehouse-victuallers' who supplied food together with ale or beer, and 'alehouse-keepers' solely retailing ale. (In the Calendar of the Worcestershire Quarter Sessions Papers for the period 1591 to 1643 there is only one mention of an alehouse providing 'lodging for man and horse and the necessaries....').[34] Much to the annoyance of bona fide innkeepers some alehouse keepers of dubious repute sought to elevate their status. In a petition to the Justices from Roger Perks who lived at the sign of the *Fish* in Whitstones near Worcester, concerning Henry Meeke who kept a 'common tippling house', Perks complained that 'one Henry Meeke that dwelleth in a house there having the sign of a *Bell* doth pretend himself to be an innholder and the reason he was suppressed by the Justices of Assizes before whom he was indicted and arrayned as accessory

---

29 Dyer, *The City of Worcester in the Sixteenth Century*, p.139.

30 Alan D.Dyer, *Probate Inventories of Worcester Tradesmen, 1546-1614*, p.46.

31 Clark, *The English Alehouse*, p.5.

32 Presentments, in this context, were sworn statements made by the constables, usually in response to specific questions they were required to answer concerning the state of their parish or bailiwick.

33 J. W. Willis Bund, *Calendar of the Quarter Sessions Papers*, p.c.

34 Ibid. p.595.

to felony in receiving goods stolen and is accounted a receiver and harbourer of lewd people as thieves and such like…'.[35]

Exactly when the Crowne Inn was established is conjectural; 'of ancient tyme' could perhaps suggest that its origins pre-dated Francis Baker by many years, perhaps even into the fifteenth century. The earliest English inns are said to have appeared in the twelfth and thirteenth centuries and were often associated with religious orders and the great pilgrimages that took place in medieval England. Many travellers relied on the 'Hospitium' or hospice of the monastic orders to provide accommodation and refreshment. Those people who did travel in medieval England were mainly pilgrims visiting holy shrines, merchants, the landed gentry, the higher orders of society and, paradoxically, the poor looking for work. A substantial majority of the populace had little necessity to travel and perhaps rarely ventured far beyond the county boundary or even the parish of their birth. By the late fourteenth century the demands on monasteries to provide hospitality had become a severe financial burden especially in centres of pilgrimage. In Gloucester Abbey the tomb of Edward II, who was brutally murdered at Berkeley Castle in 1327, became a shrine that attracted large numbers of pilgrims. Subsequently, the New Inn, which could accommodate two hundred people, was constructed by the Benedictine order. This timber-framed building, which still functions as a hotel, was said to have been one of the largest inns in the country providing great profits for the monastic order. In Tewkesbury, the Benedictine Abbey owned an inn, or large hospice, called the *Crone* (Crown) adjacent to Swilgate.[36] These inns provided the monasteries with a valuable source of income which relieved the demands on the hospitium, and by the end of the fifteenth century inns had become fairly widespread especially in the larger towns. Following the dissolution of the monasteries and the confiscation of their estates many of the monastical inns came into the possession of the Crown and were subsequently sold.

Inns would, of necessity, have been substantial buildings with sufficient rooms, bedchambers and stabling to provide adequate facilities for residential guests who arrived on horseback and were often accompanied by their servants. Beds and bedding would be required in some quantity together with tables and table linen. Catering too would have been provided throughout the day and all of these services required a number of servants to wait upon the traveller; the ostler attending to the traveller's horse; the tapster drawing his ale or wine; the chambermaid attending to the bedchamber and serving maids bringing his victuals.

Whilst the history of this building commences in the middle of the sixteenth century, life in a rural English inn at that period would have been little different from much earlier times in medieval England. For contemporary accounts of English inns we have to follow Jusserand in '*English Wayfaring Life*' who draws

---

35   Ibid. p.clxviii.

36   Anthea Jones, *Tewkesbury*, p.53.

on a manual of French conversation, written by an Englishman at the end of the fourteenth century[37]. The anonymous author provides dialogues between a servant and an innkeeper. In one example the traveller has sent his servant to enquire about lodging at the next inn; the innkeeper shows the servant the room declaring it to be "the most handsome and most respectable room and better adorned and arrayed with fine covers of gold and silk than you will find anywhere in your life". The servant replies "Truly sir I think it is well appointed and another thing that pleases me well is that the room is well prepared and swept so that I think there are no more fleas, nor nits, nor other vermin", "No, no sire, as God wills" replies the host, "for I guarantee that you will be at ease and comfortably lodged here, save that there is a great plague of rats and mice".

In the sixteenth century, apart from the Act of 1553 (*The Act to avoid the excessive Prices of Wine*), there were few statutory controls over the activities of innkeepers. It was held that the judges of assize could 'set a price upon their goods' and any innkeepers setting unreasonable rates were 'indictable for extortion'.[38] Everyday life in the sixteenth century was regulated by religious as well as secular directives and some of these impinged upon the lives of alehousekeepers and innkeepers. One such order of 14th January 1573 to the Justices of the Peace came from the Council in the Marches (originating from the Privy Council) which revealed one issue that regularly concerned the authorities, namely the non-observance of the eating of flesh during Lent:

> Whereas divers orders have been given as well as publicly by royal proclamation as well as letters from us, for the prevention of killing, dressing, selling and eating of flesh in Lent and other usual days appointed for the eating of fish. …
> … And to this end you shall provide as well by taking of bonds by obligations to Her Majesty's use as otherwise that no butcher, innholder, tippler, victualler or other person, kill, dress or suffer to be eaten within his house any kind of beef, mutton, veal or other meat commonly sold by butchers, in time of Lent, which is very convenient for the policy of this realm and the maintenance of the navy and fishing. You shall enquire for offenders at your Quarter Sessions .... and appoint persons to survey butcher's and victualler's houses from time to time. [39]

Apparently this directive was not well observed for a similar order was issued in February 1574, and in December of 1576 the Privy Council issued a further letter touching on the subject again but in rather stronger terms. The emphasis seems to have been more secular than religious: 'and considering also the great decay of

---

37 *La Manière de Langage qui enseigne à parler et à ecrire le francais.* Modèles de conversations composés en Angleterre. Publiès d'après le MS. du Mus. Brittanique. Harl. 3988.

38 Charles Viner, *A General Abridgment of Law and Equity,* (Vol. 14, 2nd Edition 1793), p.440.

39 Ralph Flenley, *The Register of the Council in the Marches of Wales 1569-1591,* p.101.

mariners and fishermen by the neglect and contempt of eating of fish, a matter very prejudicial to the strength of the navy'. The same letter also referred to the price of victuals. 'Her Majesty having late been informed that victuals within this realm are grown to most excessive prices (a matter very strange considering the long peace the realm has enjoyed through God's goodness and the Queen's providence)'.[40] The butchers, innholders and victuallers appear to have conveniently ignored these orders as the Privy Council issued yet another letter on the subject in 1578 requesting the Council to 'attend carefully to its execution'.[41]

Following his fine in 1571, John Hall's name next appeared in a list of trustees who were party to a feoffment,[42] dated 1575, which is always associated with his father, Edward Hall, and the charity of that name. Edward Hall was a person of some significance in sixteenth century Upton-upon-Severn. He was the first party named in this feoffment which involved certain lands, cottages and other property within Upton-upon-Severn, the income of which was to provide for repairing the parish church, the bridge over the River Severn and other necessary matters within the parish. The properties were transferred to the second party which consisted of fifteen gentlemen, yeomen and husbandmen who were the new trustees. In Tudor England inns were places where lawyers, merchants and the gentry could conduct their business in privacy and we can but surmise that these people met together in the Crown Inn, drinking wine from Bordeaux, to discuss the transfer of title of these charity lands. The new trustees included John Hall's brother in law, Francis Williams alias Baker, William Hall, probably a nephew, together with others, five of whom were related to the Pynnocks. Other writers have commented on the Edward Hall Charity and the nature of the connection of Edward Hall with that charity, the origins of which have eluded historians for many years. Mrs Lawson writing in *The Nation in the Parish* referred to Edward Hall and stated that: 'It was no bequest to take effect after his death, but a gift during his life; and it would seem that by this bounty Edward Hall reduced himself to poverty, for the only person of that name buried in Upton, within half a century of the feoffment is "Edward Hall a servant who died in the house of Mr. Knottisforde (in 1580)."'[43] The entry in the parish registers dated 11th December 1580 for 'Edward Hall a servant' refers to another Edward Hall, possibly the same 'Edward Haull', a servant, who was a beneficiary in William Pynnock's will of 1555. (It would appear that Mrs Lawson had drawn her conclusions concerning the charity from the wrong Edward Hall.) Edward Hall alias Oliver died in 1587 and was buried on the 8th March but, confusingly, the

40 Ibid. p.158.

41 Ibid. p.180.

42 More properly an 'Indenture of Feoffment' which described the transfer of land from one party to another. It would have been endorsed on the back with details declaring that 'Livery of Seisin' had been performed before witnesses.

43 Emily M. Lawson, *The Nation in the Parish*, p.35.

parish register used his alias name and referred to him as Edward Oliver. He left both a will and a probate inventory which show that he was no poverty stricken servant. By estimation Edward Hall was about sixty-five years of age at the time of the 1575 'Charity' document and could well have been the sole surviving trustee from an earlier generation. It is probable that the origins of the charity pre-date the Statute of Bridges of 1530 which addressed the continual difficulties with the maintenance of bridges. As a consequence of this statute the bridge over the Severn at Upton became a 'county bridge' and the responsibility for its repair was put onto the county authorities who raised a tax or levy from county tax payers. It follows, therefore, that the charity may have been established between about 1480, the supposed date of construction of the river bridge, and the date of the statute, 1530.[44]

When William Pynnock wrote his will in 1555 there were no bequests to any offspring, presumably he died childless, although there were numerous legacies to his brother, John, his two sisters, nieces, cousins and other relatives, and god-children. He owned or leased a considerable amount of land and property, including the parsonage at Powick, the Lordships of Hanley and Upton-upon-Severn; the lease of the latter was bequeathed to his brother, John Pynnock. Another bequest, for the Park at Hanley together with two mills, depended upon his wife's son from a previous marriage, John Badger, marrying one of the daughters of his brother John Pynnock. Other bequests made provision for future generations. It could be that the source of the Edward Hall Charity is to be found with the benevolent William Pynnock or his forebears.

Edward Hall alias Oliver

Edward Hall and another of his sons, Richard Hall, died within one week of each other in the spring of 1587. Richard was only about forty-five years of age and it is possible that both father and son died as a result of one of the outbreaks of typhus that occurred in that year. In Edward Hall's will he is described as 'husbandman' which is often accepted to be of lower status than 'yeoman', however in the associated probate inventory he is referred to as a yeoman. The inventory contained little of note to indicate his status apart from the 'painted clothes' which were often used by the more affluent as decorative wall hangings. The total value of his worldly goods amounted to only £28 4s 4d, a modest sum by sixteenth century standards and yet he was able to afford to keep two servants, Katerin Jones and Gabon, both of whom received bequests in his will.

The name '*Gabon*' merits further investigation. Edward's female servant is clearly referred to as '*Katerin Jones*' i.e. with a forename and a surname, but this is not the case with '*Gabon*'. There is a strong suspicion that the name could imply some connection with Gabon in equatorial West Africa. Upton-upon-Severn had always had trading links, via the river Severn, with the port of Bristol from where

---

44   See Pamela Hurle, *Upton*, pp.17-18.

merchant vessels were sailing to Africa and the Americas. By the sixteenth century Dutch, British and French vessels were all visiting Gabon. Edward Hall would undoubtedly have had connections, either directly or indirectly, with the Bristol merchants.

Research over a number of years at the Gloucestershire County Records Office by James Turtle has produced a list of references to Black and African-Caribbean people within the county of Gloucestershire, the earliest being at Bisley in 1603: John Davies 'ye black' was buried. The researcher considers that more instances are yet to be discovered, but at the time of writing, the list contains five references from the seventeenth century, twenty-two from the eighteenth and twenty-six from the nineteenth century. These unfortunate people would have arrived in England with names totally unpronounceable by their new masters and were given anglicised names as an entry from Stroud in 1801 would suggest: William Ellis, son of Qualquay Assedew, a Negro of Guinea, aged 12 years, was baptised. Many appear to have received only a Christian name such as at Driffield in 1687: Jacob, the servant of George Hanger esquire, 'a moore' was baptised; or at Sherborne in 1736: George, a black slave was baptised. Some were given a surname which would associate with the village in which they lived as an entry for Frocester in 1790 would suggest: William Frocester, supposed to be about 11 or 12 yrs old, born on the island of Barbados and now a servant of Edward Bigland, Esq. residing in Jamaica, was baptised. Other given names were Mingo (Cheltenham 1817) and Dido (Tidenham 1805) and to quote James Turtle they 'were probably thought by their owners to be the sort of names they may have had 'back home''. [45] At Stanford-on-Avon in Northamptonshire in 1734 Hannibal Gambia, 'a black boy brought from Africa', was baptised on the 29th September. [46] In the above-mentioned list there are only two references to 'slaves', their usual status or occupation was 'servant'. Wherever his origins, Gabon was certainly quite well provided for in Edward Hall's will:

> *I give unto Gabon my servant one young weaning calf, my best coat & best last. Item, I give unto my servant maide Katerin Jones one yearling beast...*

Presumably the 'last' was intended to help Gabon set himself up as a shoemaker and earn a living. There was only one bequest in Edward Hall's will to any of his sons, and that was for a 'colte' for John Hall. The will did however make provision for the four young children of his son Richard who was buried on the 1st of March 1587 a few days before his father was interred. The two daughters were under five years of age and each of the four children was bequeathed forty shillings with a similar sum to be paid when they came of age or on the day of their marriage.

---

45   http://www.irespect.net/history/Historic%20Records.htm – Site accessed 20.2.2014. See also Imtiaz Habib, *Black Lives in the English Archives, 1500-1677*.

46   Leicester & Rutland FHS Journal No.147 p.38.

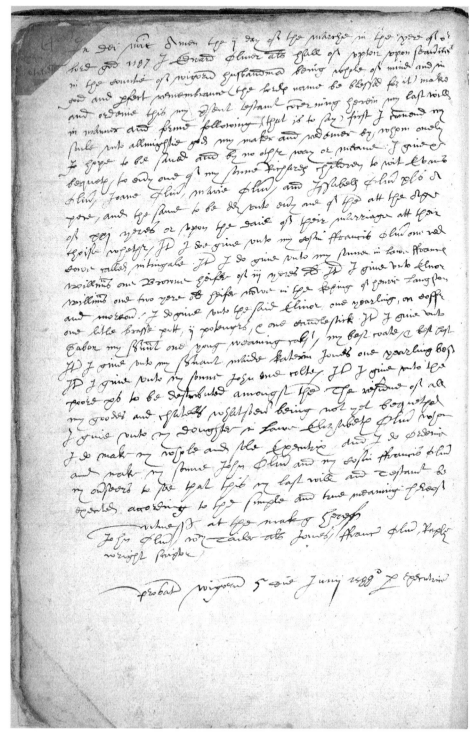

The last Will and Testament of Edward Oliver alias Hall, 2nd March 1587.

Transcription of the last Will and Testament of Edward Oliver alias Hall.

In Dei nomine Amen the ij day of the marche in the yere of our
Lord god 1587 I Edward Oliver alias Hall of Upton upon Seaverne
in the Countie of wigornia [Worcestershire] husbandman being whole of mind and
in good and perfect remembrance (the lords name be blessed for it) make
and ordeine this my present testament concerning herein my last will
in manner and forme following (that is to say) first I commend my
soule unto allmightie god my maker and redemer by whom onely
I hope to be saved and by no other way or meanes: I give and
bequeath to every one of my sonne Richard's children to wit Evans
Oliver Joane Oliver Marie Oliver and Issabell Oliver xls A
pece, and the same to be d[elivered] unto every one of them att the Age
of xxj yeres or upon the daie of their marriage att their
choise whether. Item I doe give unto my Cosin Francis Oliver one red
Cowe called nitingale. Item I do give unto my sonne in law Francis
Williams one Browne heifer of iij yeres old. Item I give unto Elinor
Williams one two yere old heifer nowe in the keeping of henrie Langdon
and moreover – I do give unto the said Elinor, one yearling, one Coffer
one litle brasse pott, ij potengers, & one Candlestick. Item I give unto
Gabon my servant one young weaning calf, my best coate, & best last
Item I give unto my servant maide Katerin Jones one yearling beast
Item I give unto my sonne John one colte. Item I give unto the
poore xs to be destributed amongst them. The residue of all
my goodes and chatells whatsoever being not yet bequeathed
I give unto my doughter in Lawe Elizabeth Oliver whom
I do make my whole and sole Executrix And I do Ordeine
and make my sonne John Oliver and my Cosin Francis Oliver
my overseers to see that this my last will and Testament be
executed according to the simple and true meaning hereof
witnesses at the making hereof
John Oliver, William Tailer alias Jones, Francis Oliver, Raphe
Wright scriptor Probatum Wigorn 5 die Junii 1588° per Executrice

It is interesting to note that he uses the surname Oliver in all of the above bequests
and in the appointment of his executrix and overseers. His daughter-in-law,
Elizabeth Oliver, was almost certainly the wife of his son, Richard who had prepared
his own will just six days earlier on the 25th of February 1587.

John Hall continued as innkeeper until his death in 1591 at the age of about
fifty-five. The parish register gives no indication as to the cause of his death, but,
at this relatively early age, the finger of suspicion points to the plague. In the

sixteenth century numerous outbreaks of bubonic plague occurred in England. In 1591 one house in Tewkesbury was suspected of being infected with plague and in 1592 there were five hundred and sixty deaths there from the disease. These outbreaks in Tewkesbury were alleged to have been brought up-river from Bristol by the Severn trowmen. An inn or alehouse would have been the first point of call for many travellers arriving via river or road exposing the occupants to whatever pestilence they carried. Several years earlier, in 1579, an outbreak of 'the sickness' had been reported in Tewkesbury, 'supposed to be the pestilence, which, by good government of the bailiffs in shutting up the houses, it began and ended in the Swan Inn. Five persons only dying thereof'.[47] It is unlikely that Upton-upon-Severn would have avoided the spread of the disease that was more prevalent in the summer months when John Hall died. He left a will for which there is an accompanying probate inventory. The will referred in some detail to the inheritance of the property situated in the High Street, Upton-upon-Severn 'nowe in the occupation of mee the said John Hall which I latelie hath & purchased of Francis Williams alias Baker unto mee the said John & Ann my Wife & unto the heires of mee the said John forever ...'.

Unfortunately no rooms were itemised in the inventory so it is not possible to be precise about the size and layout of the building. However, eight bedsteads are listed, the same number as in a later inventory of 1622 which does itemise all the rooms in the inn. Thus it could be inferred that the arrangement of the building was substantially the same as in 1622. Its construction predated that period referred to as 'The Great Rebuilding of England' which commenced in the second half of the sixteenth century – a time when many medieval buildings were replaced, rebuilt or substantially modernised. Many fine buildings and inns in other local towns date from this period, including the Feathers and the Talbot in Ledbury. The Crown Inn purchased by John Hall could have been built or rebuilt by Francis Baker alias Williams in about 1560. There would certainly have been an earlier building on the site but unfortunately the title deeds to this have not been traced.

In his will John Hall was described as 'yeoman' – a title that does not indicate any specific occupation. The terms 'yeoman' and also 'gentleman' were often used as descriptions of social status and do not give any insight into the livelihood of these men. A 'yeoman' would not necessarily be involved in agriculture or husbandry and the term could equally refer to a tradesman or merchant. William Harrison wrote at length about 'status' in English society; referring to 'yeomen' he tells us: 'This sort of people have a certain pre-eminence, and more estimation than labourers and the common sort of artificers, and these commonlie live wealthilie, keep good houses, and travell[48] to get riches. They are also for the most part farmers to gentlemen ... or at the leastwise artificers; and with grazing, frequenting of markets, and keeping of servants (not idle servants as the gentlemen doo, but such as get both their owne

---

47   William Dyed, *The History and Antiquities of Tewkesbury*, (1790), pp.93-95.

48   travail.

and part of their master's living) do come to great wealth, in somuch that manie of them are able and doo buie the lands of unthriftie gentlemen, and often, setting their sons to the schools, to the universities, and to the Ins of the Court; or otherwise leaving them sufficient lands whereupon they may live without labour, doo make them by those means to become gentlemen: these were they that in times past made all France afraid'.[49]

Transcription of John Hall's Will – 1st June 1591

In the name of god Amen the first daie of June Anno Domini 1591 & in the three and Thirtithe yeere of the reigne of our soveraigne Ladie Elizabeth by the grace of god of England France & Ireland Queene defendor of the faithe etc I John Hall of Upton Uppon Seavern in the Countie of Worcester yeoman beeing sick in bodie butt of perfecte mind and memory (Thanks bee to god) do make ordeine constitute and appointe this my last will & Testament in manner & forme followinge vizit First I geve & bequeath my sowle unto allmightie god my maker hopinge & perfectelie beeleavinge to receave enjoy and have eternall & everlastinge lief after my departure out of this worlde, by the deathe & passion of our Lord and saviour Jesus Christe, & I appointe my bodie to bee buried in the Churche of Upton aforesaid att or neere my Seates End there. Item I give & bequeath Will & devise unto Francis Hall my sonne all that my messwage or Tenemente, Backeside, garden howses, Edifices & buildinges Barnes stables easiamentes proffites Commodities Commons appurtenances & hereditamentes whatsoever scituate lyinge & beeinge in Upton aforesayd as well in the Highe streete as in the old streete[50] there & nowe in the occupacion of mee the said John Hall which I latelie hath & purchased of Francis Williams alias Baker unto mee the said John, Ann my Wief & unto the heires of mee the said John forever To have & to hold the sayd messwage or Tenemente Backeside, Garden, howses, Edifices, buildinges Barnes Stables easiaments Commons & hereditamentes whatsoever unto the sayd Francis Hall my sonne from & after the deceasse of Anne my said wief for & duringe his naturall lief & after his deceasse unto Francis Hall his sonne & unto the heires of his body lawfullie beegotten or to bee beegotten forever & for wante of suche Issue of his bodie Lawfullie to bee beegotten, unto John Hall one other sonne of the sayd Francis my sonne & unto the heires of his bodie lawfullie beegotten or to bee beegotten forever, And for wante of suche Issue of his bodie Lawfullie to bee beegotten, unto Thomas Hall one other sonne of the sayd Francis my sonne & unto the heires of his bodie lawfullie beegotten or to bee beegotten forever & for want of suche Issue of his body lawfully beegotten or to bee beegotten unto the righte heires of the sayd Francis my sonne forever. Item I give & beequeathe unto everie one of my sayd sonne Francis's Children: vizit: unto Francis Hall, John Hall, Thomas Hall & Elizabeth Hall Twenty nobles a peece of lawfull money of England to bee paied unto them & unto every one of them severallie when & assoone as they & every one of them shall severallie accomplishe the full age of one and Twentie yeeres or att the day of their

---

49 William Harrison – *The Description of England*, (1877), p.133.

50 The building in Old Street was actually a barn, and is described in more detail in a title deed of 1636.

or any of their several mariages, or else att the daie of the mariage of the said Anne my wief att their and every of their Choyces. Item, I give & bequeath unto everie one of my daughter Johans fower Children vizit unto William Jones, Richard Jones, Johan Jones & Elizabeth Jones fortie shillinges apeece of like Lawful money of England to bee paied unto them & unto every one of them severallie when & assoone as theie & every one of them shall accomplishe the full & severall age of one and Twentie Yeares Orelse att the daie of everie one of their severall mariages Item I give & beequeath unto Alice Williams alias Baker my sister my tagged Cowes Calf presently after that the same shall bee five weekes old. / All the Residue of my goodes goodes Cattelles & Chattelles whatsover above by this my present Testament & last Will nott geaven or bequeathed I give & beequeathe whollie and absolutelie unto Ann my wief to the End that shee do discharge my sayd Legacies above heerein geaven and bequeathed according to the purporte effect entente & true meaninge heereof & allso discharge my funeralles & other charges beelonginge thereunto, Which sayd Ann my wyefe I make ordeine constitute & appointe my whole and sole executrix of this my last will & Testament In wyttnes whereof I have heereunto to putt my Seale the day and yeere first above written.

Wittnesses att th'ensealinge & publisshinge of this
my last will & Testament vizit

Xpefer[51] Teale cuius signum in alta parte patet
Richard Stone cuius signum etiam in alta parte patet
Francis Hall filius predicti Testatoris
Marie uxor Thomæ Hunt
[blank] uxor Ricardi Jackson
et Willimi Jones alias Tailor scriptoris presentum

Heere followethe a note of all suche money as is owinge me vizit
Richard Beavans oweth me viili iiijs to bee payd att lamas [52] next
Mr Thomas Harewell oweth me xls to bee payd att holiroode day[53] next
[Next line deleted]
Nicholas my Brother oweth me xs
& William Hall ----------- xs

A note of all suche money as I do owe vizit
Unto my sonne Francis vjli
& unto Richard Hall my Cosen – vjli xiijs iiijd

Probatum coram Richardo Cosin per Arturo Dure__ Wigorn xxijo Martij stilo Anglie 1591
et exhibunt Inventarum ad summa xxviijli xiiijs iiijd

---

51 Xpefer = Christofer.
52 Lamas (Lammas day): 1st August.
53 Holiroode Day = Holy Rood Day = Exaltatio Sanctae Crucis – Exaltation of the Cross: 14th of September.

John Hall's inventory was valued at only £28 8s 4d, a modest sum for a yeoman. At first inspection there is little to suggest that it is anything more than that of a small farmer or husbandman cultivating a few acres of land. There would appear to be little of note in the inventory. However, an analysis of the quantity of tables, beds and bedding would suggest otherwise. John Hall's property contained the significantly large number of eight bedsteads together with five featherbeds, an expensive item in Tudor England and usually to be found in the more affluent households. A sample of inventories from the period 1545-1614 for a group of relatively wealthy Worcester merchants where the average total of their worldly goods was £67 12s 4d revealed that the average number of bedsteads was only 3.7 (two individuals had seven bedsteads).[54] Perhaps, of even more significance in the inventory was the presence of seven table-boards which is a considerably higher figure than the average of approximately 1.5 per household in Upton-upon-Severn at this period.[55] An adequate quantity of tables would have been indispensable for providing food and refreshment for the travellers calling at the inn for a nights lodging. Even when no occupational description was given, the presence of a relatively large number of beds in inventories of this period was characteristic of inns and likewise a large number of table boards was indicative of an alehouse or victualler as well as an inn. There was no mention of food, beer or wine in John Hall's inventory but this was not unusual.

Generally the appraisers of inventories ignored any perishable goods and only included preserved food items which had any saleable value. Those items appearing with any regularity in Worcestershire inventories were flitches of bacon, cheeses and occasionally butter. Wine was never mentioned in the inventories of other Worcestershire innkeepers researched for this book. John Hall's inventory also listed a number of pewter vessels and pots which were becoming popular in inns in the late sixteenth century. A later court case in Chancery dated 1623 does confirm that this was in fact the Crowne Inn and therefore the inventory itemises the contents of this inn in 1591. There was little in the inventory to suggest that John Hall was wholesaling wine, no mention of debts owed to merchants, only two outstanding debts which could possibly be for wine. From the contents of the inventory it would appear that John Hall was an innkeeper who supplemented his primary occupation with some agriculture and animal husbandry.

John Hall's will is very informative, and the directions for his inhumation are quite interesting: '& I appointe my bodie to bee buried in the Churche of Upton aforesaid att or neare my Seat End there'. Since the fifteenth century a system of pew renting had developed, with the churchwardens adopting a custom of charging rents for specific pews. This custom has been described as being 'extra-

---

54   See A.D. Dyer ed., *Probate Inventories of Worcester Tradesmen, 1545-1614.*

55   Taken from a sample of seventeen Upton inventories from the sixteenth and seventeenth centuries.

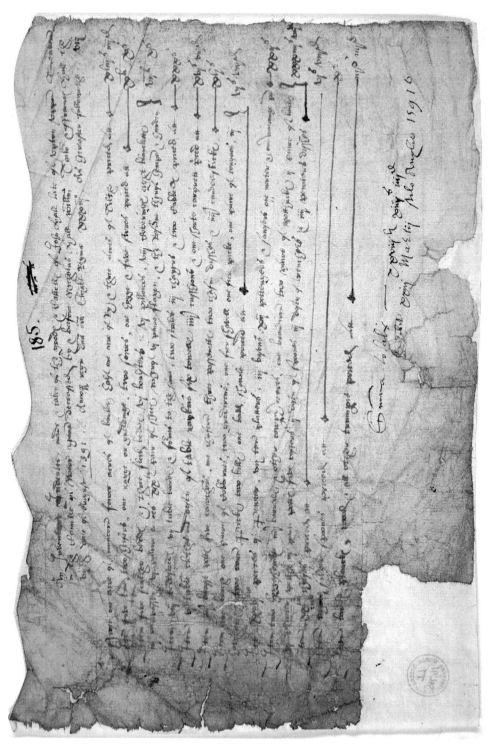

Inventory of the Goods and Cattells of John Hall, 7th August 1591.

Transcription of the Inventory of John Hall's goods and chattells, 1591

An Inventory Indented made & taken of the goods & Cattells of John Hall late of Upton Uppon Seavern in The Countie of Worcs yeoman deceased by & before Nicholas Hall William Tailor & Francis Hall the vijth daie of August 1591 Annoque regni domina nostra Elizabeth Regina xxxiij° As hereafter followeth viz

First one acre of moncorn fower acres of barley half aone acre of Ry & three acres of Tilthe priced att ____ xliij^s iiij^d

Item five kine, two heifers, one nagge one gueldinge, two sowes, one hogge & five steres priced at ____ x^{li} x^s

Item five feather bedds & three flock beds vj boulsters vj pillowes viiij Coverings eight blanketts iiij matresses vj pillowe beeres xx^{ty} paire of sheets whereof vj paire flaxyn, & the Residue though hempen & hurden } vij^{li} x^s

Item viij bedsteedes vij tableboards & formes to the same two stooles iij chayers & two Cobberds priced att ____ xxx^s

Item vj table clothes one dozen of table napkins six towells iiij cusshions & one short carprett priced att ____ xv^s viij^d

Item iiij brasse potts five cawtherns one chafern three possenotts two chafin disshes & iiij candellsticks ____ xlj^s

Item one broche one paire of Cobbernes two gredirons one fier shovell one fier picke one paire of tongues iiij hatchetts, two iron Picks two bills one badd showle priced att } vj^s viiij^d

Item xxvj^{tie} peeces of Pewter viz ten platters, iij basons xiij pottengers & sawsers one morter & one warminge pan ____ xxij^s

Item two hoggsheads iiij barrells & other cowpery wares, one brandiron two paire of potthuckes ii paire of links vj pewter potts iij pinte potts five coffers ij dozen of spoones iij dosen of trenchers & iiij pewter disshes } xxxiiij^s viij^d

Item xx^{tie} cheeses priced att ____ vj^s viij^d

Item three two silver spoones priced att ____ x^s

Item boards plancks wood & all other trumperie priced att ____ iijs iiij^d

Summa totalis ____ xxviij^{li} xiiij$_s$ iiij$_d$

[Pro]batum xxij Martii stilo Anglie 1591

Note that the Inventory was taken on the 7th August 1591 and probate was granted 22nd March (*xxij Martii*) 1591. The reason for this is that the calendar in use in the 16th Century was the old-style calendar where the year commenced on the 25th of March.

legal' and, according to one barrister at law in 1844, it was a totally 'illegal' practice.[56] It later developed into the sale of freehold pews complete with lock and key to ensure privacy for their proud proprietors. John Hall would have had to pay the churchwardens for the benefit of his own pew in the parish church, and also for interring his body near his seat.

Surprisingly, there was no mention of clothing, either in John Hall's will or within the inventory, yet we know from other inventories of this period that the innkeeper could have been a very well dressed gentleman. George Warburton, another local innkeeper who died in 1585, would have been amongst the sartorial élite of the citizens of Worcester. The inventory of his goods and chattels itemised his wearing apparel, valued at nine pounds:

The Testators Apparell

> Item one scarlett gowne faced with foynes, one Murreyd
> gowne, one blacke gowne garded with velvete, one Medleye
> gowne faced with bouge, one blacke clooke, one Jackett of
> chamlett, one Jackett of worsted, one Jacquett of mockado, one
> Doblett of satten, one Doublet of Buffyne, two payer of
> hosse one Cassocke of worsted all preised at ix[li] [£9]

(A 'gowne' in this instance refers to a loose fitting upper garment worn by men; foynes were trimmings made from the fur of a polecat or a weasel; murrey was a cloth the colour of mulberry – a purple-red or blood colour. Bouge means a fur lining. For other items see the glossary.)

John Hall was a person of modest wealth and, like his father Edward, he too would have been of some importance in the local community. In the social order of early modern England innkeepers were a degree above the other tradesmen, yeoman farmers and husbandmen. As Clark informs us in the *English Alehouse*, 'by the sixteenth century innkeepers were frequently members of the local economic élite'. The larger inns of market towns and cities could count the landed gentry and nobility among their guests. In Leicester the Angel Inn was patronised during the sixteenth century by the Earls of Shrewsbury, the Lords Derby, Talbot and Morley as well as the Marquess of Dorset.[57] A survey of the wills and inventories of Canterbury innkeepers who died between 1560 and 1640 revealed that they were amongst the ten wealthiest trades in the city.[58] Worcestershire innkeepers were no exception. In 1550 Gabryel Wyet innholder and citizen of Worcester owned property in the city and bequeathed about seventy pounds of 'lawful money' in legacies. His second

---

56   See W. E. Tate, *The Parish Chest*, (1983), 90 and John Coke Fowler, esq., *Church Pews, Their Origin and Legal Incidents with some Observations on the Propriety of Abolishing Them*, 1844.

57   Peter Clark, *The English Alehouse: A Social History 1200 – 1830*, p.7.

58   Ibid. p.7

eldest daughter, Anne Wyet, had married William Warmstry, a Notary Public and Registrar of the Worcester Diocese who died in 1581. (The name Warmstry has become better known for its association with Warmstry House where the Worcester Porcelain Manufactory was established in the eighteenth century.) Whilst the innkeeper would welcome the more affluent clientele, the 'less distinguished folk' – the tradesmen, farmers and craftsmen would also patronise these establishments.

With the growth of trade and local administration in Tudor England inns gradually evolved from their original role of providing hospitality for travellers into places of business; where merchants conducted their transactions without the regulations of the open market place and the vagaries of the English weather, and where justices and attorneys performed their duties. By the end of the fifteenth century inns were well established as commercial centres and this trading function which came to be most significant in their development, expanded rapidly during the reign of Queen Elizabeth much to the detriment of the traditional open-air markets, which led to many complaints from local magistrates. The larger inns also offered the facility of warehouses where corn, malt and other commodities could be stored. In the hop growing areas of England (which included Worcestershire and Herefordshire) inns became a centre for the hop trade. Travelling factors purchased hops from the growers which were then sold on to their customers in the comfort of the inns they frequented. Pedlars, petty chapmen and other itinerant traders often availed themselves of inns to sell their wares. A major risk in the seventeenth century for the travelling trader was the possibility of attack by highwaymen who often relieved him of his purse and goods. Consequently, many of the merchants, drovers and carriers chose to deposit their money with innkeepers along their route who acted as rudimentary bankers, drawing bills and making payments to creditors.[59]

Carriers have had a long association with inns and innkeepers. As trade and commerce expanded in the sixteenth century goods, and especially cloth, were transported across the country by a multitude of carriers who used inns as staging points. Many of these goods were transported by carts which had been the principle mode of transport since at least the fourteenth century, although use of the packhorse was commonplace especially in areas of difficult terrain.[60] A network of carriers was well established in medieval England and by the fifteenth century carriers existed in many provincial towns including Gloucester and Worcester. The increasing number of carriers requiring suitable accommodation and stabling would in part explain the increase in the number of inns in the sixteenth and seventeenth centuries. Many inns provided enclosed yards to the rear that could be made secure at night thus ensuring that the merchant's consignment would still be there when he arose the following morning. A sixteenth century carrier starting his journey

---

59 Alan Everitt, *Landscape and Community in England: The English Urban Inn*, p.173 and Dorian Gerhold, *Carriers & Coachmasters* , p.26.

60 Gerhold, *Carriers & Coachmasters*, p.4.

in Hereford would have taken a full day's travel to reach Upton-upon-Severn. He would seek refreshment, stabling and oats for his horses and a secure place to keep his load for the night. A later reference to 'loaders' in 1622 does suggest that the Crown Inn was connected to the carrying trade and there is certainly a mention of a gate across the access to the rear in 1710. Besides providing provender and stabling innkeepers also collected and delivered goods on behalf of the carriers.

If Tudor inns were rated according to the facilities they provided then the Crowne Inne in Upton-upon-Severn might have barely merited a single star. To compare it with 'three star' accommodation of that time we have to look to another Worcestershire innkeeper, Nicholas Deckles, an 'inholder' of the city of Worcester, who died in 1590 at the age of forty-one. The inventory of his worldly goods provides an insight into the furnishings of an inn in a sixteenth century provincial city. Deckles' hostelry was not exceptionally large, offering just six bedchambers, two of which were provided with window glass. In the sixteenth century glass was an expensive item only affordable by the nobility, gentry and the more affluent merchants. The furnishings appear to be relatively luxurious, the chambers hung with 'painted clothes' and the beds provided with testers and curtains. The 'great chamber on forestreet' contained 'ij standinge bedsteedes of wainscott with testernes to the same, unto one of them five Curtains of redd and greene saye, ij fetherbeddes and ij flockbeddes'. Some of the beds were 'matted and corded'[61] and provided with 'coverlyddes of arras worke lyned with canvas'. Arras was an expensive fabric, used in tapestries and wall hangings often found in the houses of the nobility.

The manufacture of mattresses, bedding and cushions was regulated by statute. In 1495, to counter the problems of 'deceitful' practices by upholsterers using unsuitable materials, an Act was passed: *What Stuff upholsters shall put in bolsters, feather-beds and pillows'* (11, Henry VII, c.19). Devious 'upholsters' had been using 'horse-hair, fen-down, neats-hair, deers-hair, and goats-hair, which is wrought in lime-fats[62], and by the heat of man's body the savour and taste is so abominable and contagious, that many of the King's subjects [have] thereby been destroyed'. This practice was forbidden and upholsterers were obliged to stuff feather-beds, bolsters and pillows with 'dry pulled feathers, or else with clean down', and quilts, mattresses, and cushions could only be filled with clean wool or clean flocks. Homemade articles were exempt from the statute provided they were not sold at fairs or markets. This was followed nearly sixty years later by a similar statute: *An act for stuffing of feather-beds, bolsters, mattresses and cushions,* (5 & 6 Edward VI, c. 23). Happily no record has been found of any of his majesty's subjects being destroyed by their bedding in Worcestershire.

---

61 matted and corded: the bedsteads had an arrangement of ropes across the frames with a mat to support the mattress – an improvement on beds with wooden slats.

62 vats.

In the list of contents of one room in Deckles' inn was a 'bread grater', a seemingly mundane article yet further investigation reveals that grated bread was a common ingredient in sixteenth century cuisine. The ubiquitous potato had yet to overwhelm the English diet and root vegetables such as carrots and turnips together with cereals were the source of carbohydrates. 'A Book of Cookrye', published in 1591 provides the mouth-watering delights that 'mine host' could provide for the hungry traveller:

Cony with a Pudding in his Belly:

'Take your Cony and fley him, & leave on the eares and wash it faire, and take grated Bread, sweete Suet minced fine, corance and some fine hearbs, Peneriall; winter savery; percely, Spinage or beets, sweet margeram, and chop your hearbs fine, and season it with Cloves, Mace and Sugar, a little creame and salt and yolks of Egs, and Dates minst fine. Then mingle all your stuf togither, and put it in your Rabets belly and sowe it up with a thred, for the broth take mutton broth when it is boyled a little, and put it in a pot wheras your Rabet may lye long waies in it, and let your broth boile or ever you put it in, then put in Gooceberies or els Grapes, corance and sweet Butter, Vergious, Salt, grated bread and Sugar a little, and when it is boyled, lay it in a dish with Sops. And so serve it in.'

Other items in Deckles' inventory suggest that even the more prosperous city innholders had secondary occupations or were employing artisans. In the 'olde kytchin' are listed a number of woodworking tools; in the stable are 'oken boards'; and in the 'Backside' are listed a number of objects normally associated with a wheelwright, 'spokes' and 'fallayes for wheels'. These could imply that Deckles was involved in the repair or manufacture of carts and agricultural articles, including ploughs, as the entry for 'vj thaves and throkes' would suggest. There is little doubt that Deckles had connections with the carrying trade and the construction and sale of carts would have complemented his innkeeping activities. The carriers were important to the cloth merchants of Worcestershire who relied upon them to distribute their merchandise, for cloth was almost exclusively transported by road.[63] In common with many city residents Deckles does not appear to be involved in husbandry apart from two sows kept in the back yard. In comparison with this splendid city inn the accommodation at the Crowne Inn at Upton-upon-Severn would have been barely adequate. There was no mention of window-glass or tester beds with hangings, or even painted clothes about the rooms. The chambers would have been mean, cold and draughty places, merely provided with shutters to the windows to keep out the elements.

John Hall's children were of full age when he died (his only son, Francis, was thirty-one years old) and under the terms of his will the inn remained in the

---

63   Dorian Gerhold, *Carriers and Coachmasters*, p.40.

possession of his wife Anne until her demise. In the sixteenth century it was expected that a husband should make some financial provision for his widow so that she did not become a liability upon the parish. He also had to provide for the possibility that his wife would remarry and the implications of the legal status of married women in early modern England. At that time 'By marriage, the husband and wife are one person in law; that is, the very being or legal existence of the woman is suspended during the marriage, or at least is incorporated and consolidated into that of the husband; under whose wing, protection and cover, she performs everything; and is therefore called in our law-french a *feme-covert* …'.[64] If Anne Hall were to remarry then once the matrimonial knot was tied all her household items, personal possessions, money and property would have come under the control of her new husband. Everything she owned would become his and all legal transactions were done in his name. (The status of married women remained thus until the Married Women's Property Act of 1882). Consequently, the prime intent of John Hall's will was to ensure that the inheritance of the inn and the other freehold property eventually came to his male heirs. In effect, this created a 'fee tail'. (The agricultural land referred to in the inventory would most likely have been copyhold tenure held according to the custom of the manor.)

The will also specified bequests amounting to more than £34 to be paid to eight grandchildren when they came of age. The four children of John Hall's sister, Joan Jones, were each bequeathed forty nobles (£13 6s 8d), to be paid when they too came of age. In anticipation of the prospect of his wife's remarriage John Hall gave his grandchildren the option of claiming their inheritances '*att the daie of the marriage of the said Ann my wife*'. The bequests in the will amounted to more than the total of his movable goods listed in his inventory which would suggest that income was arising from other sources. Other wills of this period show instances of land or property being reserved for the specific purpose of providing bequests for young children when they married or came of age.

In the above 'last will and testament' the word 'testament' refers to the deceased's personal effects whereas the 'will' devises the property and land. It is important to note that John Hall did not sign the document and the significance of the words '*I have here putt my Seale.....*' at the end of the will. A will relating to property or land empowered the devisee to gain instant access to the property once the will had been proved in the Probate Court. The use of a seal was particularly advisable in any will which devised property. This was because it was actually a deed or conveyance transferring the estate to a new owner and thus required a seal.[65] John Hall's seal was adequate testimony to authenticate the document and his signature was not deemed necessary. (Regrettably the seal has been detached from this will.) This document is, in effect, the earliest extant title deed for the Crowne Inn.

64   Sir William Blackstone, *Commentaries on the Laws of England* (1765-1769), Book 1, p.442.
65   Anne Tarver, *Church Court Records*, p.57.

2.

Aqua Vitae

AFTER the death of John Hall in 1591 the ownership of the property remained with his wife, Anne, who continued as innkeeper for another thirty years. Anne Hall never re-married and it is almost certain that her son, Francis, also lived in the inn with his wife and four young children. This would have been a family concern with three generations involved in the running of the hostelry. Francis Hall, who would have anticipated inheriting the property after his mother's demise, doubtless took charge of the husbandry and evidently was responsible for purchasing wine from the Bristol merchants; his name appears in the Upton parish registers as churchwarden and yet he would turn out to be something of a rogue. His two daughters, Elizabeth and Anne, spent many years living in the inn, presumably as serving maids waiting upon the travelling guests. Anne Hall had kept the inn throughout the final years of Tudor England.

This was a time when news was regularly circulated by word of mouth and it has been said that a usual greeting for travellers arriving at any alehouse or inn was 'What news?'. In early March of 1603 rumours were heard concerning the health of the ageing Queen Elizabeth and finally news arrived telling of her death on the 24th of that month. The age of the Tudors had come to an end. Soon, further reports arrived in Upton-upon-Severn declaring that James, the first of the Stuart monarchs, had succeeded to the throne.

The new reign saw the introduction of new Acts onto the statute book concerning the degenerate condition of many inns and alehouses, the first being in 1603, '*An Act to restrain the inordinate Haunting and tipling in Inns, Alehouses and other Victualling-houses*' (1 James I c.9):

> 'WHEREAS the ancient and true principal use of Inns, Alehouses and Victualling-houses was for the receipt, relief and lodging of wayfaring people travelling from place to place, and for such supply of the wants of such people as are not able by greater quantities to make their provision of victuals, and

not meant for the entertainment and harbouring of lewd and idle people to spend and consume their money and their time in lewd and drunken manner.'

This was followed within a few years by '*An Act to restrayne the Utterance of Beer and Ale to Alehouse Keepers and Tipplers not licensed*' (4 James I c.4), and in 1607 '*An Act for repressing the odious and loathsome Sin of Drunkenness*' (4 James I c.5) came on to the statute book:

> 'WHEREAS the odious and loathsome sin of drunkennes is of late grown into common use within this real me, being the root and foundation of many other enormous sins, as bloodshed stabbinge murder swearinge fornication adultery and such like, to the great dishonour of God and of our nation, the overthrow of many good arts and manual trades, the disabling of divers workmen and the general impoverishing of many good subjects, abusively wasting the good creatures of God.'

Any person convicted of drunkenness must 'for every such offence forfeit and lose five shillings of lawful money of England… and if the offender be not able to pay the said sum of five shillings, then the offender shall be committed to the stocks, there to remain for the space of six hours'.

William Harrison commented most graphically on the subject of drunkenness: 'I know some aleknights so much addicted thereunto, that they will not cease from morow until even to visit the same, cleansing house after house, till they defile themselves and either fall quite under the boord, or else not daring to stir from their stools, sit pinking[66] with their narrow eyes halfe sleeping till the fume of their adversary be digested that he may go to it afresh'. On the same page he referred to the dubious practice of adulterating beer with salt: 'As for the force of the salt, it is well known by the effect, for the more the drinker tipleth, the more he may, and so dooth he carrie a drie drunken noll[67] to bed with him, except his lucke be better'.[68] Worcestershire was not without its own aleknights as an entry in the Upton parish register revealed:

> 'John Gravell of Busheley died sodenly, as some suppose with taking over much drinke and was buried the third daie of February Anno Predicto [1586]'.

(It is not clear whether the rector is describing the speed of his demise or the depth of his intoxication.)

---

66   blinking.

67   soul.

68   William Harrison, *The Description of England.* (1877), pp.160-161.

Whilst the legislation was perhaps directed towards the more infamous alehouses some inns of this period had very dubious reputations indeed. Even in fifteenth century Canterbury, which attracted large numbers of pilgrims to the shrine of Thomas Becket, Katherine Borach was providing more earthly pleasures and keeping a common brothel with assistance from the innholder of the Rose and his wife.[69] But such activities were more commonly associated with the alehouse as was told by the presentment of the constable of Whistones near Worcester:

> 2 October 1637. Presentment by Marmaduke West, Constable of Whistones, that "Henry Meeke sells ale without licence and sells with pots that are not full measure contrary to the Statute. John Ashbie sells ale and beer with potts that are less than full measure. The said John Ashbie keeps a lewd woman in his house called by the name of Elizabeth Hodges and suffers divers lewd persons to keep the said Elizabeth company in the night time and also suffers the said Elizabeth to be unlawfully begotten with child in his house and upon his own bed where he did usually lie and his wife put her apron before the window to shadow them which the said Elizabeth and others of the said Ashbie's tenants hath divers times confessed being then present in his house and his resetting of her hath been a great charge to the tything".[70]

In seventeenth century England gold and silver coin was the currency of business and the banking system was yet to be established. The use of cheques was not introduced until 1659 and large sums of money were often carried in the ordinary way of business. The innkeeper would welcome the way-worn traveller but, as Trevelyan has observed, 'alas, the willing servants and the jolly host himself are often in league with highwaymen'. The servants of the inn, running to attend the new arrival, would handle every article of baggage, gauging that the heavier the bag, the more likely it was to contain coin. Showing an interest in his journey they would learn his route and pass on the information to their accomplices waiting outside. 'The inn keeps its good name, for no robbery is done within its walls; the thieves spring out from a thicket some miles off upon the road'.[71] One such Worcestershire inn was the *Rose and Crown* on the Lickey Hills near Bromsgrove. The landlord, William Manley, was involved with a notorious gang of highwaymen but eventually his nefarious activities were exposed and he was subsequently tried and executed at Stafford in 1732.[72]

Such unscrupulous innkeepers were, perhaps, more in the minority. Fynes Moryson, the son of a Lincolnshire gentleman, travelled around many European

69   Canterbury Cathedral Archives, CC/JQ/237/3.

70   J. W. Willis Bund, *Calendar of the Quarter Sessions Papers,* p.647.

71   George M. Trevelyan, *English Social History* (1946). p.161.

72   Alan Everitt, *Landscape and Community in England – The English Urban Inn*, p.200.

countries from 1591 to 1595, sampling the facilities of various inns. Moryson's comments about the English innkeeper were rather more complimentary:

'.... the World affoords not such Innes as England hath, either for good and cheape entertainement after the Guests owne pleasure, or for humble attendance on passengers, yea, even in very poore Villages, where if Curculio of Plautus, should see the thatched houses, he would fall into a fainting of his spirits, but if he should smell the variety of meates, his starveling looke would be much cheared: For as soone as a passenger comes to an Inne, the servants run to him, and one takes his Horse and walkes him till he be cold, then rubs him, and gives him meate, yet I must say that they are not much to be trusted in this last point, without the eye of the Master or his Servant, to oversee them. Another servant gives the passenger his private chamber, and kindles his fier, the third puls of his bootes, and makes them cleane. Then the Host or Hostesse visits him, and if he will eate with the Host, or at a common Table with others, his meale will cost him six pence, or in some places but foure pence, (yet this course is lesse honourable, and not used by Gentlemen): but if he will eate in his chamber, he commands what meate he will according to his appetite, and as much as he thinkes fit for him and his company, yea, the kitchin is open to him, to command the meat to be dressed as he best likes; and when he sits at Table, the Host or Hostesse will accompany him, or if they have many Guests, will at least visit him, taking it for curtesie to be bid sit downe: while he eates, if he have company especially, he shall be offred musicke, which he may freely take or refuse, and if he be solitary, the Musitians will give him the good day with musicke in the morning. It is the custome and no way disgracefull to set up part of supper for his breakefast: In the evening or in the morning after breakefast, (for the common sort use not to dine, but ride from breakefast to supper time, yet comming early to the Inne for better resting of their Horses) he shall have a reckoning in writing, and if it seeme unreasonable, the Host will satisfie him, either for the due price, or by abating part, especially if the servant deceive him in any way. ... ... a Man cannot more freely command at home in his owne House, then hee may doe in his Inne, and at parting if he give some few pence to the Chamberlin & Ostler, they wish him a happy journey.' [73]

There is no suggestion of any disreputable activities in the Crown Inn and Anne Hall doubtless kept a more orderly house that should have contented Fynes Moryson.

During the sixteenth and seventeenth centuries many inns were built or rebuilt and some very splendid buildings survive to this day. Whilst many of these inns were no larger than village 'public houses', those located in the great coaching towns were notable for their size and splendour. In early surveys, buildings were often recorded

---

73   Fynes Moryson, *The Itinerary of Fynes Moryson*, Vol IV, (1908), pp.174 -175.

as being of so many 'bays' (a 'bay' was the distance between two sets of principle posts that made up the structure, between fifteen and twenty feet in width). The Rose and Crown in seventeenth century Northampton was thirteen bays in width and three storeys high whilst in other towns inns could be found extending to over twenty bays in width.[74] The Crown Inn in Upton was very much at the lower end of this scale – extending to about three bays in width and two stories high with stabling at the rear for a few horses. Clark describes three categories of inn that had developed by the eighteenth century: the 'splendid 'county' inns – often in the heart of a town and catering for the landed aristocracy and the like; secondary inns, also large, but marginally less exclusive and serving the urban élite as well as the gentry; and market or carrier inns, the most numerous group, somewhat smaller and closely involved in inland trade'.[75] Upton-upon-Severn was essentially a place of trade; a small town at a crossing point of roads and river and it is to the third category of inn that the Crown would have belonged.

Some inns incorporated a gallery overlooking the courtyard where guests could watch the performances of travelling players. These entertainers were sometimes sponsored by the innkeeper. Whilst the Crown may not have been so sophisticated in design it is known that travelling performers did visit the town in the early seventeenth century. In 1630 John Jones, a labourer of Bedwardine, was indicted for performing at Upton-upon-Severn 'under a so called licence from Sir Henry Herbert, Master of the Revells'. The licence, which 'authorisedd Jones, his wife, Richard Payne, Richard Jones and their assistants to set forth divers feats and to pass with their show through all towns, cities and boroughs within the realm of England, they behaving themselves honestly and not exhibiting on the Sabbath day', was purported to be 'false and counterfeit'. Jones had either procured or forged the licence. (From the Tudor period onwards 'no one could legally hold any show or play or exhibit any athletic sports, such as tumbling, vaulting, sleight-of-hand and other such like feats of activity, without a licence from the Master of the Revels, who, by the King's Commission under the Great Seal, was authorisedd to grant such licences; all unlicensed shows were to be put down'.)[76] In a similar vein John Haye of Anserwick, a labourer, was indicted for 'allowing unlawful games to wit dancing in his house during Divine service and for lodging persons of ill fame'.[77]

Inns have been the subject of surveys for military and monetary purposes on at least two occasions. The earliest of these was a detailed survey of Alehouses, Taverns and Inns of July 1577 when the Privy Council directed local justices to inquire as to the numbers of victualling houses in every shire, together with the names of their occupiers. As it would appear from a letter sent by the Privy Council, the primary

---

74 Alan Everett, *Landscape and Community in England – The English Urban Inn*, p.165.

75 Clark, *The English Alehouse*, p.7.

76 J. W. Willis Bund *Calendar of the Quarter Sessions Papers*, p.lxxxvi and p.470.

77 Ibid. p.101.

objective of this survey was purely fiscal: 'Whereas the Queen's Majesty, finding the havens of the realm, situate on the narrow seas, barred and as yet altogether decayed, ...' and '... the port of Dover, where the haven is in such utter decay that without some large contribution, the money requisite to make it a fit harbour for Her Majesty's ships cannot be levied, Her Majesty hath willed us to think on some method of levying a convenient sum ... we find, after long consideration, no better means than some small fine to set by way of license upon all alehouses, inns and taverns throughout the realm.'[78] Although the returns of this survey are incomplete they do give some indication of the numbers of victualling houses. There were more than 15,000 alehouses, 2,161 inns but only 339 taverns out of a total of 17,595 drinking houses listed in thirty of the English counties surveyed. The figures for Worcestershire were included in a separate survey that was instigated in the same year of 1577 by the Council in the Marches of Wales. Worcestershire was the only English county to provide a return to the Council in the Marches but the county magistrates did not provide a breakdown of the individual figures, only a total of 447 drinking houses. This possibly infers a figure of about thirty inns within the county, a number comparable with the neighbouring county of Warwickshire which had twenty-nine inns. A later survey of 1686 did provide figures for Upton-upon-Severn – the accommodation in the town then comprised twelve guest beds and stabling for nine horses. The comparative figures for Ledbury were forty-three beds and stabling for thirty-five horses whilst the city of Worcester could provide 271 guest beds with stabling for 350 horses. The twelve beds listed for Upton-upon-Severn would have included the other inn in the High Street and possibly some alehouses.[79]

Anne Hall was about eighty years of age when she died in December of 1622. The inventory of her goods and chattels gives a more detailed insight into the contents and furnishings of this small Worcestershire inn at the beginning of the seventeenth century. The building has changed considerably over the past four hundred years but the individual rooms listed in the inventory can be used to establish a probable arrangement of the building in 1622. It would have been of timber-frame construction with a wattle and daub infill to the panels, typical of the many 'black and white' buildings still to be found in Worcestershire, but certainly not painted black and white. The origins of the building are possibly medieval although 'improvements' have left only vestiges of the original structure. There is still evidence of a timber-frame underlying later construction; some timbers remain embedded in later brickwork on the ground floor, and above the sales area the first floor still has timbers in the characteristic style of that period. It would certainly have been similar to other vernacular buildings from the Tudor period and constructed in an L-shape. Many surviving Tudor buildings adopted this

---

78   Ralph Fenley, *The Register Of The Council In The Marches Of Wales 1569-1591*, (Letter from the Privy Council 20th July 1577), p.168.

79   TNA WO 30/48, *Inns and Alehouses: Return of Accommodation for Men and Horses.*

arrangement with two possible variations: either a range of rooms of two or three stories, possibly containing a shop or workshop, fronting onto the street with the hall, kitchen and domestic rooms running down the plot, or alternatively with the hall running parallel to the street and another range of rooms at right angles. It is probable that the Crown Inn adopted the second arrangement thereby providing its patrons with the benefit of a large hall opening on to the High Street (the hall was a large room with a hearth and chimney where food and drink were served). The inns were basically of two groups, the 'courtyard' and the 'gatehouse'. The latter had a central gateway giving access to the rear of often extensive buildings, the courtyard type followed the plan of many town houses of the period with a side access to stables at the rear of the building.

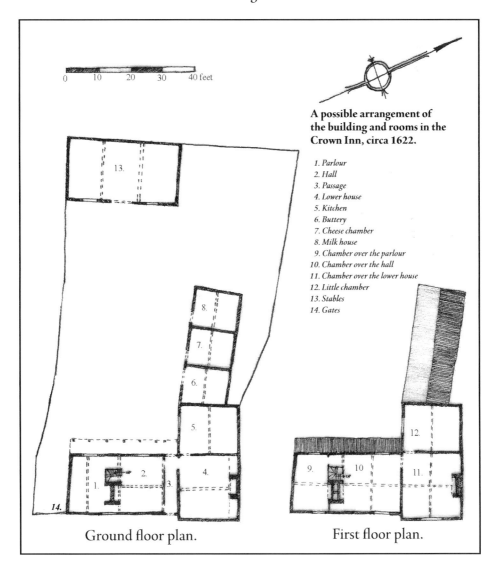

A possible arrangement of the building and rooms in the Crown Inn, circa 1622.

1. Parlour
2. Hall
3. Passage
4. Lower house
5. Kitchen
6. Buttery
7. Cheese chamber
8. Milk house
9. Chamber over the parlour
10. Chamber over the hall
11. Chamber over the lower house
12. Little chamber
13. Stables
14. Gates

Ground floor plan.

First floor plan.

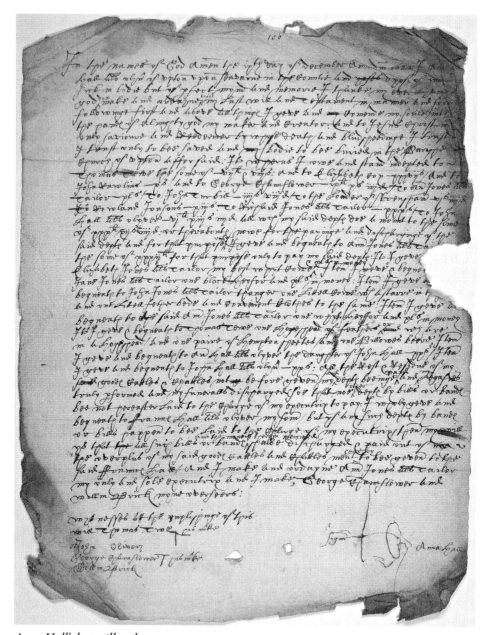

Anne Hall's last will and testament.

Transcription of the last will and testament of Anne Hall alias Oliver – 9th December 1622

In the name of God Amen the ixth day of december Anno d*omi*ni 1622 I Anne
Hall al*ias* Olyv*er* of Upton upon Seaverne in the Countie and dyo*c*ese of Worce*ster*
sick in bodie but of p*er*fect mynd and memorie I thanke my ever lyving

god doe make and ordayne this my last will and Testament in manner and forme
followinge first and above all things I geve and Comende my soule into
the hands of Almighty god my maker and Creator and to Jesus Christ my
only savioure and Reedeemer by whose death and blud sheeding I trust
I trust (sic) only to bee saved and my bodie to bee buried in the Parishe
Church of Upton afforsaid: Item wheras I owe and stand indepted to ~
Thomas Tewe the some of vij^li viij^s: And to Elizabeth Cox xxxvij^s And to
John Rawlins x^s And to George Chamflower ix^li x^s iiij^d To Anne Jones alias
Tailor xl^s To John Turbill iiij^s viij^d To the Loader of Strensham xj^s iiij^d
To Rowland Jonsons xiij^s To Richard Jones alias Tailor xxx^s To John
Hall alias Olyver vj^li xiij^s iiij^d all which my said depts doe a mount to the some
of xxx^li xij^s viij^d or therabouts nowe for the payinge and discharginge of the
said debts and for that purpose only I geve and bequeath to Anne Jones alias Ta[ilor]
the some of xxxij^li for that purpose only to pay my said depts. Item I geve [& bequeath to]
Elizabeth Jones alias Tailor my best whyt Cowe & xl^s in money. Item I geve & beque[ath to]
Jane Jones alias Tailor one black heyfor and xl^s in money. Item I gave [and]
bequeath to John Jones alias Tailor the yonger one littell Cowe with a starre in ....
and one littell fether bede and Convenient Clothes to the same. Item I give a[nd]
bequeath to the said Anne Jones alias Tailor one whyte heyffor and xl^s in money
Item I gave and bequeath to Thomas Tewe one hogeshead of feathers or which are
in a hogshead and one paire of hempton sheetes and one Pillowes beere Item
I geve and bequeath to Anne Hall alias Olyver the daughter of John Hall xx^s Item
I geve and bequeath to John Hall alias Olyver xx^s: All the Rest & Residue of my
~~said~~ goods Cattles & Chattles not before geven my said depts beeinge paid and my legasies
truly performed and my funeralls discharged soe that noe other depts by bills or bands[80]
bee not hereafter laid to the Charge of my executrix to pay: I wholygeve and
bequeath to Frances Hall alias Olyver my sonne but yf any such depts by bands
or bills happened to bee laid to the Charge of my executrix then my will
ys that all such bills or bands (and the monies therein mencioned) shalbe discharged & paid out of
the overplus of my said goods Cattles and Chattles ment (hereby) to bee geven to the
said Francis Hall And I make and ordayne Anne Jones alias Tailor
my only and sole executrix and I make, George Chamflower and
William Brick myne overseers:

Wyttnessed att the puplishinge (sic) of this   Signum X Anna Hall
Will: Thomas Tewe x his mark
John Oliver
George Chamflower x his mark
William Brick

(The right hand side of this document had suffered some damage but it was possible to
deduce most of the writing that was lost.)

---

80   A band was a legal document giving security for a debt.

Anne Hall's Inventory

A comparison with the earlier inventory of her husband dated 1591 suggests that under Anne Hall's tenure the inn had continued to prosper. There was a notable threefold increase in the value of the beds, bedcovers, linen goods, tables and all other household furniture (these items were valued at £31 15s 4d in Anne Hall's inventory compared with only £9 15s 7d in her husband's inventory). The inventory also listed the large number of nine 'table boards', most of which were of the more 'modern' form of the framed or 'joined' table which had appeared by the sixteenth century. The top of the table was fixed to a frame consisting of the legs, stretchers and top rails. Prior to this innovation tables were formed from wooden 'table boards' supported on trestles. Of all the rooms listed in Anne Hall's inventory the parlour appears to be the better furnished, providing 'one joynd bedsteade with a Testerne over & curtens' and ten 'cushins' which were once a luxury item but by the seventeenth century were becoming more commonplace. (The 'parlour' had it origins in medieval houses, the root of the word *parlour* is the Old French *parleur* 'to speak'. The parlour was a smaller room used for private conversation and 'functioned as a more intimate version of the open hall'. In the later sixteenth century the parlour became a ground floor bed-chamber but by the end of the seventeenth century it had assumed its more modern form, a room with tables, chairs and other furniture.)[81] There was also an improvement in the bedchambers, the bedding being more comfortable with most of the rooms enjoying the more expensive feather beds. Two of the rooms had truckle beds that were stored under the 'joyned' bedsteads when not in use. In his diaries, Samuel Pepys wrote about truckle beds which were used on occasions to accommodate his servants. One such occurrence was in 1668 when Pepys and his wife were journeying to the West Country: 'And there with great difficulty come about ten at night to a little inn, where we were fain [obliged] to go to a room where a pedlar was in bed, and made him rise; and there wife and I lay, and in a truckle-bed Betty Turner and Willett but good beds, and the master of the house a sober, understanding man...' (Deborah Willett was servant to Mrs Pepys.) The diary entry for the following morning read: 'Up, finding our beds good but lousy, which made us merry.'[82]

---

81 Kowaleski and Goldberg: *Medieval Domesticity,* n. p.137.
82 Samuel Pepys Diary 11th & 12th June 1668.

Inventory of Anne Hall's Goods and Chattels, 1622.

A true & Lawfull Inventory Indented
& made the xvth day of December
Anno Domini 1622 of all the goodes
Cattles and Chattles of Anne Hall
alias Olyver Late of Upton upon
Seavarne wydowe deceased taken
and appraised by and before
Francis Hall alias Olyver, Robert
Richards George Chamber : Thomas
Tewe: William Brick

Imprimis in the Hall one table bord & Tressells & one Joynd forme	iiij^s
Item one other Littell table & frame	iij^s
Item one Joynd Cubberd & a Littell table & one Chaire	viij^s
Item ij paire of Linkes j paire of Cobberns } ij paire of Pott hookes: ij fyershovels } ij gridirons j pare of Tonges j iron } Barr j iron plate j paire of bellowes } ij broches }	vij^s
Item in the parlor ij table bords ij } frames v formes one Cobberd } ij Chaires }	xxxiij^s iiij^d
Item x^{en} Cushins	viij^s
Item one Joynd bedsteede with a Testerne } over, one Feather bed iij blankettes } j Coverlett j boulster j pillowe & } one Truckelbed & Curtens }	iiij^{li}
Item in the Chamber over the lower howse ij bedsteeds one with Curtens } ij Featherbedes iij boulsters ij paire } of blankettes ij Coverlettes ij tablebordes } ij frames ij stooles ij formes }	vij^{li} iij^s iiij^d
Item in the Chamber over the Hall } j Joyned bedsteed j truclebed ij } Feather bedes j Table bord & frame } j boulster j forme iiij pillowes j } Coverlett }	iiij^{li} x^s
Item in the Littell Chamber j bedsteed } j flocbed & one Littell tabell bord }	xiij^s iiij^d
Item in the Chamber over the parlor } ij bedsteedes j featherbed j boulster } iij blanketes ij quiltes j Coverlett } v Coffers }	iij^{li}
Item one peece of newe flaxen Cloth	xij^s
Item in the Cheese Chamber xxxv^{tie} Cheeses	xxx^s
Item j Coffer & trumperie in the Cheese Chamber	x^s
Item in the milk howse butter and other thinges	xl^s
Item in the lower howse j table bord with a frame j bedsteede and other thinges	xxxj^s iiij^d
Item Pewter ^ 36 peeces	li^s iiij^d
Item one warminge pann	ij s

Item in the kychin Trumperie } other thinges }	xx^s
Item iiij brasse pottes iiij kettles iij } Chafingdishes j chaforne iij postnotes } ij skymers j brasse Candlestick. }	iij^{li} vj^s __ ^d
Item j limbeck	iijs iiij ^d
Item in the buttree Certen Implem^{ts}	xx^s
Item in the Sellor j hogge of bacon } metheglinge beere & other thinges }	iiij^{li} iiij^s
Item vij swyne	iij^{li}
Item ix table Clothes & vj towells	xxxv^s vj^d
Item vj Towells	ix^[s] viij^d
Item v pillowe beeres	vij^s
Item ix flaxen sheetes	xlvj^s
Item xij hempton sheetes	xlviij^s
Item x hurden sheetes	xxx^s
Item xx^{tie} table napkinges	viij^s
Item wood	vj^s viij^d
Item for ladders dunge & other } thinges in the backsyde }	vj^s viij^d
Item Hay and strawe	iiij^{li}
Item iij kyne	vj^{li}
Item one lease for viij yeares	xx^s
Item one furnis	vj^s viij^d
Item j paire of potthookes and one } drippinge pann }	ij^s
Item lynen yarn	vij^s
Item Corne on the grownde	xxiij^s iiij^d
Item her wearinge apparell	iij^{li}

Summe ys 60^{li} 16^s 9^d [£60 16s 9d]
which the
deptes owinge owede

Imprimis to Thomas Tewe	vij^{li} viij^s
Item to Elizabeth Cox	xxxvij^s
Item to John Rawlins	x^s
Item to George Charmflower	ix^{li} x^s
Item Ann Jones	xl^s
Item to John Turbill	iiij^s viiij^d
Item to the Loader of Strensham	vj^s iiij^d
Item to Rowland Jonsons	xiij^s
Item to Richard Jones	xxx^s
Item to John Hall	vj^{li} xiij^s iiij^d
Item for Rent	xx^s
Item the funerall expences	xl^s
Item geven to the poore	xx^s
Item to William Brick for scole wages	ij^s vj^d

Summe ys xxxiiij^{li} xv^s ij^d xviij^s xiij^d
Exhibitum Wigorn 30
December 1622 per Anna
Jones alias Taylor executirix
Examinatur

The only items of food appraised were thirty-five cheeses, one hogge of bacon, and butter. Wine was not mentioned yet there is evidence from the 1571 indenture and from a later Quarter Sessions presentment of 1634 that wine was being sold in the inn. The only beverage mentioned is a quantity of metheglin beer in the cellar. (Metheglin was a spiced or medicated variety of mead, said to have originated in Wales.) Whilst inns were noted for supplying wine they also supplied ale to their patrons. Many innkeepers at this time who brewed beer or ale sold any surplus to local alehouse-keepers. Anne Hall was almost certainly brewing beer as the '*furnis*' (furnace) valued at 6s 8d suggests. The 'furnis', a boiler or cauldron, probably set in brickwork, was used either for brewing ale or, with an alembic, for the distillation of spirits – see below. The presence of seven swine could also suggest that beer or ale was being brewed on the premises for in the seventeenth century it was quite usual for alehouse-keepers and other brewers of ale to keep a number of pigs which were fed on the spent mash from the brewing process. The production of malt and brewing of ale were significant activities in the local economy at this time and the excessive consumption of ale was the cause of some disquiet to central government. This was not solely because it resulted in drunkenness and disorder but, more importantly, because it resulted in a shortage of food. The authorities tried to control the production of malt, which was produced from barley, as this was the grain upon which people most depended for their bread. On his travels Fynes Moryson observed that many people lived on barley bread at this time: 'The English Husbandmen eate Barley and Rye browne bread, and preferre it to white bread as abiding longer in the stomack, and not so soone digested with their labour, but Citizens and Gentlemen eate most pure white bread, England yeelding (as I have said) all kinds of Corne in plenty'.[83] If the activities of the maltsters and brewers of ale were not curtailed then in those years when the harvest was poor there was a very great danger of insufficient grain for baking bread. Worcestershire Quarter Sessions Records contain letters from the Privy Council to the Justices of the Peace in the years 1625 and 1631 (when there appeared to be a considerable fear of famine) instructing the Justices to take 'all care to prevent any vain or unnecessary consumption of grain'. The Justices were particularly opposed to the sale of strong ales as these required much more malt to brew them.[84] The inventory also differentiated between various grades of sheets. The better quality flaxen sheets were priced at 5s 1d each, whilst the 'middling' hempen sheets were 4s each and the poorest quality hurden sheets were 3s each. (Hurden was a coarse fabric made from the hards of hemp or flax, the hards being the coarser fibres separated in the hackling or combing process in the production of flax). The travelling guests, seeking hospitality for the night, would have had the benefit of flaxen sheets, whilst hurden sheets sufficed the ostler and serving maids.

83   Fynes Moryson: *The Itinerary of Fynes Moryson,* Vol IV (1908), p.171.
84   J W Willis Bund, *Calendar of the Quarter Sessions Papers,* p.cv.

Artist's impression of the Crown Inn in the early seventeenth century.

The reference to the 'Loader of Strensham' in the list of Anne Hall's debts is obscure. The Oxford English Dictionary gives one definition of 'loader' as a 'carrier' (an obsolete or dialect word). William Harrison in his *Description of England* refers to 'loders and common carriers' and gives a definition of 'loders' as equivalent to 'laders'- i.e. those who freight ships. With the proximity of the River Avon the 'Loader of Strensham' could equally refer to a carrier of goods by road or a lader of the vessels which plied the river system down to Gloucester and Bristol. It is quite possible that this points to the inn having some connection with the carrying trade. The debt of two shillings and sixpence owing to William Brick for 'scole wage' is probably nothing to do with a school, it is more likely to be a re-imbursement for him drawing up the will and inventory. William Brick was without doubt one of the few people in Upton-upon-Severn sufficiently literate to be able to write out wills and inventories – his name appears as witness to other local wills of this period.

One particularly notable item in the inventory is the 'limbeck' – an alembic or still was used for the preparation of spirits such as aqua vitae or aqua composita; the 'furnis' could have been used for heating the still. By the late sixteenth century the distillation of these spirits, often for medicinal purposes or cooking, was well established in England. The fashion for drinking spirits is said to have been attributed to Elizabethan soldiers billeted in the Low Countries who had acquired a taste for 'Hollands' or gin. By 1572 a victualling establishment called the 'Aqua Vitae House' had been opened in Barking (Essex) and by the beginning of the seventeenth century spirits were widely available.[85] Stills appear in other local probate inventories of this period: they include that of Hugh Robinson, a brewer of Worcester, who died in 1608 and Alice Jarrett, innholder of Warwick, who died in the same year. For these individuals the production of spirits would have been a secondary activity. There is one instance of a distiller in Worcestershire, a John Gyles of Worcester who died in 1611.[86] The contents of his 'Still House' and cellar suggests that Gyles was trading strong liquor in an extensive way:

The Ale and all other licour there to distill		iij^{li}
One great Tubbe, Tenne other vessells	}	
and some other small implements there	}	xx^s
Twoe ffurnaces and the pypes thereto	}	
belonging	}	xx^s

His tavern (here referring to the cellar) contained barrels and about seven gallons of aqua vitae. Spirits were by this date being distilled on a larger scale, especially in London; substantial quantities were exported to the American colonies, spirits travelling better than beer on the long voyage across the Atlantic. The distillation

---

85   Clark, p.95.
86   Alan D. Dyer, *The City of Worcester in the Sixteenth Century*, p.140.

process was relatively crude and unsophisticated, using rudimentary equipment and home made liquor, or the dregs of ale or beer, which produced spirits that were 'notoriously rough'.

The property next door to the Crown Inn (on the south side) was occupied by Thomas Goodyer, a yeoman, who died in 1641 (earlier entries in the Quarter Sessions records show that he was previously a tailor by trade). The probate inventory of his worldly goods listed 'the brass and a still in the kitchen' valued at £6 13s 4d and 'distilled waters in ye hall'. The last item refers to spirits which appear to have been produced from fermented malt liquor. The only other items in Goodyer's inventory suggesting any occupation or trade were barley, malt, a malt mill and 'iij great fates' (three large vats). The relatively high value (£3 6s 8d) of table boards, stools, formes and chairs may well suggest that Goodyer was running an 'aqua vitae' house and retailing spirits (a higher than average number of tables and chairs were to be found in drinking establishments). Some years earlier in 1611 Thomas Goodyer was recorded as being the 'Bailiff of the Town of Upton'. The lords of Upton-upon-Severn were then the Bromleys whose Worcestershire seat was at Holt Castle, north of Worcester, and they would have appointed officers to oversee the running of their manor. The steward and the bailiff had divers duties which included holding the manorial courts, administering local justice and managing the lords estate. The town bailiff, an important local official, was responsible for collecting rents on the four quarter days, collecting fines and keeping accounts. Perhaps he was not the most popular person in the community for in 1611 Francis Olyver and Thomas Olyver, both of Upton-on-Severn, were indicted for assaulting their neighbour, Thomas Goodyer. (The indictment was annotated 'A true Bill'.)

One particular bequest in Thomas Goodyer's will was quite remarkable, for he left only two shillings and six pence to each of his four daughters. He explained 'the reason why I make them no larger bequest is for that God hath dealt mercifully and liberally towards them in the things of this life so that they stand in no need of my poore helpe'. Thomas Goodyer must have had four most eligible daughters, two of whom had married clergymen. Jane Goodyer married a 'Mr Timothy Rogers, clerk' and Margaret married a 'Mr Nehemiah Rogers, clerk' ('clerk' here denotes 'cleric'). There are only two clerics with these names listed in the Church of England Database at this time, Timothy and Nehemiah Rogers, two of the sons of Vincent Rogers, rector of Stratford-le-Bow in Middlesex. Vincent Rogers was said to be the probable grandson of John Rogers, the compiler of the first authorised English bible, a pioneer of the English reformation and a protestant martyr whose religious inclinations were not to the liking of Mary Tudor. He was burnt at the stake at Smithfield on the 4th February 1555. Timothy Rogers was a protestant clergyman of some repute who had published several theological works. These included '*The Righteous Man's Evidence for Heaven, Or, a Treatise Shewing how Every One, While He Lives Here, May Certainly Know what Shall Become of Him After His Departure*

Out of this Life. This work proved to be very popular. [87] Nehemiah was a more celebrated clergyman than his elder brother. He was a friend of the renowned William Laud, Archbishop of Canterbury, whose religious policies were opposed by the puritans and who was executed in 1645. Nehemiah Rogers was described as an 'uncompromising royalist' and was the author of numerous theological works. The inevitable question arises as to how the daughters of the bailiff in a small Worcestershire town came to marry such relatively distinguished clerics from distant Middlesex. The answer is to be found with Anne, Lady Bromley of Holt Castle in Worcestershire, the fourth wife of Sir Henry Bromley. Sir Henry had purchased the manor of Upton-upon-Severn in 1593. Lady Anne had contributed to the funding of Timothy Rogers' education, first at the Merchant Taylors' School and then Emmanuel College, Cambridge where he graduated with a BA in 1608. When Timothy Rogers wrote '*Good Newes from Heaven*' in 1627 the book was dedicated to 'The Right Worshipfull and vertuous Ladies, the Lady Anne Bromley of Holt in Worcestershire; and Lady Marie Eden of Bollidon Hall in Essex'. He described his patron, Lady Anne, as 'a bountifull friend unto me in time of my minoritie, and all the while I was at the Universitie many years together'. Henry Bromley's fourth wife was Mrs Anne Offley née Beswick, the widow of William Offley 'merchant of the staple and citizen of London'.[88] The connection may lie with the Offley family who were related to a David Rogers, a wealthy grocer of London, who died in 1582. Lady Anne would certainly have been acquainted with the daughters of her husband's bailiff and presumably had acted as intermediary in pre-marital arrangements. Nehemiah's second son, John Rogers, (he being Thomas Goodyer's grandson) had differing religious views to his father who subsequently turned him out of his house. John Rogers was a troublesome cleric who preached violent political sermons in support of the Long Parliament. Eventually he was imprisoned for his sermons denouncing Oliver Cromwell.

Of Thomas Goodyer's other daughters, Joane married Francis Burford, son of Charles Burford of Little Malvern. There is a feoffment dated 1618 from Charles Burford and his wife Margery of 'a messuage called Bruars, land and appurtenances in Littell Malvarne, being a settlement upon the marriage of the said Fraunces and Johan'. One of the witnesses to this document was another cleric, James Burford, rector of Earls Croome and minister of Little Malvern. For three of these daughters the waters of life took a troubled course and, considering his earlier pronouncement,

---

87 See Oxford Dictionary of National Biography – Timothy Rogers (1589 -1650) and Nehemiah Rogers (1593-1660). Some biographies appear to be in error, giving Nehemiah Rogers' wife as Margaret, sister of William Collingwood, canon of St. Paul's. Jane Rogers (née Goodyer) died sometime between 1630 when her father wrote his will and 1641 when the will was proved. A Jane Rogers was buried on 13th July 1639 in All Saints church in Sudbury, Suffolk. In 1636 Timothy Rogers had been appointed to the vicarage of this same church.

88 Some biographies are in error giving Anne Beswick as Bromley's third wife – see Nash, *Collections for the history of Worcerstershire*, Vol. 1, p.595.

it is ironic that when Thomas Goodyer's will was proved in 1641 Jane, Margaret and Joane, were all deceased. The fourth daughter, Ellinor, married a John Wyn (possibly also of Little Malvern).

After a long life as an innkeeper Anne Hall was laid to rest in the parish church at Upton on the 15th December 1622, most probably buried alongside her late husband John Hall. The ownership of the inn then came to her son Francis. He was sixty-two years of age when he finally received his inheritance and became innholder in his own right, yet his tenure of the inn would last scarcely three weeks.

3.

A Cause in Chancery

ACCORDING to the terms of the will of John Hall the elder it was directed that following the death of his wife, Anne, the inheritance of the inn was, at first, restricted to his legitimate heirs in the male line. His only son Francis was next in line to inherit followed, in turn, by his three grandsons Francis, John and Thomas Hall. The 'younger' Francis Hall was born in 1584 and his brother John in 1587. Anne Hall's granddaughters were found employment in the Crown Inn and several of her grandsons became cordwainers (shoemakers). Francis Hall alias Oliver the younger and his brother John are most probably those persons indicted at the Quarter Sessions in 1611 together with their cousin William:

> Indictment of William Jones alias Taylor of Upton on Severn, John Oliver and Francis Oliver of the same, Cordwainers for spoiling the grass in Richard Damanne's meadow at Defford. (Not a true Bill).

The endorsement 'Not a true Bill' denotes that the Grand Jury considered that no further proceedings should be taken on the matter and the court would have discharged the accused. The younger John Hall had previously been brought before the justices at the Quarter Sessions – the record for 25th September 1603 mentions 'John Halle alias Oliver, yeoman, for keeping his peace towards Edwarde Kinge'.

As a younger son, John Hall must have been resigned to the injustices of primogeniture and so did not anticipate any significant inheritance from his father, however within the space of three years events had dramatically changed this prospect. His elder brother, Francis, had pre-deceased his grandmother in 1619 and was 'likewise dead without issue of his body' at the age of only thirty-five. Consequently, in accordance with his grandfather's will, John was next in line to inherit the Crown Inn after the decease of his father. A terrible accident would soon befall the township of Upton-upon-Severn and in particular the Hall family.

Within the burials listed in the Upton parish register for January 1622 is to be found the following entry:

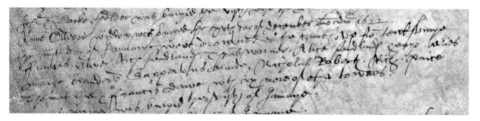

Anne Olliver widdow was buryed the xvth day of December An*no* D*omi*ni 1622
the iiijth day of January were drowned as they came up fro*m* Tewksburye
Francis Oliver Rich*ard* Sandlands Thomas Warner Alice Sandlands George
   Balies
Marye brandard Sapperton's maide Nicholas Roberts Rich*ard* Price
Thomas Hill & Francis Dawe with ix [9] more of other townes.

Many of these ill-fated people died without making any will and hence the Worcestershire probate records list several 'Grants of Administration' to the relatives of the deceased.

The elder Francis Oliver alias Hall (John Hall's father) had drowned in the River Severn with nineteen other people many of whom were inhabitants of Upton-upon-Severn. There is no record of any burials within the Upton registers, presumably their bodies were never recovered from the river Severn and were swept out into the Bristol Channel. This small group of people had been travelling on one of the many vessels that plied their trade along the river in the seventeenth century. As a consequence of this tragic event the younger John Hall unexpectedly came into possession of the Crown Inn.

A trow sailing towards Tewkesbury in the eighteenth century.

The Quarter Sessions records confirmed that John Hall alias Oliver was himself the innholder and had not installed a tenant. He was mentioned in the Sessions record for 18th March 1623: 'Recognizance by William Barnes of Upton upon Severn, woollen draper, John Durston of Upton upon Severn, innholder and John Hall alias Oliver, innholder for appearance of William Barnes'.[89] Innkeepers, being persons of some repute and wealth in the community, regularly appeared in the Sessions recognizances providing sureties for their neighbours who were summoned before the justices. John Durston was the innkeeper of the only other inn in Upton-upon-Severn at that time. It is possible that John Hall was also a merchant, selling wine by wholesale, for he was described as a 'vintner' in letters of administration granted to him in 1623 following the death of his younger brother Thomas.

The course of events suggests that John Hall preferred not to follow his father and grandfather into the victualling trade and wished to dispose of his new inheritance. However, he was not in possession of the title deeds relating to the property. These documents were in the hands of either John Kettleby, 'gentleman, Cittisen and merchant of London', or one Richard Griffiths of Bristol. A 'black box' containing the title deeds had at some time been pawned against a debt due to one of the antecedents of John Kettleby, and Richard Griffiths had been instructed to recover the debt on Kettleby's behalf. This lack of documentary evidence would have questioned the validity of John Hall's title to the inn and hindered his ability to transfer the title to another party.

John Hall had not only inherited the inn but had also acquired the problem of this long-standing debt. Evidently he was not prepared to settle with John Kettleby in order to reclaim the title deeds and so, in common with many other people of this period, he turned to the courts of law in an attempt to resolve the issue. In the early modern period, or even in medieval England, our predecessors were no strangers to litigation and were always ready to turn to the law to seek remedies for their grievances. At this time there was no shortage of attorneys for the law was often the career of choice for those younger sons who declined the option of a clerical vocation. Even as early as the thirteenth century legal advice was readily available both in the capital city and in many towns of England. There were numerous courts of law to which the litigant could turn to address his particular cause. On the civil side, courts ranged from the local manorial Court Baron dealing with minor issues to the higher courts of the King's Bench and the Court of Chancery. Parallel to this were the ecclesiastical courts dealing with their own range of cases under canon law. Whilst the sixteenth and seventeenth century litigant was ready to go to law he was equally prepared to discontinue the action if a satisfactory settlement was reached without the cause running its full course through the courts. In those proceedings commenced in the Court of Chancery the majority of cases failed to run to a final hearing and decree. It was not uncommon for a defendant in a case to commence a

89   WAAS 1/1/46/23.

suit in another court in order to attempt to limit, by injunction, the original action against him. Litigants were known to have pursued their cause through more than one court to gain some advantage over their adversary. William Powell, a Welsh vicar, being a somewhat extreme example from 1630, launched twenty-six suits in six years in seven law courts against one unfortunate parishioner. As far as has been ascertained the Crown Inn in Upton-upon-Severn only became involved with two of these courts, the Court of Chancery and the Court of Common Pleas.

The Court of Chancery

The Court of Chancery had its origins during the reign of Edward I and evolved into a separate court of law dealing with petitions addressed to the Lord Chancellor. By the beginning of the seventeenth century it was one of the principal courts dealing with a wide range of disputes; its jurisdiction covered England and Wales. It became a court of equity where plaintiffs could bring cases where they would have difficulty in securing a remedy under Common Law. The Court heard disputes concerning land and property, business, debts and bonds, inheritance and wills, trusts and marriage settlements, although the majority of suits concerned land and estates. Whereas the Common Law courts had strict rules and harsh penalties, Chancery had different procedures for resolving disputes. The Court of Chancery placed a threshold on the value or extent of property or land that came under its jurisdiction – a minimum of ten pounds in value, a yearly income of forty shillings or six acres in area. For property of value below these thresholds, litigants, often poorer men and women, had recourse to the Court of Requests which handled smaller claims. Complainants sometimes had other motives for bringing a suit in Chancery – namely blocking actions brought in other courts, as a means of compelling an opponent to disclose information under oath, or in collusive actions which often occurred where the trustees or administrators of a valuable or complicated estate were reluctant to proceed with the disposal without the formal decree of a Master in Chancery.

The Court of Chancery had its own set of procedures for conducting its business:

1. The First Stage was the **Pleadings:**
The case would be instigated by a written **Bill of Complaint** from the plaintiff (described in the bill as '**Your Orator**') addressed to the Lord Keeper of the Great Seal. A **Subpoena** could then be issued which ordered the defendant to appear before the court and to answer, under oath, the Bill of Complaint. The Chancery clerks would make a copy of the Bill of Complaint to be despatched to the defendant who would respond with a written **Answer**, sworn under oath (in the answer the defendant usually referred to the plaintiff as '**the complainant**').

There were alternative responses, such as the **Disclaimer**, the **Demurrer** and the **Plea** (the Plea was used to reject the Bill on some legal ground, e.g. that the case should be heard in another court of law). There could possibly be a further series of actions by either of the parties: a **Replication** or **Exception** by the Plaintiff, a **Rejoinder** by the defendant, a **Rebuttal** by the plaintiff and a **Sure-rebuttal** by the defendant. (In the case of the defendant these were often devices to delay the course of the action through the Court.)

If the proceedings had reached thus far through the court (although as noted above many did not follow the full course) then the case reached the next stages of the action:

2. The Second Stage: a possible **Injunction**:
If the plaintiff had asked for an **Injunction** in his original bill, or at a later date in the legal process, then the Court could proceed accordingly, and issue an injunction against the defendant.

3. The Third Stage was the **Proofs: Interrogatories, Depositions and Exhibits.** The Court of Chancery did not operate in a manner with which we are familiar today. The Court would direct a list of **Interrogatories** or questions to be drawn up and these questions would then be put to the witnesses. Each party produced their own witnesses but they could have questions put to the witnesses of the opposing side. The witnesses were placed under oath and examined in secrecy before the Examiners or Commissioners appointed by the court. Each witness simply answered (where he was able) the list of questions or interrogatories which were put to him (or her) and their **Depositions** (answers) were recorded in writing. Witnesses were not cross-examined by either party to the case. **Exhibits** were documents such as title deeds and other property documents, inventories or schedules and account books submitted to the court as evidence.

In the case of witnesses not residing within or near the city of London, the responsibility for taking testimony was delegated to commissioners, appointed under a *Writ of Dedimus Potestatem* ('we have given the power'), who often came from the particular locality involved. The depositions would be returned to the Court of Chancery in London where the case would continue its progress. Frequently, parties to the case died before there was a hearing in which case a **Bill of Revivor** became necessary to reinstate the cause. If the case still continued through the Court (and this could take many years) it would then proceed to a **Hearing**, a **Master's Report** and finally a **Decree**. The majority of suits instigated never proceeded to the stage of a hearing and some were dropped after the depositions had been taken and consequently no decree was issued. The Court of Chancery made its rulings or decrees based upon the statements made by the complainant, defendant and witnesses to the case and any documents that had been produced as supporting evidence. The author of the publication '*Family Feuds*' has commented that 'both the Bill and Answer seem utterly believable when you read them, and some fascination with Chancery Proceedings comes from the fact that you know that one party *must* be lying!'[90] (or at best being 'economical with the truth'). If a case in Chancery did not run its full course to a Master's Decree it is difficult to establish the truth; in those cases where there was only a Bill and corresponding Answer it is often impossible, without other evidence, to come to any conclusion – it is simply the word of the plaintiff against the defendant, both 'utterly believable'. If the case did proceed as far as the taking of depositions from witnesses it then becomes possible to perceive some truth emerging from the fog of testimony.

The three Chancery Cases which involved the Crown Inn in Upton-upon-Severn only went through a limited number of the legal processes outlined above. The earliest case of 1623 produced a Bill of Complaint from the plaintiff and an Answer from the defendant. The second case dated 1637 produced a Bill of Complaint and an Answer as well as two sets of Interrogatories with the associated Depositions from the witnesses for both of the parties to the dispute. (The appended memorandum to the earliest title deed (dated 1636) relating to this building refers to the third stage of the court process – the examination of the witnesses.) A third case dated 1720 produced a Bill and four Answers with Pleas. No other Chancery records concerning the building have yet come to light. Three occupants in the latter part of the seventeenth century became directly or indirectly involved with Chancery cases concerning other property and one occupant from the nineteenth century became involved in a long series of cases concerning a complicated inheritance.

The Court of Common Pleas

Some of the litigants involved with this property in Upton also resorted to the Court of Common Pleas. By the thirteenth century this court had become differentiated from the Curia Regis (The King's Court) and in 1272 it was granted its own Chief Justice. It was originally known as the Bench or 'Banco' and dealt primarily with civil litigation at common law. The records of this court are kept under division 'CP' of The National Archives and the most useful documents are the 'Final Concords'. These are the records of property lawsuits retained by the Court of Common Pleas, copies of which were kept by the parties to the suit.

The First Chancery Case: Hall alias Oliver v. Griffiths

Not long after John Hall had taken possession of his inheritance he instigated a cause in the Court of Chancery against Richard Griffiths in an attempt to recover

---

90   Susan T. Moore, *Family Feuds: An Introduction to Chancery Proceedings.* p.9.

the errant title deeds to the inn.[91] The preamble to the Bill of Complaint established that John Hall was in possession of an inn, 'knowne by the name of the Crowne' in Upton-upon-Severn. He stated that as his grandmother Anne, his father and his brother, Francis, were all deceased, then, as by right, the inheritance of the inn had come to him. The Bill continued to relate that by some means John Kettleby or Richard Griffiths had come into possession of the title deeds to the inn and John Hall was taking action through the Court to recover them. The sworn Answer from Richard Griffiths, dated 19th January 1623, divulged that one John Hopkins 'late of the City of Bristol, alderman' had died and his estate had passed first to his wife Elizabeth and then, in 1619, to his three grandsons, John, Charles and Thomas Kettleby. John Kettleby was executor of his grandmother's estate and had discovered amongst her papers a debt of thirty pounds that was still due from Anne Hall alias Oliver or from her son Francis:

> '...which debt was never paid to this defendant nor to any other to this defendants knowledge but still resteth unpaid, neither hath the said John Ketlebye any Remedy to Recover the said debt, but only by keeping the said writings in pawne as they were delivered to the said John Hopkins his said grandfather....'.

The title deeds to the inn had been surrendered to John Hopkins as some form of security and in August of 1622 John Kettleby had instructed Richard Griffiths, as his agent, to recover the outstanding debt. The precise circumstances of the debt were only revealed in the documents relating to a second Chancery case that commenced in 1637. No depositions from the 1623 case have come to light but, in the depositions relating to this later case of 1637/8, the witnesses stated that in about 1608 it was Francis Oliver alias Hall (the elder) who had run up a debt with his wine merchant, a Captain Hopkins. He was unable to settle his account and had pawned the title deeds to Hopkins. Elizabeth Sandlands of Holly Green (granddaughter of Anne Hall) in her deposition of 1638 stated that she 'doth believe it to be true that Francis the sonne of the said John Hall alias Ollyver after the death of the said John had gotten into his custody from the said Anne [Hall] the deeds of the said house made by one Francis Williams alias Baker unto the said John Hall alias Ollyver and pawned them to one Captayne Hopkins a merchant in Bristol for wynes...'. There was an air of subterfuge surrounding Francis Hall's actions. The witness statement suggested that his mother, Anne Hall, was not party to his actions and that by some devious means Francis had taken possession of 'a blacke boxe of wrytings' (the title deeds) and pawned them. Perhaps Francis Hall had

---

91 TNA C 2/JAS/H5/44. In the Complaint John Hall refers to the defendant as Richard Griffin. It is possible that Richard Griffiths also used an alias for there is a reference in Bristol Record Office, dated 1616, to *'Richard Griffith alias Griffin of Chepstowe, gent.,'* (BRO P/St.P and J/D/8(j)). A Richard Griffiths is mentioned in 1622 as secretary to the Company of Merchant Venturers.

been a little profligate with his purchases of wine from Bristol – the amount of the debt probably represented a quantity in excess of 250 gallons of wine (about 1500 modern 75cl. bottles). Francis Hall also owed money elsewhere. In 1605 he was mentioned as owing £3 13s 4d. and one acre of grass to David Morris of Upton. Richard Griffiths continued with his Answer and offered to deliver the writings (i.e. the deeds) into the Court: 'and therefore humbly offereth … … to deliver the said writings into this highe and honorable Courte of Chancery to bee delivered to whome the said Court shall award …'.

If we now turn back several months and reconsider the will of John Hall's grandmother, Anne Hall, the directions for the disposal of her estate assume a new significance. The instructions within the will provided for the implications of the actions of her son Francis. The will listed Anne Hall's debts and she provided thirty-two pounds specifically for her executrix to discharge the 'said debts and for that purpose only'. These debts were also itemised in her inventory and there was no mention of any outstanding amount due to John Hopkins. However, the will did make one further and final provision that if there were to be a claim on her estate as a result of any unsettled debt then it should be discharged and paid out of Francis Hall's share of the estate: 'but if any such depts by bande or bills happen to bee laid to the charge of my executrix then my will is that all such bills or bands and the monies therin mencioned shalbe discharged and paid out of the overplus of my said goods Cattles and Chattles ment hereby to bee geven to the said Francis Hall' (a 'band' was a document giving security for a debt). Obviously Anne Hall was not prepared to acknowledge the debt as her own responsibility but nevertheless she did have to make some provision in her will for the eventuality of any further claim against her estate.

Mrs Hall must have had some very choice words for her son when she discovered the box of 'writings' was missing and that he had pawned the title deeds to the Crown Inn. In the second Chancery Case of 1637 Anne Hall's granddaughter, Elizabeth Sandlands, disclosed that there had been a domestic dispute concerning the inheritance of the inn. Elizabeth deposed that she knew 'of speeches that have fallen out about who should have the said house or Inne after the decease of the said Anne her grandmother' and she further testified that she might have expected to inherit the inn herself: 'that the said Anne might give the same (i.e. the inn) to this deponent'.

Captain John Hopkins

Captain John Hopkins and his family deserve more than a passing mention. John Hopkins was a dignitary of considerable importance in the city of Bristol. He is recorded as being a colourful, larger than life character, a man of many talents, a merchant, a smuggler and a 'privateer'. (He has also been described as a fishmonger but this is probably not correct.) He held numerous civic posts in Bristol: Sheriff

1586 – 1587, Alderman, Mayor 1600 – 1601, Member of Parliament in 1601 and was appointed Master of the Merchant Venturers in 1605.[92] His career has been well documented and in 2004 he was the subject of an MA thesis by William Jessop at Bristol University. [93]

John Hopkins was born about 1547 and apprenticed at fourteen years of age to a Bristol merchant called George Higgins; he was made a Freeman of the city of Bristol on 10th September 1570. Jessop cites a letter dated 27th October 1569 referring to a siege at St Jean D'Angely in southern France which relates that an English merchant by the name of John Hopkins had been captured by the French and ransomed for 100 crowns.[94] It is quite likely that he was already involved in the wine trade, visiting the ports of La Rochelle and Bordeaux from where considerable quantities of wine were being shipped to Bristol. However, it is as a privateer that John Hopkins was most renowned. Jessop asserted that 'The admiralty records show that he was one of the greatest privateers of the outports and was arguably the leading privateer in Bristol'.[95] Captain Hopkin's privateering activities took place during the war with Spain from 1585 to 1604. Privateering often descended into outright piracy as states actually encouraged attacks on vessels of other nations even during periods of peace – for all intents and purposes they were 'state registered pirates'. The motives of the privateer were primarily to make a profit for the promoters of the venture by capturing cargoes of enemy shipping rather than destroying their ships.

In October 1585 John Hopkins, together with several other merchants, was charged with smuggling wheat and grain out of Bristol. The cargo was delivered by Hopkins to San Lucar in southern Spain aboard his vessel *The Mary Fortune*.[96] This incident occurred during hostilities with Spain and three years before the Spanish Armada of 1588. Two years later in 1587 he was charged with exporting prohibited goods to Spain 'to the great hurte of her majestie and the utter undoing of her Highness realme if such abuse be not addressed'. On this occasion he had furnished and freighted a ship called the *Jonas* which was sold to the Spanish with four cast pieces and all her sails and tackle for three hundred pounds.[97] John Hopkins participated in one of the great events of the Anglo-Spanish war when, in 1596, he sailed with the Earl of Essex, Sir Walter Raleigh and Lord Howard to attack the Spaniards and participated in the sack of the port of Cadiz. He returned

---

92   Alfred B. Beaven, *Bristol Lists*, (1899) p.296.

93   William Jessop, *Privateering in Elizabethan Bristol: A Case Study on John Hopkins*. 2004.

94   Ibid. p.31.

95   Ibid. Abstract.

96   TNA, E 134/27&28 Eliz/Mich8: The Queen v. John Yardley, John Newton, John Hopkyns, Andrew Brown, and a ship called *"The Mary Fortune,"* of Bristol. What wheat or other grain was transported in said ship beyond seas or elsewhere?

97   Jean Vanes, ed., *Documents illustrating The Overseas Trade of Bristol in the Sixteenth Century*, (1979), p.141.

home with the spoils of a great victory over the Spanish and the event was described in the Annals of the City of Bristol:

> 'John Hopkins, fishmonger, mayor of the city for the year ending Michaelmas 1601 had gained great renown in 1596 by having equipped a ship, which sailed under his command and took part in the memorable sack of Cadiz. On his return says a local chronicler, "he was with much joy met by the citizens on Durdham Down" who conducted him home in triumph and lighted "all their tallow candles and a great bonfire at the High Cross, very beautiful to behold".'[98]

At the beginning of the seventeenth century Hopkins supported the various Virginia enterprises in the Americas and he was one of a number of Bristol merchants who contributed to Martin Pring's voyage to the New World on the ship *Speedwell*. The merchants of Bristol raised £1000 to promote this voyage. Pring sailed for North Virginia in 1603 with the objective of collecting medicinal plants and trading for furs. In 1605 Hopkins' name appeared with other Bristol merchants in the charter granted to the 'Spanish Company' established for the advancement of trade with Spain and Portugal and a few years later John Hopkins and his son-in-law, John Kettleby senior, were named in the second 'Virginia Charter' of 1609 which sanctioned the establishment of a colony 'in that parte of America comonlie called Virginia'. This charter was granted to the Virginia Company of London, a joint-stock company set up by wealthy gentry and merchants with the objective of establishing a trading colony in America in anticipation of future profits. The name John Kettleby also appeared on the Third Virginia Charter of 1612 but Hopkins did not subscribe to this charter. He died in 1616 and the bequests in his will imply that Mary, his only daughter, had predeceased him.

Mary Hopkins had married John Kettleby, esquire, from Cotheridge in Worcestershire. In 1641 a Captain John Kettleby was appointed Governor of Nevis Island but it is not clear if this could be the elder or the younger John Kettleby.[99] There is little doubt that the father of the elder John Kettleby was Francis Kettleby who, on Friday 8th November 1605, together with Sir Richard Walsh, sheriff of Worcester, and two hundred armed men in a *posse comitatus,* arrived at Holbeach House in Shropshire. Here they captured the traitors Robert Catesby, Thomas Percy and Thomas Winter who were involved in the Gunpowder Plot. Catesby and Percy died from their injuries during the assault on the house, but Winter was captured alive. Francis Kettleby was awarded a knighthood at about this time, and from 1607 to 1615 he was one of the Justices of the Peace for Worcestershire.

---

98 J. Latimer, *Annals of Bristol in the 17th Century*, p.15. Jessop suggests that Latimer is in error with the description 'fishmonger' and has confused two of several John Hopkins living in Bristol during this period.

99 V.E. Oliver, *Caribbeana* Vol II, p.5.

John Hopkin's wife, Elizabeth, died in 1619 and the estate passed to her grandsons John, Charles and Thomas Kettleby, all of whom were still under the age of twenty-one years. As well as bequests of property each grandchild was left the sum of two hundred pounds. The younger John Kettleby was appointed executor of her estate and by the time of the 1623 Chancery case he had established himself as a merchant in London.

John Hall continued as innkeeper at the Crown for several more years as his cause slowly proceeded through Chancery. The authorities in Westminster continued to enact statutes concerning victuallers and innholders and the continual repression of drunkards. In 1623 came '*An Act for the better repressing of Drunkenness and restraining the inordinate haunting of Inns, Alehouses and other Victualling houses*'. (21 James I c. 7) and then '*An Acte concerning Hostlers and Inholders*' (21 James I c. 20, 21) which contained the section:

> 'AND be it further enacted, That no Hostler or Inholder shall at any tyme after the end of this Present Session of Parliament make Horsebread in his Hostery nor without, but Bakers shall make it, and the Assize shalbe kept, and the Weight reasonable, after the price of Corne and Graine in the Marketts adjoyning: and the Hostlers or Inneholders shall sell their Horsebread and their Hay Oates Beanes Pease Provender and alsoe all kinde of Victuall both for Man and Beast for reasonable gaine, having respect to the prices for which they shalbe sold in Marketts adjoyning, without taking anything for litter'.

The penalties for infringement of this statute were quite severe:

> 'And the Hostler or Inneholder for the first offence shalbe fined according to the quantitie of the Offence; And if being once convicted he shall againe offend, for the second offence he shalbe imprisoned for the space of one Month without bail or Mainprise; And if he shall a third time offend, being convicted, he shall stand upon the Pillory without being redeemed for money; And if he shall offend after the Judgement of the Pillory given he shalbe forejudged for keeping any Inne againe'.

This was followed in 1625 by '*An Act for the Further Restraint of Inns, Alehouses and Victualling houses*'. (1 Charles I. c.4) The Worcestershire innkeepers do appear to have observed these regulations for there were few indictments of innkeepers in the Worcester Quarter Sessions at this time.

In the seventeenth century, town halls and county offices did not exist and many inns became places where meetings for county administration and various judicial assemblies were held, the more important business being conducted in the larger inns of the shire towns. Records survive from the sixteenth century of meetings of the Quarter and Petty Sessions which took place in Worcestershire inns. 'Petty Sessions, "Monthly Meetings" they were called, seem to have been held once a month, as there are frequent references to these Monthly Meetings of the Magistrates in the different places in the County, and it would appear that they were usually attended by 3 or 4 Magistrates'. [100] In 1627 the Worcestershire Justices of the Peace summoned witnesses and jurors to meet 'on the 15th December at the Talbott in Sydbury, Worcester on Saturday next at 10 of the clock in the morning to give evidence on his highnesses behalf concerning a riot committed at Grafton Flivord..'.[101] The Talbot was an old Worcester coaching inn, and would have had the facilities to accommodate a large gathering (the jury consisted of twenty four men). Many of these individuals would have attended on horseback and an inn was one of the few places that could provide stabling and feed for their mounts. The jury was sworn in to enquire into this riot, but 'by some sinister practice between the parties complaining and the rioters' no witnesses appeared.[102] There was a further instance in 1627 when the Sessions were held at the house of Edward Walker another Worcestershire innholder. In later years, enclosure and bankruptcy commissioners and turnpike trustees would also meet in an inn to conduct their business.

The Crown Inn would have been an important building in the small town of Upton-upon-Severn; inns in rural towns were centres for local business and places where provincial politics were argued over. These smaller inns dealt with local affairs and minor judicial matters. Such meetings were held wherever it was more convenient for the parties involved. Two years earlier in 1625 the Petty Sessions were held in Upton when the justices met to examine the parties involved in a matter concerning *certain foul and scandalous speeches* which had been uttered in a local alehouse by Thomas Halsey and John Kayse. There can be little doubt that this meeting of the Petty Sessions was held in one of the two inns in the town. These 'speeches' had been uttered in the alehouse of Gilbert Cornwell (or Cornwall). Thomas Halsey's words had come to the attention of the justices of the peace; the subject of Halsey's outburst being Sir Henry Spiller, himself one of the justices. This incident illustrates some of the social attitudes prevalent in the seventeenth century. At this time it was a crime to speak 'evil' of those in authority (a *scandalum magnatum*) and 'it then constituted an offence under the Act, 12 Richard II. c. 11, which forbade using reproachful words to the great men of the realm'.[103] Society, in the seventeenth century, was a hierarchy descending by degrees of quality from nobles, to gentlemen of greater or lesser status, citizens or burgesses, then yeomen, with artificers or labourers and the poor at the bottom of the pile. The gravity of

---

100 J.W. Willis Bund, *Calendar of the Quarter Sessions Papers*, Vol I, p.xxxi.

101 Ibid. p.431.

102 Ibid. p.xxxi. The Talbot appears to have been a regular meeting place for the justices – another jury was summoned here in 1627 to inquire into a riot at Berrow Wood, Ibid. p.430.

103 Ibid. p.cxiv. This Act was a re-enactment of a statute of Edward I.

the offence depended not so much on the words spoken but the social standing of the person to whom they referred. Speaking wicked or disgraceful language against peers, judges or other great officers of the realm was a far more serious offence than outrageous words directed at persons of lesser quality. Halsey and Kayse were brought before the justices at the Petty Session in Upton on the 21st October 1625. Gilbert Cornwell was called as a witness to give evidence concerning this offence:

'The informacions of Gilbert Cornewell taken the xxith of October 1625

He saith that on Wednesday last, Thomas Halsey (amongst others) being at this Informants house in Upton upon Severne, speeking of Sir Henry Spyller, & the suite betweene him and the said Halsey, he the said Halsey said if Sir Henry had had his ox for a Herriott then the said suite had been ended, whereupon he the said Halsey further said, that if the hornes of his oxe were in the said Sir Henry his belly it were noe matter, for then there would be an end of the suite. These words were spoken in the presence of Mr Woodford, Mr Thomas Jefferies, John Pyke and others, and Mr Woodford and Mr Jefferies did then reprove the said Halsey for the words he spoke against the said Sir Henry'.

Gilbert Cornwall [104]

Mr Woodford was William Woodford who had recently been appointed rector of the parish of Upton-upon-Severn. The 'heriot' was a feudal due payable to the lord of the manor who usually took the best beast belonging to his tenant as payment. This would explain why Halsey had uttered such strong words against Sir Henry. Halsey and Kayse were bound over by the justices 'to their good behaviour'. [105] It is apparent that there may have been extenuating circumstances for these outbursts against Sir Henry Spiller. Willis Bund enlarged on this incident and commented that 'It is difficult to see what was the precise offence of which Kayse was guilty, and the Justices seem to have felt the same difficulty, for they did what it appears was their practice when in doubt, and they were uncertain what to do, they bound over Kayse to be of good behaviour. Spiller was an unpopular person, being the grantee of various monopolies. He also seems, if the proceedings in the Long Parliament are to be relied on, to have been a strong-minded, violent person, for he stopped a prosecution of a Clergyman at Quarter Sessions for refusing to give a parishioner the Sacrament; or, as it was put, "denied him justice at Quarter Sessions." Unfortunately, no trace of this is to be found among the existing documents. Spiller was arrested by order of the Long Parliament and committed to be kept in safe custody. He was also accused of releasing and conniving at Popish Priests. Subsequently he was liberated on bail'. [106] Halsey was a repeated troublemaker and a warrant was issued

---

104 WAAS 1/1/48/164.

105 Willis Bund p.394.

106 Ibid. p.cxv.

for his arrest in 1634 in 'order to his entering into his recognizance with sureties for his appearance at Sessions and in the meantime to be of good behaviour'.

A Fine sur Cognizance de Droit Come Ceo

By 1626 John Hall's case in Chancery was still unresolved, John Kettleby was probably more concerned with his own trading activities and his agent, Richard Griffiths, had almost certainly delayed the course of this bill through Chancery. Although Kettleby held the title deeds to the inn, this alone would not have been sufficient to confer ownership of the property on him. In the eyes of the law possession was still vested in John Hall, the reason being that no formal transfer of the property recognised in law had taken place. In the early seventeenth century there were several methods of conveying freehold property – the 'Feoffment', the 'Bargain and Sale' and by 'Fine' or 'Recovery'. Some of the owners of this building used the feoffment, which incorporated the medieval 'Livery of Seizin', as a means of conveying freehold. The term 'Livery of Seizin' means 'transfer of possession' and was carried out by means of a formal ceremony in front of witnesses where the vendor or feoffor declared the transfer of ownership to the purchaser or feoffee. The ceremony would be finalised by the feoffor handing a symbolic object such as a piece of turf, a twig or key to the feoffee before the purchaser entered his acquisition. It was eventually realised that some record of the event was required (if the witnesses had subsequently died this would be especially important). This was achieved by means of a written document confirming the seizin. The written deed (or feoffment) was simply an account of what had occurred but the actual legal transfer of ownership was still enshrined in the act of 'Livery of Seizin'. The missing title deeds would have confirmed the past transfers of ownership and were written proof that Livery of Seizin had once been performed.

For John Hall the inability to recover the deeds was perhaps more of a very irritating inconvenience that would have to be resolved. He was proposing to sell the inn to John and Edward Flook of Deerhurst in Gloucestershire but without secure title he would obviously have some difficulty in conveying the property to the other parties. The prospective purchasers would require some assurance that the title to the property they were about to acquire was secure. Consequently, John Hall returned to his attorney for further legal counsel and was advised that a suitable course of action was available to redress the situation – a legal procedure known as a 'Fine sur cognizance de droit come ceo' through the Court of Common Pleas. The word 'Fine' is derived from the Latin 'finis', meaning 'end'. This was an alternative method of conveying freehold that had developed by the reign of Henry II. A 'Fine' is 'an amicable agreement or composition of a suit, whether real or fictitious, between the demandant[107] and the tenant,[108] with the consent of judges, and inrolled among the

---

107 plaintiff.

108 i.e. the owner of the property.

records of the court where the suit is commenced, by which lands or tenements are transferred from one person to another, or any other settlement is made respecting them'.[109] In effect it is a fictitious or collusive law suit for the conveyance of land or property and was resorted to in cases where alternative methods of conveyance were not available or were defective at law. The person to whom the property was to be conveyed would sue the owner for wrongfully depriving him of possession; the defendant (or cognizor) would then acknowledge the right of the plaintiff (or cognizee) to the property; the judgement was then entered in the records of the court. The details were copied out in triplicate onto a parchment which was cut, along wavy lines, into three parts two of which were handed to the parties to the suit and the third part referred to as the 'foot of the fine' was filed amongst the rolls of the Court of Common Pleas as an official record of the suit, hence the term 'Feet of Fines'. William Blackstone explained: 'a Fine is so called because it puts an end to the suit, which, once decided, puts an end not only to that suit, but also to all other controversies concerning the same matter'. In 1626 John Hall sold the inn to the Flooks by this legal process of the '*Fine sur cognizance de droit come ceo*'. By the use of the '*Fine*' John Hall not only established a change of ownership acknowledged in law and enrolled in the Court of Common Pleas but also annulled the earlier deeds still in the possession of Richard Griffiths.

The sale was completed on the 30th January 1626, between John Hall alias Oliver together 'with Marjery his then wife and one Richard Teale and Elizabeth his wife who had some former estate with the said premises' and John Flook and Edward Flook 'for and in consideration of the some of one hundred and thirtye pounds'[110] It is not apparent why Richard Teale and his wife were involved in this transaction, but perhaps, as was stated in a later Chancery case, they were cited 'for the better Conveyance of the said house or Inne'.

109 William Cruise: *A Digest of the Laws of England*, Vol V, 1805, p.5.

110 TNA C 2/CHAS1/B15/40 – Answer of John Best 1638.

4.

Two Flooks and a stir in the churchyard

JOHN Flook and Edward Flook were joint owners of the property for a period of ten years from 1626 to 1636. There were several families by the name of Flook living in Gloucestershire and south Worcestershire and John Flook, a yeoman, was probably one of the wealthiest individuals leaving bequests in his will to his children and grandchildren amounting to nearly one thousand pounds. His wife, Margery, left substantial bequests amounting to over three hundred pounds and his brother, Edward, an affluent blacksmith, owned land and property in Deerhurst. The Flooks were not innkeepers themselves but had let the Crown Inn to a tenant under a ten-year lease at the yearly rent of £12 (this yielded a very respectable 9.2% return on their investment). The name of one of the past tenants and the terms of the tenancy were written in the 1636 purchase deed:

> 'All such Estate & Terme for yeares as was heretofore granted unto one John Bradwell deceased of the said bargained premisses by the said John Flook and Edward Flook not exceeding the term of Tenn years from the time of granting thereof and for and under the yearely Rent of Twelve pounds of lawfull money of England…'

The name of John Bradwell (or Brodwell), the first tenant innkeeper, appeared in a Court Baron of Henry Bromley in Upton-upon-Severn dated October 1625. Whilst the Justices at the Quarter Sessions had jurisdiction over the regulation and licensing of alehouse keepers and innkeepers the manorial courts also exercised some control over their activities, in particular the prices and quality of victuals, especially bread and ale. The two innkeepers in the town together with the alehouse keepers had been summoned to appear before the court to answer charges of overcharging for victuals and for not being licenced (from the constables presentments it is evident that there were two innkeepers and eleven alehouse keepers at this date). Bradwell was listed twice in this court record, firstly as a juror and secondly with the other victuallers. The entire assembly was fined four pence each by the court:

'And that John Brodwell [4d] John Durston [4d] Gilbert Cornwell [4d] Henry Mowshall [4d] Ed. Pomfrey [4d] John Baylis [4d] Jun*ior* William Payne [4d], George Sandlande [4d] Thomas Noake [4d], John Knighte [4d], John Anthonye [4d], John Caffold [4d], and Thomas Hunte [4d] have sold victuals [at] excessive costs and illicit keeping there; therefore themselves in mercy, just as appears above the margin of them, whomsoever'. [amercement 4 shillings 4 pence] [111]

It has been suggested that such charges brought before the manorial courts were merely a fiction in order to extract licence fees from the proprietors of the various drinking houses in the town.

John Bradwell died in 1631 and although he left a will unfortunately it does not contain any mention of the inn. Following his decease the tenancy was taken by a John Teffe (or Tiffe), who was mentioned in the presentment for the Worcester Quarter Sessions in April 1634:

'April the 10th The presentment of the Constable of Upton super Sabrinam made against this next generall Sessiones of the peace houlden for this countie Tuchinge all the Articles given me as followeth Anno Domini 1634:
Imprimis as concerninge Taverners or Vintner wee have not any within our Constablewick.
Item I doe present that for bakeres wee have but one that is Humfery Smith and who selleth not other rate than Thirteen to the dussen.
Item I present that within our parishe there are none that keep ordinary tables.
Item as concerninge Inkeepers there bee within your Constablewick two the first is John Tiffe and he selleth wine and Beere and hee doeth victuall and hee keepeth horsemeat .... for beere hee selleth a full ale quart .... second for horsemeat hee doeth not exceed the rate in the Articles and for victuallinge hee doeth not [exceed] neither, the other Inkeeper is John [Durston] hee selleth noe wine but beere ... he selleth the full measure and does not exceed in his rates for horse meate neither in [oats] nor in hay.
Item I doe present that there are noe wanderers received or Lodged within your Constablewick.
Item I doe present that I Punnished all the wanderers that came within your Constablewick and let none passe bye unpunished.
Item I present that your watch and warde it is duely kept

---

111 WAAS 705:46 BA104/4.

I doe present as Tuchinge alehowse keepers [Unlicensed] John Tanner Thomas Hope Ralph Jacion licensed Gilbert Cornwell Antony Sermon William Fell Edmund Pewsey John Baylice John Antony and Thomas Hunt dwell in convenient places keep good order and selleth a full ale quarte of the better and strongest ale for a penny, neither do they in time of devine service nor att undue times of the night. John Browne alehowsekeeper licensed and he selleth at undue times in the night and shott one man himself with a piece in the night about the middle of the night and he keepeth odiouse and sinful drunkenness in his howse at all times so that his neighbours cannot rest for time in their howses for the odious noyse of drunkenness and [voices] of drunken men. Contrary to the statute made in the fowerth yeare of his majesties raigne Contrary to the statute made in the 7 yeare of the kinges majesties raigne Item as Tuchinge your heigh wayes and Bridges they are are well repayred and in bee good repayre.

per me John Cotterill Constable' [112]

John Browne was indicted and brought before the Justices of the Peace for permitting drunkenness in his alehouse. The two innkeepers were John Teffe born February 1573 in Bredon, Worcestershire and John Durston, born Upton-upon-Severn in 1594. The presentment also suggests that following the departure of John Hall the new proprietors had not continued the trade of vintner. The statutes appear to refer to those passed in the reign of James I. The statute made 'in the fowerth yeare' would be *An Act to restrain the Utterance of Beer and Ale to Alehouse Keepers and Tipplers,* (4 James I, c.4) and the other *An Act for Reformation of Alehouse Keepers* of 1609, (7 James I, c.10).

In his presentment, the town constable, John Cotterill, declared that 'there are none that keep ordinary tables'. In the seventeenth century 'ordinary' in the context of victualling had several meanings; it could refer to a meal provided at a fixed price in a victualling house or the actual building. It could also refer to the dining room where this meal was served. In this instance it referred to the meal itself, which was perhaps more like a '*plat du jour*'. Samuel Pepys mentioned the 'ordinary' when he took his wife 'to a French house to dinner, and so enquired out Monsieur Robins, my perriwigg-maker, who keeps an ordinary; and in an ugly street in Covent Garden did find him at the door, and so we in; and in a moment almost had the table covered, and clean glasses, and all in the French manner, and a mess of potage first, and then a couple of pigeons à la esterve, and then a piece of bœuf-à-la mode, all exceedingly well seasoned, and to our great liking; at least it would have been anywhere else but in this bad street, and in a perriwigg-maker's house;'.

---

112 WAAS 1/1/24/91.

This meal cost Pepys six shillings.[113] The 'horse meat' referred to was definitely not meat for human consumption but a mix of oats and barley or other cereals for feeding horses. The rates charged by innkeepers were regulated by statute. In the early seventeenth century presentments, it seems that the charge for a gentleman at an inn was two shillings per day and eight pence for his servant. The charge for a horse for a night was 6d, a peck of oats for the horse was 6d and 'for standing a horse at hay for the space of a day' the charge was 2d.[114]

The lives of alehouse-keepers and innkeepers in Upton-upon-Severn were little different to those in other small towns and villages in Worcestershire where there must have been much competition for trade and customers. In the village of Crowle, a few miles east of Worcester, where two alehouses were already well established, a local surgeon, James Carless, had persuaded the Bishop of Worcester to grant him a licence to sell ale for the benefit of his patients who came to him for treatment. Having acquired his licence Carless' 'surgery' then 'became the resort of all the idle beggars that came to Crowle'. This prompted a local resident to write at length to the Justices of the Peace. This letter, dated 1633, from Thomas Cocks to Sir Robert Berkeley, one of the Justices of the Quarter Sessions, vividly illustrates life in a rural community and some of the problems encountered by honest tradesmen:

"I beseech you give me leave amongst your many well wishers (though unworthy to be ranked in the number of your meanest friends) to pray as heartily as any that you may happily enjoy your rising fortunes. I hear you intend a Session at Worcester this day about the mending of highways which is a very charitable and good work and so it is also (if you think good) before your going out of the County to take some course concerning putting down of the superfluity of alehouses and common tippling houses of which kind we have no less than three in Crowle and that is two too many for one little village as I find by experience to my loss of servants and they very often to the loss of their money and wits. The nearest of these alesellers is James Careless and therefore the worst. The next in propinquity of neighbourhood is Richard Brinton a tenant to Mr Symons of Aston and upheld by him in that capacity. Careless petitioned my Lord Bishop for a licence to sell ale because he was a surgeon and had many patients come to him for help and found it a great inconvenience for them to go to remote places for their diet and drink and in that respect obtained a licence (as I understand) with a limitation to sell ale to none but his patients. But now of late especially he far exceeds his bounds and entertains all comers as well by night as by day high and low rich and poor beggars and none excepted. For example a poor wandering fellow came not long since to my door counterfeiting himself to be blind lame and taken most perilously with a shaking palsy which part of an infirm man in these

113 Samuel Pepys Diary, 12th May 1667.

114 J.W. Willis Bund, *Calendar of the Quarter Sessions Papers*, p.cii and p.643.

several particulars he performed so artificially that he made my wife to take great compassion of him for besides meat and drink she gave him money and a piece of bacon which he had no sooner had than he went away with a snail's pace halting downright and shaking and groping with his staffe till he thought he was out of sight and then he was an upright man on the sudden and without any lameness blindness quaking or quivering could find the way to Careless's house presently where he called for a pot of ale a pipe of tobacco and a pennyworth of eggs to fry with his bacon and Careless rose up from other company and sat down by him where my two witnesses left them who heard and saw all their passage and after told it to me and my wife. Another poor fellow professed himself an extraordinary carder and spinner of woollen or linen was of late set a work by my wife to card and spin coarse wool for blankets and when he had gotten some money for his work to Careless he goes and there with another of my men spent the greatest part of the night till it was three o'clock in the morning or thereabouts and then they parted but the spinner made his way through the churchyard when finding two beggar women in the church porch gave a groat to the younger to lie with him when there was such a stir between them that there was taken out of his pocket about 16s which he presently missed by feeling in his pocket for his money and made so great a noise in chiding and brawling one with another that being near my chamber I woke my wife who called up all my men to go into the churchyard and see what the matter was and by searching with a lantern and a candle there was found a crown of it which he had again the rest was lost. In the meantime whilst the search was made I sent for the Constable to put the spinning man and the young woman in the stocks and so was ridden of them and their disorder and many more (which is too much to set down in a letter) Careless' ale distributed to all comers privately and being enjoyned to march to Sessions whether a well governed alehouse it is. I will now most humbly take my leave and receiving pardon for being so tedious .... Will end.

Your poor neighbour and servant to command

Crowle 12st Sep. 1633   Tho. Cocks[115] "

At the beginning of the seventeenth century there were thirteen premises selling ale, beer or wine out of a total of one hundred or so dwellings in Upton-upon-Severn

115 Taken from J W Willis Bund, *Calendar of the Quarter Sessions Papers*, pp.529-31 with amendments from the original document which has deteriorated since Willis Bund examined it. The Catholic family of Cocks had been settled in Crowle for some time and caused the Constable continuing problems. In 1634 the Constable presented Thomas Cocks Esq., his family and servant for not going to Church and for not receiving the Sacrament. They were presented in 1635 as 'Popish' recusants and were all indicted in 1636 for 'not going to church'. They were still refusing to attend church in 1638. The head of the family, Thomas Cocks, had been included with the 244 persons who, on the 14th April 1640, were indicted at Westminster for recusancy; he is described as "Thomas Coxe, late of Crowle, County Worcester, Gentleman, and late of St. Andrews in Holborn, in the County of Middlesex." – Ibid. pp.cc-cci.

(Nash, in his history of Worcestershire, says there were one hundred and thirteen families living in the town in the reign of Elizabeth I – about 600 individuals).[116] Alehouse keepers were often associated with the lower strata of society and many of these alehouses would have been meagre drinking places run by alewives, subsidising their livelihood by alehouse-keeping (or tippling as it was known). But not all of them were paltry establishments; some were providing food and lodging as well as selling ale. Exactly how many of these alehouse-keepers were providing lodging for travellers is difficult to determine, but from the sixteenth century they were under pressure from the local officials and justices to do so.[117] Four of the Upton alehouse-keepers, Gilbert Cornwall, John Baylis, Anthony Sermon and William Fell, all left wills with accompanying inventories. Gilbert Cornwall's alehouse was the smallest comprising three principle rooms and John Baylis' establishment was a little larger with five rooms.

The alehouses of Sermon and Fell were much more extensive premises, each with seven rooms and several bedsteads which suggest that they were accommodating overnight guests. William Fell also had a brewhouse and stabling facilities available for travellers. Many small alehouse-keepers would have readily accepted the few extra pence from the lodger even if it meant following the example of Evan ap Rice of West Ham who, in 1584, was accused of 'lodging strange men in his bed with him and his wife'.[118] The value of the goods and chattels of these four alehouse keepers suggests that they were all making a reasonably good living from their trade which appears to have been their sole or primary occupation.

A noteworthy event that affected the lives of many innkeepers occurred on 31st July 1635 when, by royal proclamation, Charles I made the Royal Mail available to the public. The Royal Mail had been started by Henry VIII in 1516 for the purpose of carrying official correspondence; 'posts' were set up, usually roadside inns, where fresh horses were provided for the couriers transporting the royal mail. After 1635, 'Letter Receiving Houses', or public post offices were usually housed at inns with the innkeepers acting as provincial postmasters. After the Postage Act of 1657[119], which fixed rates for sending letters, the postmasters (or innkeepers) were responsible for accepting and handing out letters, exchanging mailbags and providing fresh horses or stabling for the Post-Boys; they were remunerated according to the amount of mail they handled, the postal charges being paid by the recipient.

In the autumn of 1636 John and Edward Flook agreed to sell the inn to John Best, another 'yeoman' of Upton-upon-Severn, and the transaction is recorded in the *Deed of Purchase* of that date. This document is not the original but a copy made sometime later, probably when the property was sold in 1710. The

---

116 Nash, *History of Worcestershire*, Vol II, p.446.

117 Peter Clark, *The English Alehouse*, p.135.

118 Ibid. p.135.

119 *An Act for settling the Postage of England, Scotland and Ireland*, 9th June 1657.

feoffment was not in the usual form of conveyance as in vendor 'A' to purchaser 'B' because a sitting tenant was in possession of the premises. At some time during the ownership of the Flooks the name of the inn had changed to the King's Arms, presumably in celebration of the accession to the throne of James I. The location of the 'King's Armes' together with the various neighbours was described in some detail:

> *'That John Flook and Edward Flook ... Have Granted bargained sold alienated enfeoffed delivered released and Confirmed ~ and by these Presents Do and either of them Doth Grant bargain sell alien enfeoffe deliver Release and Confirme unto the said John Best his heirs & assignes for ever. All That Inn Messuage or Tenement with th'appurtenances Scituate lying and being in the town of Upton upon Severne in the said county of Worcester in a Street there called the High Street commonly called or known by the name of the Kings Armes and Scituate lying and being between the Land in occupacion of Margarett Durstian widow on the Northeast side and the Land in Occupacion of Thomas Goodyeare on the Southwest side And also all that dwelling house with th'appurtenances Scituate in Upton upon Seavern aforesaid wherein one Thomas Powell now liveth being heretofore a Barne and lyeth in the old street there between the Parish Land of Upton upon Seavern aforesaid on the Northside and the Land of Thomas Jessope at Bucknell on the Southside. Together with a small piece or Butt of arrable Land whereon the said dwelling house doth stand lying in a feild called Berrefeild conteyning by estimation halfe an acre or thereabouts be the same more or less And all houses Outhouses Edifices Buildings Courtyards Banksides and Gardens to the said Inne ...*

The above extract defines the boundaries of the property, and it is interesting to note that barn conversions are not a present day phenomenon as the reference to the residence of Thomas Powell reveals: *'heretofore a Barne'* (this was a separate building in Old Street). The title deed was dated 2nd October 1636 but the actual livery of seizin did not occur until the 5th of December of that year. The sum involved was *'One hundred and fifty pounds of lawfull money of England'* and a memorandum on the title deed confirmed the ceremony of seisin:

> *'Memorandum that possession & seizin was given & executed in due forme of Law by John Durstan & Christopher Wynbury the Attornies within named unto the within named John Best in their proper persons att which time John Teffe & Thomas Powell the tennants of the premises did attorne Tenant by delivery of Six pence in Silver a peece Unto the within named John Best in name of attornement the fifth day of December Anno Domini 1636 Anno Regni Regis Caroli Duodecimo*

In the presence of John Teffe. Tho: Powell. Jo: Durstan Christopher Wynbury John Knight Jo: Thorneton.

Sealed & Delivered in the presence of Richard Dowdeswell, Charles Dowdeswell, Nicholas Philpotts. Jo: Cowley. John Morris John Portman John Hunt'.

To '*attorne tenant*' meant to formally agree to become tenant of the new landlord and '*delivery of Six pence in Silver a peece*' represented the legal acknowledgement of the new tenancy. (The Deed of Purchase in this instance was actually a document known as a 'Bargain and Sale with Feoffment'. This method of conveyance incorporated elements of the earlier 'Feoffment' with the 'Bargain and Sale', an alternative means of property transaction which, by the sixteenth century, had developed for the sale of real estate.)

John and Edward Flook did not attend the ceremony of seisin themselves but had appointed attorneys to act on their behalf. Richard Dowdeswell is believed to be the same Richard Dowdeswell, an attorney, who owned Pull Court in Bushley near Tewkesbury. Christopher Wynbury was a prosperous mercer and John Portman was brother-in-law to the new proprietor John Best who, like John Hall before him, would soon become entangled in Chancery proceedings.

5.

Inheritance Lost

THE evidence indicates that the new proprietor, John Best, was the son of Robert and Anne Best. Their names appeared together at a Court Baron of Henry Bromley dated 29th of March 1626 when Robert and Anne surrendered lands *(sursum redditio)* unto the lord of the manor:

> 'To this Court have come Robert Best and Anne, his wife, and Anne herself by the Steward aforesaid in form of Law examined, and John Best, their son, in their own persons and in open Court have surrendered into the hands of the Lord one messuage, with appurtenances, lying next to The Grange of the Lord, next to the Town in that place, and one kitchen-garden in that place, with appurtenances, with a garden adjacent, and likewise two acres of land lying in Bury field, called Stockes ground, and one half acre of meadow-land lying in Overham'.[120]

These parcels of land were copyhold tenure held of the manor of Upton-upon-Severn, but the reason for the surrender was not explained.

In the previous year John Best's parents had been summoned to appear before the justices at the Worcester Quarter Sessions to answer a charge of riotous assembly:

> '1625: Indictment of Robert Best the elder Yeoman, Anna Best wife of the said Robert Best, Shoemaker, Anthony Best, Labourer, Richard Southerne, Shoemaker, William Sandlands, Shoemaker all of Upton upon Severn, Anthony Best the younger of Dumbleton in the County of Gloucester, Yeoman, Joan wife of William Hayward of Twyning, Yeoman and Roland Johnson of Upton upon

---

120 WAAS 705:46 BA104/4.

Severn, Labourer for riotously assembling at Upton on Severn and assaulting Robert Farley'. [121]

(This indictment was annotated a 'True bill'.)

John Best came from a family of shoemakers although he himself was referred to as 'yeoman'. His mother, Anne, and also his brother, Robert Best, were described as shoemakers, an activity often associated with the lower orders of society. The son of a shoemaker was perhaps an unlikely candidate to be an innkeeper, but not all shoemakers were poverty-stricken individuals. One Worcester shoemaker who died in 1574 was worth more than £115 and other shoemakers did achieve modest levels of wealth by diversification into other business activities or by purchasing land.[122] John Best was born about 1600 and had at least two children, Anne and John, by his first wife, Anne, who had died in about 1635. The younger John Best, was born in 1629 and the rector, William Woodforde, described the event in the parish register with his customary attention to detail: 'John Best sonne of John Best was borne on Thursday the 26th day of November about fowre of ye clock in ye morning'. There is no further mention of the younger John Best which presupposes that he died in infancy. John Best soon remarried; his second wife was Katherine Portman, the daughter of John Portman of Twyning in Gloucestershire. The Portmans were a family of prosperous yeomen and husbandmen who had lived in Twyning for many generations; John Portman left bequests in his will amounting to over three hundred pounds; Richard Portman of 'Twinning', who died in 1683, gained an MA at Oxford and was ordained in 1674.[123] John Best's new wife, Katherine, had 'some fortune or portion in money' and 'itt was so agreed on his marriage to purchase some Estate whereof to make some provision in nature of a Joynture[124] for his second wife and for the heirs of such second marriage and the said John Best did sometime after such his second marriage purchase one messuage or tenement in Upton-upon-Severn called the King's Arms and another messuage or tenement in Upton-upon-Severn …'.[125] John Best and Katherine produced another five children – John, Katherine, Mary, Margaret and one other daughter. Of these children, Mary Best eventually inherited the High Street property and Katherine married one of the sons of the infamous Captain Thomas Bound whose ghost is said to still haunt the streets of Upton-upon-Severn. The other children all predeceased their mother who died in 1692, all three dying without issue.

---

121 WAAS 110 BA1 48/6.

122 Alan D. Dyer, *The City of Worcester in the Sixteenth Century*, p.122.

123 CCED – Richard Portman, ID 81362.

124 Jointure: an estate settled by a husband for benefit of his wife after his decease – 'a competent livelihood of *freehold* for the wife of lands or tenements, to take effect after the death of the husband for the life of the wife at least …' (Thomas Coventry, *A Readable Edition of Coke upon Littleton*, s.41).

125 TNA C 11/993/18 – Answer of Mary Towne.

The Second Chancery Case: Baker alias Williams v Best, 1637-1638.[126]

In this small community it cannot have escaped the attention of John Best that his title to the High Street property was being disputed. It must therefore have been of little surprise when, in 1637, a Bill of Complaint was issued against him out of the Court of Chancery in a cause instigated by fifty-five year old Richard Baker alias Williams, a younger son of Francis Baker alias Williams the former owner of the building (hereinafter mention of the surname Baker refers to 'Baker alias Williams'). This Chancery case produced several documents, including a Bill of Complaint from Richard Baker and the corresponding Answer from John Best. The dispute was that Richard Baker maintained that the title to the inn belonged with his family, that the Halls had been merely tenants with no right to sell the property to a third party (i.e the Flooks) and consequently John Best's title was defective.[127] At this point the earlier title deeds were possibly still in the hands of Richard Griffiths and John Best's title to the inn rested on two documents: John Hall's will (and the declaration that he had purchased the property from Francis Baker) and the 1626 *Fine sur cognizance de droit come ceo* enrolled in the Court of Common Pleas. For Richard Baker's claim to succeed he would have to prove that his father had not conveyed the inn to John Hall alias Oliver.

Francis Baker had married Alice, sister to the elder John Hall alias Oliver. They had three sons Francis, Richard and Thomas and several daughters. The younger Francis Baker had four children, two sons and two daughters. By 1622 the elder Francis Baker was deceased and his son Francis had also died leaving his four orphaned children of 'tender years'. By 1637 these four children had also died leaving Francis' younger brother, Richard Baker, as the next heir to any estate of their late father Francis. Richard Baker asserted that the earlier owners, Francis Hall or his son, John Hall, had by some nefarious means obtained the title deeds to the inn and thereby deprived these ill-fated orphans of their rightful inheritance. By applying the legal principles of entail and primogeniture he claimed that the title should have passed first from his father Francis Baker, the elder, down to his brother Francis and then in turn down to Francis' sons. Accordingly, as Francis' sons had all died in childhood without issue, Richard Baker then claimed that the ownership of the inn should now come to him. Consequently, in November of 1637 he instigated a cause in Chancery against John Best to establish his rights to the property. In his Bill of Complaint Richard Baker stated: 'the sayd premises discended and came as of right they ought by virtue of some deed of entayle formerlie made or otherwise to the first heire male of your Orators sayd father'. Furthermore he claimed that John Hall had come to some dubious

---

126 TNA C 2/Chas1/B15/40.

127 There is a discrepancy regarding the name of the inn, for this Chancery Case still refers to the property as the Crowne Inn. Presumably Messrs Flook had renamed the inn after they had purchased it from John Hall in 1626 but the plaintiff still used the former name in his Bill of Complaint.

financial arrangement with the Flooks concerning the purchase of the inn. The Bill described the sad plight of his nephews and nieces:

> 'the sayd Francis Baker alias Williams your Orators eldest brother allsoe died leavinge behind him Richard his eldest Sonne and Francis his younger sonne and two daughters beinge all Infants[128] of tender years after whose decease [i.e. Francis Baker alias Williams, brother to the orator] by virtue as aforesayd the sayd howse or Inne with the premisses thereto discended and came to Richard his eldest sonne as of right the same ought to discend and come during whose mynoritie the sayd John Oliver alias Hale sonne of the sayd Francis [Hall] being in possession of the sayd premisses by means as aforesayd and having by himself or by his sayd father by some indirect meanes obteyned into his or their hands or to the hands of some other by their privitie alle the deeds or writtings with the sayd deeds of entayle concerninge the sayd premisses and knoweinge the sayd Richard Baker alias Williams to be an infant of tender yeares and having few or noe friends to looke after him or take care of him pretended title to the said Inne or house with the premisses and challenged and claymed the same as his alone...'

> '...and the sayd Richard the infant to whom of right it did belong beinge of tender years and as yt were left friendless [and they] did combine with one John Fluke and Edward Fluke or one of them to purchase the sayd Inne or howse of him with the premisses thereto belonginge att and for some easie rate or undervalue with the said Flukes or one of them unconscionably to make theire or one of theire advantages ... accordingly doe after which pretended purchase of the said Flukes or one of them That is to say about [omitted] years since the sayd Richard Baker the Infant died without yssue after whose decease the sayd premisses descended and came by virtue aforesayd to [Francis] Baker his younger brother whoe alsoe with his sayd two sisters are since dead without yssue being all the yssue which your Orators sayd brother Francis left of his bodye lawfully begotten...'

On receipt of the Bill of Complaint John Best travelled to Tewkesbury to consult his attorney and subsequently replied with his written Answer which produced a considerable amount of information; it reiterated that John Hall alias Oliver the elder had died in 1591 and recited the terms of his will which dealt with the inheritance of the inn. In his Answer John Best went to great lengths to establish his title to the inn but did not provide any evidence of title deeds prior to the conveyance of 1626. The defence rested in part on the establishment of good title ascribed to the previous owners of the inn, John Hall alias Oliver and his descendants. It

---

128 An infant in Common Law was someone who had not attained the age of twenty one years.

also appears that some emphasis was placed on establishing the legitimacy of the younger John Hall's claim to the inn. The third Interrogatory put to the witnesses deposing on John Best's behalf asked:

> 'Item did you know the said John Hall als Oliver first named that purchased the said howse or Inn from Francis Baker alias Williams deceased, had the said John a sonne whose name was Francis and had that Francis a sonne called Francis likewise and another sonne called John.
>
> And did the said John last named survive the said Francis his brother and is it not the note or wryteing now shewed you att the Tyme of your Examinacion a true Coppie takenout of ye Church booke'.

Depositions of Witnesses.[129]

The witnesses were summoned to appear before the commissioners on two occasions, the first being on the 31st August 1638 when they appeared on behalf of the plaintiff, Richard Baker alias Williams. The first page of the deposition commenced:

> 'Depositions of Witnesses taken att the howse of John Durston in Upton upon Seavern in the County of Worcester upon the last day of August in the fowerteenth yeare of the reign of our Sovereign Lord King Charles of England Annoque Domini 1638. By and before Anthony Ludford Esq., William Millington, John Hollins and Christopher Canner gents. By vertue of A Commission out of his highness' high Court of Chancery in a cause there depending at issue Betweene Richard Baker alias Williams plaintiff and John Best defendant to them in that behalf directed as followeth vizit'.

John Durston was one of the two 'attorneys' present at the ceremony of seisin when John Best had purchased the inn. Durston was the other innkeeper in Upton-upon-Severn at this period and it is likely that his 'howse' was the present day White Lion Hotel. Events like this would have been most remarkable in such a small community causing considerable interest and gossip, and doubtless a crowd of interested spectators arrived to hear what questions had been put to the witnesses. The case must have caused tension within several families as some of the deponents giving evidence for the two parties were related. The defendant, John Best, would have anxiously watched the proceedings from the opposite side of the High Street as the deponents assembled, each waiting to be called by the commissioners to answer the questions to be put to them. There were five interrogatories listed (some consisting of more than one question) which the deponents had to answer. The deponents appear to have been chosen for their longevity as their average age was

129 TNA C 22/10/16 and C 22/599/38.

a remarkable seventy-one years. The oldest, Henry Pennystone, aged 'fower score years and tenn or thereabouts', was born about 1548 during the reign of Edward VI. The outcome of the case depended on events that had occurred seventy years earlier and so it was important to have witnesses with some memory or knowledge of those events.

The first witness to be called was seventy-seven year old Johane Brick, daughter of the elder Francis Baker and elder sister to the plaintiff (the document gave her age as 'lxxx years'), who deposed that she 'believes that the Inheritance of the said Messuage with the appurtenances doth lawfully descend & come to the plaintiff if the said Francis Baker alias Williams the elder, Francis Baker alias Williams the younger or his children have not conveyed or passed the same away'. Next to be called before the commissioners was Johane Edwards who 'sayeth that she doth not knowe what estate the said Francis Baker alias Williams, the plaintiffs father, had in the howse or inne nowe in question but sayeth that the said Francis Baker alias Williams and Francis his eldest son being about five and forty years since upon ... occasion att this deponants house uppon some conference then and there between the said Francis the elder (in this deponants hearing) did tell the said Francis the younger his sonne that the house or inne nowe in question .... was or should be his immediately after the death of him the said Francis Baker alias Williams the elder or to that effect'. Other witnesses produced similar depositions and whilst their evidence showed that there was no doubt that Richard Baker was rightful heir to his father's estate there was nothing to support his claim to the title of the inn or anything to suggest that the Halls did not have sufficient title thereto.

At the second examination (this document was damaged, but presumably it was held on the following day and once again at the house of John Durston) eight witnesses were summoned to testify on behalf of the defendant, John Best. On this occasion the first witness called to give evidence was Mr William Woodforde who had been appointed rector of Upton-upon-Severn in 1625. Mrs Lawson described him as someone who 'lived among his people, concerned himself with their daily troubles, and knew of each incident which stirred the course of parochial life' and 'he was strict in observing the rules and rites of the Church'. His testimony must have been incontestable. It was he who was responsible for copying the details taken from the parish register to be shown to the deponents in their examination. He testified that he had never heard a 'contrary' word to suggest that the 'Olivers' were not the lawful owners of the inn. In his deposition he stated:

> '[To] the third Interrogatorie he saith that the note or wryting now shown unto
> him this deponant at the tyme of his examination subscribed with his name is
> a true note or coppy taken out of the Churchbooke or register of Upton upon
> Sevearne in the countie of Worcester And further saith [that] Johane Hall al*ias*
> Olliver in the note mencioned was (as this deponant hath byn informed) the

wyfe of one Hall al*ias* Olliver of Berryend in the vill of Upton upon Seaverne aforesaid And that the name Joane (being the name of a woman) is usually wrytten ye booke or Register Johane, in severall places...'

It is not clear why this point was raised or who Joane Hall alias Oliver was; possibly the plaintiff was attempting to establish that there was some discrepancy in John Hall's genealogy.

Robert Clay, the curate, also testified about the entry in the parish register, but at the age of seventy he had some difficulty in reading the entry: 'this deponants sight being not very good'. However the most revealing evidence came from the deposition of Thomas Portman:

'Thomas Portman of Twyning in the County of Gloucester yeoman aged about xxviij [28] years sworne & examined sayth: ... that about whitsontide last he this deponent being at the Citty of Bristol with the defendant John Best did heare one Mr Griffith of the said Citty confesse to the said defendant that about Thirty yeares since [1608] one Frances Oliver [i.e. Francis Hall alias Oliver the elder] of Upton upon Seaverne in the County of Worcs did pawne to one Mr Hopkins of Bristol aforesaid for money which he had runne behind for to him for wyne a blacke boxe of wrytings, which wrytings were deeds of purchase of the house or inne mencioned or meant in & by the First Interrogatory from Francis Williams alias Baker to John Hall alias Olliver & Anne his wyfe joynt purchasers therein And allsoe sayth that the said Griffith then likewise told the said defendant, that the same wryting or deeds came into his possession & hands after the death of the said Hopkins, uppon perusall of the wrytings of the said Hopkins And that afterwards one John Hall alias Olliver sonne of the said Frances conceived or brought a suite in the Chancery against the said Griffith for recovery & returning of the said wrytings of the said wryting or deeds of purchase in which suite the said Griffiths did make his answer upon oath and set forth the whole truth of the premisses And this deponent further sayeth that the said Mr Griffith did then allsoe say to the deponent John Best in this deponants hearing that he the said Griffith saith he had the said deeds or writing in his hands & was willing to deliver them.....and thereuppon made search for them ...... and other wrytings but could not find the same'.

The other deponents included Elizabeth Sandlands and Anne Fisher, the granddaughters of the elder John Hall (Elizabeth and Anne had lived in the inn with their grandmother, Anne Hall, for many years). Another witness was Thomas Tewe who confirmed the evidence of the earlier deponents. He revealed further details concerning the plaintiff, Richard Baker, who was 'lyveing a poore man in ... Upton upon Seavern ... for the tyme of twenty years' and that Anne Hall would give him 'meale, meat and drinke'. He continued with his testimony: 'but did never know him in all that tyme demand any right to the said house or any penny of rente for the same which this deponent doth believe if he had had any right thereunto considering the poverty he lived in for a good while...'.

The evidence of these deponents confirmed that in about the year 1608 Francis Hall alias Oliver had got himself into debt with a 'Mr Hopkins', a wine merchant from Bristol. To extricate himself from this predicament he had somehow obtained the black box containing the deeds to the inn which were in the possession of his mother, Anne Hall alias Oliver, and pawned them to Hopkins. It also revealed that around Whitsuntide in 1637 John Best had travelled to Bristol with Thomas Portman to meet Richard Griffiths in an attempt to resolve the difficulty he was having with the disputed title and, more importantly, to recover the title deeds to the inn. Four of the witnesses testified that the Halls had been in possession of the earlier deeds that were pawned but none testified that they had seen any deed or conveyance giving title to the plaintiff.

This second Chancery case raises several issues. First and foremost is the whereabouts of the title deeds before they were appropriated by Francis Hall – were they actually in the possession of his mother, Anne Hall, or did Francis take advantage of those poor friendless orphans? Secondly, why did Richard Baker wait so long before instigating his Chancery case? Did he genuinely believe that he had a valid claim to the inn, and how was an individual of reduced means able to afford litigation? (It was necessary for the complainant's attorney to sign the Bill of Complaint thereby attesting that he believed that the 'Orator' had a genuine grievance against the defendant.) Richard Baker was probably aware that the original title deeds to the inn were missing and thus John Best's title could not be supported by earlier documents; he may also have heard a rumour concerning the legitimacy of the elder John Hall's heirs (rumours being the life-blood of small towns!). No further documents relating to Richard Baker's case have been traced, so presumably it did not run its full course through Chancery. As to the true legal title of the property we can only speculate.

Which party was in the right we will never know but the testimony of the witnesses called to give evidence appears to substantiate the validity of John Best's title and, as the saying goes, 'possession is nine points of the law'. The inn continued in the ownership of John Best and his family until the early years of the eighteenth century when it was sold by his daughter Mary and grandson John Towne. As to the present whereabouts of the black box of deeds and its contents, it may not have survived and all records of owners prior to Francis Baker alias Williams could have been lost.

John Durston – Innholder

John Durston, the other innkeeper in Upton-upon-Severn, died in 1640 just prior to the Civil War. His will and the inventory of his goods and chattels give a further insight into the lives of seventeenth century innkeepers. (See Appendix A.) He was born in 1597 and was almost certainly the son of Thomas Durston of Upton. It is possible that his father kept the inn before him (the White Lion is said to date from the seventeenth century).[130] Whilst his will described him as 'yeoman' he was referred to as 'gentleman' in the Chancery records. The inventory of John Durston's effects makes an interesting comparison with those of the earlier innkeepers at the Crown (or King's Arms). There was no specific reference to an inn in either his will or the inventory and only by examining the nature and quantities of individual items does it become apparent that this was not a list of the goods and chattels of an ordinary yeoman farmer. Foremost, was the relatively large quantity of eight beds, four of which were 'joyned bedsteads'. The first room to be 'prized' was the 'Best Chamber'. Presumably this was reserved for the more refined paying guest and the description of the bed suggests it was a 'tester' complete with 'greene curtains and a fringe'. This chamber was well furnished, provided with eighteen cushions, chairs, tables and a 'trundle' bed for the servants. Other notable items in the inventory were seven table boards and eight table cloths, but perhaps the most remarkable item was the 'glasse cupboard with the glasses therein'. The glass-making industry was very much in its infancy in the first half of the seventeenth century and this was quite an early date to find drinking glasses in such a modest establishment and points to some degree of refinement. It is quite likely that this was the first time that many of the inhabitants of the town had become acquainted with a 'drinking glass'. The list of rooms in the inn suggests that the building, with only three bedchambers, was a little smaller than the Crown on the opposite side of the High Street. In common with many innkeepers of this period Durston was brewing ale or beer for his customers, albeit on a small scale. Barley was being malted in the 'Noast Chamber' (this was a room which functioned as an 'oast house'). Agriculture was still an important element in the household economy; Durston held some land and kept a few cows, heifers and some swine, sufficient to supply the household with milk, cheese and bacon. The quantity of books to the value of twenty shillings suggests that John Durston had had some formal education, but unfortunately the appraisers did not itemise the books and so there is no record of his reading matter. In common with other innkeepers of this time he would certainly have been of some stature in local society – a 'gentleman', and able to afford a good education for his children. His younger son, William Durston, attended Magdalen College, Oxford, gaining a B.A. in 1642 and becoming a *Doctor of Physic* after achieving a D.Med in 1660. (In the seventeenth century a university education, often followed by a career in the church, medicine or law, was the direction taken by many younger sons of gentlemen.)

---

130 A.W. Coysh, *Historic English Inns* p.165.

William Harrison made some pertinent observations on the social mobility of his era. Referring to those aspiring to be a 'gentleman', who 'can live without manuell labour, and thereto is able and will beare the port, charge, and countenance of a gentleman, he shall for monie have a coat and arms bestowed upon him by heralds (who in the charter of the same doo of custome pretend antiquitie and service and many gaie things), and thereunto made so good cheape, be called master, which is the title that men give to esquires and gentlemen...'. He continued in the same vein, that it is 'to be reprehended in all states of gentilitie, and which in short time will turne to the great ruine of our countrie, and that is, the usual sending of noblemens & meane gentlemens sonnes into Italie, from whence they bring home nothing but meere atheisme, infidelitie, vicious conversation, and ambitious and proud behaviour, whereby it commeth to pass that they return far worse men than they went out'.[131]

After the demise of her husband it is possible that Anne Durston continued to keep the inn but thus far no further records have come to light.

The English Civil War and Upton-upon-Severn

John Best was the innkeeper of the King's Arms during the four years of the first Civil War (1642-1646) and, like other tradesmen and townspeople, he would have witnessed events unfolding with a certain degree of apprehension. Upton-upon-Severn was situated at a strategic crossing point of the River Severn and the bridge was an important element in two battles during the conflict: 'Unwalled and defenceless, it lay at the mercy of any party which might choose to occupy it, and thus secure the bridge which was a necessary link on the road from East Worcestershire to Herefordshire.'[132] Upton's first notable encounter with the civil war was on the 13th of April 1643 when the Parliamentary troops commanded by William Waller were defeated at the battle of Ripple Field by the Royalists led by Prince Maurice, the younger brother of Prince Rupert. Both the Parliamentarians and the Royalists passed through Upton-upon-Severn on several occasions and with allowance for a little poetic licence Emily Lawson eloquently describes one such 'episode':

> Late one spring afternoon the course of life in the little town went on smoothly as usual; the housewives were kneading the flour, or stirring the plum porridge for the evening meal; the maidens had been to purchase fine lawn or sad-coloured cloth from Philip Bound, or their cherry-coloured and blue breast knots from Christopher Winbury, according to the political bias of their families; .... Suddenly, everyone was startled into excitement. Some husbandman hoeing the young wheat on the Palace Farm, or some herdsman

---

131 William Harrison, *The Description of England*. Ch. V. pp.128-9.

132 Emily Lawson, *The Nation in the Parish*, p.58.

tending his cows on historic Raven Hill, had seen a sight in the distance which sent him in hot haste to Upton. Glancing towards the hills, he had noticed dark masses of men moving slowly down the steep road by Little Malvern in regular order. They were partly hidden by clouds of dust, but an occasional glint of steel in the western sunlight showed they were armed men. As they drew nearer, anxious watchers could discern from their banners and uniform that these were the soldiers of Parliament. There was barely time for the startled Royalists in the town to hide away their plate in the coal-cellars, and their cash under a loose board ... before Waller's detachment marched in by Ale-house Green and Stocks-yat. They were eighteen hundred men, cavalry and infantry all told; men who believed both in themselves and in the officers who had led them to victory on many a well-fought field. Sir William Waller was one of the ablest generals of his time, a good man and a gentleman, while his second in command, Colonel Massey, is equally well known for his successes ... On the first tidings of the approach of the Parliamentarians, messengers had been despatched to the chief parishoners, and Lawyer Hackett would hurry in, armed with a long list of townspeople, classified according to their options. By this list orders for billeting the soldiers were rapidly made out, and the house of every Royalist was soon crowded from basement to garret with unwelcome visitors; while the Puritan gentry and tradespeople received as many as their rooms would comfortably accommodate. ... The detachments of Sir William Waller and Prince Maurice at this period seem to have troubled themselves very little with camp equipage, but moved rapidly about the country, trusting to the enforced hospitality of the towns. ... The troops of the Parliament were generally kept in good order, and restrained from the violence and cruelty which characterised earlier civil wars. It is to be feared that the Royalist soldiers were far more lawless ... Far into the night Upton was full of turmoil and clamour, poultry and little pigs being caught and slaughtered, furniture and bedding being dragged from one house to another, shops and store-rooms ransacked for bread and meat, while in every inn barrels of ale and cider were set running to supply the moderate potations of the Puritans.[133]

On those occasions when Upton-upon-Severn became embroiled in the conflict the military forces would have readily availed themselves of the facilities of the two inns. Much of the burden of billeting fell on alehouse-keepers, victuallers and innkeepers, and whilst the 'Petition of Right' of 1628 was supposed to have granted private householders exemption from having soldiers quartered on them, this was not always respected. In towns and villages the population was expected to provide 'free quarter' for the soldiers; there were set rates for feeding and lodging troops, and providing fodder for the horses. When no money was available the

133 Emily Lawson, *The Nation in the Parish*, pp.58-61.

reluctant host was issued with a voucher to be redeemed at a later date although many had great difficulty in being reimbursed. Naturally there would have been some selection as to who had the benefit of the better facilities, with the lower ranks being consigned to the alehouses, taverns and cottages. Even though the Puritans abhorred drunkenness and high-living they were by no means abstainers from alcoholic refreshments and if Sir William Waller and his officers were partial to a glass of claret they could have patronised John Best's hostelry. Perhaps Cromwell's general and his colonels sat in the inn, drinking his finest Malmsey wine or Claret to wash away the dust of the Malvern Hills whilst discussing the tactics of Prince Maurice and his Royalist army; their host undoubtedly reflecting on whether or not he was to be recompensed for the 'refreshments' recently delivered from the port of Bristol or once again would he be contributing to 'the war effort'. There is no indication as to which party John Best favoured during the hostilities. Certainly he was well acquainted with Richard Dowdeswell, described as 'a zealous loyalist' and with Christopher Wynbury who, according to Mrs Lawson's account, was also with the Royalist cause. John Best probably kept his own counsel for he must have been well known to supporters on both sides of the conflict.

The numerous encounters with the opposing forces in the Civil War could have been uncomfortable for the proprietor of an inn displaying a sign with Royalist connotations. Inn and alehouse signs were often an expression of political opinion. John Taylor, a poet, proprietor of the *Crown* at Phoenix Alley in London, and fervent royalist renamed his alehouse the *Mourning Crown* after the execution of Charles I. The Parliamentarians did not appreciate this public display of royalist sympathy, Taylor was obliged to replace the sign with a portrait of his own head and the *Mourning Crown* then became the *Poet's Head*. Richard Flecknoe, who penned his '*Aenigmatical Characters*' in the seventeenth century, devoted one character to the Puritans entitled '*Of your Fanatick Reformers*'. Referring to the enforced change of signs with 'unsuitable' connotations he wrote: 'As for the Signs they have pretty well begun their reformation already, changing the sign of the *Salutation of the Angel and our Lady* into the *Soldier and Citizen,* and the *Katherine Wheel* into the *Cat and Wheel*…Such ridiculous work they make of their reformation, and so zealous they are against all *Mirth* and *Jollity*, as they would pluck down the Sign of the *Cat and Fiddle* too, if it durst but play so loud as they might hear it'.[134] There is no mention of any such change of name at the King's Arms in Upton-upon-Severn.

The Civil War disrupted commerce throughout the country and several towns in the lower Severn valley were particularly affected. Bridgenorth, Worcester and Upton-upon-Severn were all involved in the conflict. Tewkesbury, to the south, situated near another strategic river crossing, suffered extensively at the hands of the opposing forces, being occupied by both Roundheads and Cavaliers. The wine

---

134 Richard Flecknoe, *Aenigmatical Characters*, London, p.83 (1665) and also Larwood and Hotten, *English Inn Signs*, pp.8-9.

trade was badly disrupted; importers and vintners all felt the effects of war; many of their customers were amongst those landed gentry who had been deprived of their estates or forced into exile. Innkeepers, depending to a considerable extent upon merchants and carriers for their livelihood, would have been particularly affected by the hostilities. The import of wine from the continent was interrupted, and the port of Bristol, where wine arrived from France, Spain and Portugal, was twice under siege from the opposing armies; in 1643 Bristol was taken by the Royalist armies and in August 1645 it was retaken by the Parliamentarians. The merchant ships were commandeered and the wine trade was severely reduced. As the conflict continued Parliament found that it could not fund the civil war from Royal revenues and resorted to further taxation. Wine had always been subject to customs charges and parliament increased the duty payable. Prior to the hostilities the duty on wine which had been three pounds per tun, increased to nine pounds and retail prices rose accordingly. Spanish wines sold at eighteen pence a quart and French wine seven pence.[135] Such drastic price inflation would certainly have adversely affected trade at the King's Arms in Upton-upon-Severn.

John Best died in 1645 towards the end of the First Civil War. He did not leave a will and letters of administration were granted to his widow, Katherine. He was described as a yeoman, both in the purchase deed and in the inventory of his goods. There is no specific mention of John Best being the innkeeper and the Quarter Sessions records do not make any reference to inns in Upton-upon-Severn during the period of his occupancy. The evidence from the inventory of John Best's effects shows that he was in fact an innkeeper as there are certain anomalies that once again point to the fact that the goods and chattels were not characteristic of a yeoman farmer. Firstly, there was the quantity and quality of the beds and bedding (one bedstead had all the curtains and curtain rods to accompany it), and secondly the cellar contained a large quantity of beer (over two hundred gallons), which on its own is perhaps not significant. However, the two most notable items were the large quantity of seven table boards and the total of seventy-eight table napkins, the latter being an unusually high number for a yeoman farmer. (In other inventories for some Worcestershire gentlemen of this period the average quantity of napkins was nineteen). Hence, unless John Best was entertaining his friends on a prodigious scale it is safe to assume that the inventory relates to the King's Arms. The few cows and ten acres of corn are indicative of John Best, like his predecessors, being involved in husbandry, albeit on a small scale. (His inventory is shown in Appendix B.)

After the death of John Best the ownership of the inn passed to his wife, Katherine, who within two years had taken a new husband, Henry Symes. Symes then became 'possessed' of all his wife's freehold and other property. He was mentioned in a Rent Roll of freeholders for Upton-upon-Severn dated 1647: 'Henry Simes, *in jure uxoris*, 1s' ('*in jure uxoris*' meaning he held the property 'by right of his

---

135 A.D. Francis, *The Wine Trade*, p.57.

wife').[136] Katherine and Henry Symes were innholders during the period leading up to the battle of Worcester in 1651. On the 30th January 1649 Charles I was beheaded by the Parliamentarians and on the 1st January 1651 his son Charles was officially crowned King of Scotland at Scone. Charles II with his Scottish allies marched south into England and by 22nd August of that year his forces were at Worcester, a city with Royalist sympathies. As a defence against the Parliamentarians the Royalists were preparing to destroy several of the Severn bridges leading to the city. Consequently, the bridge downstream at Upton-upon-Severn assumed strategic importance. On 25th August the Royalists despatched Major-General Edward Massey towards Upton with a force of 300 troops of the 5th Cavalry Brigade, and for his headquarters, he requisitioned Severn End at Hanley Castle, the home of the parliamentarian Nicholas Lechmere. Doubtless, the officers made themselves comfortable, once again billeted in the two inns in the High Street in Upton-upon-Severn. The Royalists destroyed the arch of the stone bridge nearest the town, and following normal procedure, left a plank in place to allow passage of friendly troops but remarkably did not mount a guard on the crossing. Cromwell had ordered Major-General John Lambert with his dragoons to Upton on the 27th of August. The King's Arms would have been a close witness to the events of the morning of 28th August, certainly much closer than any of the inhabitants of the town would have wished to be. The parliamentarians were able to send a small force across the unguarded plank and arriving at the lower part of the High Street established a bridgehead on the west bank of the river. This allowed the cavalry to ford the river and by the end of the day 12,000 Roundheads had crossed to the west bank of the Severn. The hostilities and destruction of the arches of the bridge must have curtailed the activities of merchants and trades people in the area. Once again innkeepers would have been affected. It is quite possible that as a consequence of a decline in trade during the civil war Katherine Symes had let out part of the inn to a tenant as a 'sales shop'. Certainly, at sometime before 1710 a sales shop had been established in the premises. The ground floor rooms of many inns situated in town centres were often let as shops for they provided valuable retail space fronting on to the high street. By the end of the Civil War the King's Arms may have seen better days and one contemporary caricature of an English inn could be an intimation of its reduced circumstances:

136 WAAS 705:46 BA104/1.

Of an English Inne
Made Anno 1654

An English Inne is a House of so ancient standing, as 'tis ready to fall down agen; onely its Sign-poast is new, and in that consists its greatest Gallantry. Within 'tis a great Machin of four wheels, Ostler, Cook, Tapster and Chamberlain, with mine Hoast and Hoastis, the main Springs that move all the rest. Being entred, they all fall to couzening[137] you in their severall Vocations; the Ostler your Horses, the rest you; the Cook with meat so tough and raw roasted, as spite of your teeth y'are forc't to leave it to the house, the Tapster in so miscounting his stone Juggs, as you may as well count the Stoneage as them; then the Chamberlain uses such couzenage with his Faggots, as the fire it self can scarcely bring to light. For your Chamber, it seems the Pressyard[138] by the pillars of the bed, with a Teastern so heavy, as if it fall on you, Lord have mercy upon you, and for more exquisite torment and in lingring pain; you have a heavy Tapestry for Coverlet, in Summer kills you with heat, and in Winter with cold as well as weight; with a Feather-bed, whole feathers (as if you flounc't into the water) part on either side, and you in the midst to sink unto the bottom. For mine Hoast and Hoastis, who were wont to be good fellows in the dayes of jollity, their humours are spoild in this time of godliness and stumm'd Sack[139] and Religion has quite marr'd their mirth; onely mine Hoast will make a shift still to be half drunk every day, and on Market dayes out-right, when he is wonderous kinde; and his kindeness chiefly consists in a pint of Sack to the Master, and a double Jug to the Servingman, alwayes in order to the Reckoning, which as a Warning-piece being discharged once, there follows a whole volley of Welcomes, like small shot discharg'd on every side, and you are discharged too.

(Richard Flecknoe, *Aenigmatical Characters*, p.104: *Of an English Inne. Made Anno 1654*, London, 1665.)

---

137 cozen – to cheat, deceive or defraud.

138 Pressyard is a reference to a courtyard in the old Newgate Prison where the torture of *'peine forte et dure'* was supposed to have been carried out.

139 stum: in this context, to renew wine by mixing with stum or must and start a new fermentation.

Another, less popular, public duty attached to the innkeeper was that of 'office keeper' for the Excise. Excise Duty, introduced in 1643, was a levy on many home-produced goods and Excise Offices were set up in all market towns. These Excise Offices were usually located in inns, where a room was provided for the officers to conduct their business.[140] They held regular 'sitting days' to gather the excise duties; these collections occurred eight times a year. The innkeeper or 'office keeper' received entries and notices submitted by those traders who were obliged to pay the duties,[141] a practice that did not cease until the nineteenth century.

Inns have long been associated with parliamentary elections and following the death of Oliver Cromwell in 1658 writs were issued summoning Parliament to meet at Westminster on the 27th January. Nicholas Lechmere and Thomas Foley were 'chosen' as representatives for Worcestershire. Lechmere complained of the very costly expense of hiring 'severall Innes in Worcester for the entertaynment' of their friends the total cost being 'noe lesse than six hundred and fourteen pounds'.[142]

Following the restoration of the monarchy in 1660 parliament granted Charles II an annual income of £1.2 million, derived mainly from customs and excise duties. These duties alone were insufficient to provide this sum and in 1662 the Hearth Tax Bill or Chimney Money Act was passed by parliament to supplement his income. This very unpopular tax was imposed upon those householders whose dwellings exceeded the yearly value of twenty shillings. A tax of two shillings per annum was payable for every hearth in their house and was collected twice yearly. Several Hearth Tax rolls exist for Upton-upon-Severn listing names of householders and the number of taxable hearths. The earliest roll, dated 1662, gives some indication of the comparative size and status of the King's Arms in Upton. This roll shows that out of the total population of the town there were about 130 householders liable to pay tax on a total of 278 hearths. Of these eligible households 48% possessed just a single hearth and 30% had only two hearths. Henry Symes, being the taxable householder of the King's Arms, had five hearths. Only five buildings in Upton possessed more than five hearths, these included Henry Bromley, the lord of the manor, with ten, the parsonage with seven, Thomas Bound[143] with six and Phillip Bound with fourteen hearths. A later roll for Upton lists several hearths as having been 'demolished' and by 1672 Henry Symes was paying tax on only three hearths. The taxation list for January 1675 shows that Henry Symes was by then deceased and 'Widdow Symes' was again paying tax on five hearths. Her neighbour, Samuel Phillips, had just one hearth. There was considerable objection to paying the Hearth Tax and it was finally repealed in 1689 when William and Mary acceded to the throne.

---

140 Graham Smith, *Something To Declare* p.14.

141 Ibid. p.28.

142 *Hanley and the House of Lechemere*, p.28.

143 This person was most probably 'Captain' Thomas Bound.

The younger Katherine Best, one of the daughters of the late John Best the innkeeper, was a person of some social standing, and as to be expected she had married accordingly, a Mr. Thomas Wilson in Croome d'Abitot in 1667. (In the seventeenth century the title 'Mr' or 'Master' was a declaration of status, used by gentlemen and esquires.) Their marriage only lasted two years, for Katherine was widowed in 1669. Thomas Wilson had died intestate but the inventory of his worldly goods is both interesting and unusual. Clearly he was not living in his own property and only one room was mentioned: 'his Lodgeing chamber' which contained his bed, furniture and other articles. The remainder of his effects was found 'In other rooms dispersed'. There was no mention of agriculture or husbandry and the only suggestion of any occupation or trade came from 'seven little wine runletts' (a 'runlet' was a small cask for holding wine or other liquor), 'four dozen of napkins' and a quantity of drinking pots of varying size. It is conceivable that once married, he and Katherine had moved into a chamber in the King's Arms in Upton-upon-Severn and lived in the inn with Katherine Symes and her husband Henry, and participated in the running of the hostelry.

Thomas Bound – a Relative Complaint

In 1672 Katherine Wilson (née Best) married a second time, her new husband was Thomas Bound of Upton-upon-Severn and it was not long before he too became entangled in Chancery proceedings. Two years later, in 1674, he was the Orator in a cause against three of his relatives – his uncle, Phillip Bound, Giles King and his wife, Mary, the latter being Thomas' half sister (Giles King was from Stratton in Gloucestershire).[144] This case had its roots in the extensive matrimonial activities of his late father, the 'infamous' Captain Thomas Bound whose ghost is said to haunt the streets of Upton-upon-Severn. Much has been written about Thomas Bound, the father, some of it fact and some of it most probably fiction. Stories have been passed down from generation to generation, each telling and re-telling embellishing and enlarging the tales. One such account, as re-told by Mrs Lawson, relates that 'Captain Bound was a desperately wicked man, very cruel, and covetous, and hard to the poor. He had some land in the Ham, and he used to ride down there on a grey horse, when folk were not about to see him, and remove the land-marks, so as to get more land for his self. He was married to three wives, but the poor creatures had a hard time of it, and he made away with two on 'em. He lived for a good bit at Soley's orchard, and he had some fields nigh the house, but he wanted more. There was an old lady who lived at Southend, and owned the farm, and it ought to have come after her to some relations who were in poor circumstances. When she was a-dying Captain Bound was there, and he watched his chance, and as soon as she died he put a pen into the hand of the corpse, and guided it so as her should sign a will which left all to him. Then he went and took up his abode at Southend; but

---

144 TNA C 6/211/9, *Bound v. Bound.*

the old lady's ghost appeared there very soon, and, what with that and, it may be, things going contrary, he grew so miserable that he could not wait for the Lord to send him death, but he went and drowned his self in the pool by the Causeway (the raised path which connects the Rectory-lane and Southend).'[145] There is at least one inaccuracy in this account, for Captain Bound was married four times. The story of his suicide led to the myth that he was denied a Christian burial and was buried in unconsecrated ground – 'the shadowy funeral of the Captain going from the town to the Causeway pool'. Mrs Lawson continued: 'One lady still living declares that, in her childhood, she met this phantom array, a coffin covered in a black pall, and three or four men following in black cloaks; that she thought it was an ordinary funeral, and only marvelled that it should be going from, instead of towards, the church'.[146] These ghostly legends were enlarged after Thomas Bound's death and 'his awful presence haunted Soley's orchard and Southend'.

In contradiction of these tales Captain Thomas Bound was actually given a Christian burial. The parish register records his funeral and, after the preamble in his will, he directed: 'in the yeare of our Lord God one Thousand six hundred sixty six in manner and forme as followeth First I bequeath my soule unto the hands of my mediator my lord and saviour Jesus Christ hoping to receave the benefitt of all his merritts and to praise the lorde for his free Grace forever more for my body I desire it may be buried under some stone in our parish Charnell that my first wife Mary that was the daughter of Mr Cooke of Longdon was buried & now lyeth over her grave. And that five pounds may be given to our poore...'. (Five pounds was about seven hundred pounds today.) In the early part of the nineteenth century, when a vault was being constructed in the parish church for a member of the Beale family, a statue of De Boteler was discovered and lying beneath it was the gravestone of Captain Thomas Bound.

Thomas Bound's Chancery suit of 1674 involved the disputed ownership of several properties and lands in Upton-upon-Severn and elsewhere which had been in the possession of the elder Thomas Bound. In particular it concerned the wording or the 'declaration' of a '*Deed to Declare the Uses of a Fine*', a legal document connected with the '*Fine sur cognizance de droit come ceo*', which explained the true intention of the 'Fine' and was prepared at a later date. (A '*Deed Leading to the Uses of a Fine*' was a similar document produced prior to the Fine.) As usual the Bill and Answers provided a lot of genealogical information, some of which conflicted with previous histories of the Bounds. It is very difficult to ascertain the true facts in this particular case. Not only was the complainant making charges against the three defendants, but the two co-defendants, Giles King and his wife, Mary, were making accusations against the other defendant, Phillip Bound. In their Answer, Giles and Mary King stated that they believed that the complainant (Thomas Bound) and Phillip Bound

145 E. Lawson, *The Nation in the Parish*, p.182.
146 Ibid. p.184.

'subtilly combined together against these defendants to coasin[147] & defraud these defendants of their just right in the said lands'. They also asserted that Phillip Bound was the 'promoter' of the court case.[148] As to be expected with any Chancery case, there would be at least two versions of prior events – one version according to the Bill issued by the Orator and the other (or others) in the Answers from the Defendants. Phillip Bound's Answer gave a perfectly satisfactory (and believable) version of events prior to the Complaint.[149]

Captain Thomas Bound (hereinafter 'Thomas Bound the elder' will refer to Captain Thomas Bound) had inherited land and property in Upton-upon-Severn from his father, also called Thomas Bound. In 1639 Thomas Bound the elder had married Mary Cooke, daughter of Mr Cooke, of Chambers Court in nearby Longdon, a 'gentleman of good position and fortune'. Mary died one year later following the death of their only child, Thomas, who was just two months old. Thomas Bound the elder subsequently married Mary Higgins, from Tewkesbury, who came with a considerable marriage portion of fifteen hundred pounds or thereabouts (about £220,000 today). A settlement for the benefit of Mary Higgins was arranged prior to their marriage. The sole issue of this union was a daughter, Mary, who later married the defendant, Giles King. Eight years later Thomas Bound was again widowed when his second wife, Mary, died in 1647 but he soon re-married. In 1648 he 'took to wife Margaret Nourse', a widow (other sources say he married a Margaret Batherne but one of these surnames could well be her maiden name). Margaret produced six children two of whom died in infancy. Their eldest child was Thomas Bound junior, the Orator in this present Chancery case.

According to the Bill of Complaint, Thomas Bound's third wife, Margaret, was 'seized and possessed' of real and personal estate to the value of at least one thousand pounds which increased her husband's fortune to over three thousand pounds. With the agreement of his wife these lands were sold and the monies raised were used to buy other lands 'which he gave away and disposed of amongst his other children and to other uses'. However, the version given by Giles King and his wife differed – they 'have heard and doubteth not to prove that Margaret Nourse was indebted' and that her property was 'mortgaged for two or three hundred pounds'. Their version agreed with that of the Orator in respect of Margaret's lands being sold but they stated that considerable sums of money were laid down for the purchase of Harvington Manor near Evesham. There is some truth in this version of events. In 1652 Thomas Bound the elder purchased the Manor of Harvington from the Commissioners responsible for the sale of the lands of the Dean and Chapter of Worcester. The manor was charged at a yearly rent of £3 6s 8d which was paid

---

147 coasin = cozen: to cheat or defraud.
148 Giles King and Mary King issued a separate Bill of Complaint against Philip Bound, Thomas Herbert, gent, Thomas Cooke, gent and others. (C 5/511/6 *King v Bound*).
149 TNA C 6/214/10, *Bound v Bound*.

towards the maintenance of the Free Grammar School in Worcester. According to Phillip Bound, the greater part of these lands was settled by jointure on Margaret Bound.

Margaret Bound died in 1658 three months after the birth of their sixth child, Sara, who had died in infancy. Once again Thomas Bound was a widower and once more he acquired a new wife, a widow, Mary Collier, whom he married in November 1661. In his Bill of Complaint Thomas Bound junior said that about this time his father was indebted to several persons for 'sommes of money for which … … Phillipp Bound, his brother, stood engaged as his surety'. (Phillip Bound was in occupation of certain lands and property in Upton as tenant to his brother Thomas – the Hearth Tax returns show that this included a substantial property with a large number of hearths). It was claimed that for various reasons it was expedient for Thomas Bound the elder to take a *Fine sur cognizance de droit come ceo* in the Court of Common Pleas. This *Fine* did not convey the freehold but declared the 'Uses for Lives' of certain messuages and lands in Upton-upon-Severn and elsewhere. The 'Use' was for the lives of Thomas Bound the elder and his brother Phillip and to 'the longer liver' of them and then to the heirs of the elder Thomas Bound. If the younger Thomas Bound were to outlive his father and his uncle he would then inherit these lands and property. According to Thomas Bound's Bill of Complaint the defendant, Giles King, had somehow got hold of the deeds or indentures and put them 'in his pockett or bagge and refused to deliver them to him'. There were claims and counterclaims concerning these documents, the most significant being that Thomas Bound the elder had declared the 'Uses of the Fine' to bar his fourth wife, Mary Collier, from 'her dower or title to her dower' (dower was a common law right of a widow to one third of her husband's estate for her life). It was also argued that Thomas Bound the elder did not have the power to impose such a bar on his wife's dower. The documents do not provide any explanation as to why he would choose to impede his wife's rights after his death. It was also claimed that in the event of the decease of the elder Thomas Bound the rental income from these extensive lands and properties was to be applied to payment of his debts. In his Answer, Phillip Bound referred to these 'troublesome times' and revealed that following the restoration of the monarchy the Manor of Harvington was taken from Thomas Bound the elder by the Dean and Chapter of Worcester. As a consequence of this re-possession Captain Bound lost a considerable portion of the money that he had paid for the purchase of the manor.

The elder Thomas Bound died in 1667 leaving other properties in his will to his daughter, Mary, by his second wife, and to his son, Samuel, and daughter, Ann, both children by his third wife, Margaret. The executors named to dispose of his estate were his brother, Phillip, and daughter, Mary. Phillip Bound was to have the benefit of the rent from certain property in Upton for his life. There was no mention of the younger Thomas Bound in his father's will but, as the eldest son, he stood to inherit the lands and properties cited in the *Fine sur cognizance de droit come ceo*. According to the Orator's bill of complaint Phillip Bound then took possession of all the goods and chattells as well as all the messuages and lands of Thomas Bound the elder and received the rents thereof, allegedly to pay off the debts of the deceased.

Three years later, when the younger Thomas Bound came of age, he was 'suddenly acquainted' by his uncle Phillip that there were insufficient monies available to settle all his late father's debts and that there was a considerable deficit of at least five hundred pounds. This statement was clearly contradicted in the Answer from Giles and Mary King who declared that they understood that there had been sufficient personal estate to pay off these outstanding debts. (Phillip Bound still stood surety for the debts of the deceased Thomas Bound the elder.) It was then suggested to Thomas Bound by his uncle that the possession of certain property and lands 'would much creditt him' and his uncle would then be able to 'proffer him in marriage'. (For a young gentleman seeking a suitable spouse in the seventeenth century land and property were an essential pre-requisite to convince the bride's family that he was of sound financial standing. Any encumbrance on the estate may have been conveniently forgotten.) Thomas junior 'readily embraced' this offer and to accommodate his uncle's scheme he 'immediately entered into a Recognizance or Statute Merchant taken before the Mayor and Towne clerke of the City of Worcester to ye said Phillipp Bound for five hundred pounds'. (A 'Statute Merchant' was a form of bond which provided tradespeople with a process at law for recovering a loan where the borrower was in default, although eventually it came to be used by the public at large.) Whilst this land and property were in Thomas Bound's name he was bound by the Statute to pay his uncle five hundred pounds which, they both hopefully anticipated, his new wife would provide as her marriage portion. It is quite possible that some of this land and property may have been bequeathed to Mary Bound, now wife of Giles King.

In his Bill, Thomas Bound continued: 'Phillipp Bound in a seemingly friendly manner went with your Orator to severall treatyes as touching your Orators marriage to severall persons of good fortune' – his uncle confirmed this, saying that he went on several journeys with his nephew in search of a suitable bride. Unfortunately, their physical attraction did not match their personal fortunes because Thomas ignored his uncle's advice and fell for the charms of a young woman, recently widowed – Katherine Wilson née Best. Thomas and Katherine were married by licence in Upton-upon-Severn on 22nd April 1672. Katherine gave her age as 'twenty five years and upwards' – she was probably nearer thirty five years of age. The newly wedded couple may each have been disappointed with what their respective partners brought to their marriage. Thomas' property was still subject to his uncle's bond and Katherine appears to have had little in the way of 'ready money', and so when payment came due to his uncle he was unable to pay the full five hundred pounds cited in the Statute Merchant. Phillip Bound then promptly issued a *Writ of Capias Si Laicus*[150] against his young nephew and, as Thomas related, 'thereon arrested your Orator's body' and took possession of all his 'goods chattels lands and tenements lyeing in Worcestershire'. Phillip Bound kept his nephew in prison for about eighteen months, during which time he sold off all his personal possessions. Eventually, 'being weary of lying in prison' Thomas, with the aid of friends (i.e. his family), pleaded to be able to meet with his uncle to discuss his wretched plight. After much discussion and negotiation Phillip Bound finally agreed to allow Thomas Bound to mortgage the properties for six hundred pounds and thereby relieved his nephew from his obligations in the Statute Merchant that he had previously signed. The mortgage was to be in the name of Phillip Bound's son, another Phillip. According to Phillip Bound's Answer, within about twelve months Thomas Bound had paid four hundred and fifty pounds as a part payment of this mortgage. The Bill of Complaint does not mention this payment but continues to recount that the title deeds or indentures were never released to Thomas Bound who then commenced his action in Chancery.

Perhaps Phillip Bound had devised some villainous scheme to deprive his nephew of his inheritance, taking advantage of his age and inexperience or it could have been a scheme to defraud Giles King and his wife Mary of her inheritance. Thomas Bound was eventually re-united with some of his land and property; the 1675 Hearth Tax Roll for Upton lists 'Thomas Bound, gent.', with six hearths and also 'Mr Bound for ye Folly' (this could be 'Sillies Orchard'), seven hearths and 'Mr Bound for Pinnocks', two hearths. Phillip Bound was charged for six hearths. When Thomas Bound died in 1677 his will mentioned several properties among the bequests to his wife, Katherine; he owned freehold land in Buryfield and elsewhere in Upton-upon-Severn; he held a lease on property called Sillies alias Sollies Orchard also in Upton, and freehold land in Monmouthshire.

This case seems to have spawned a number of subsequent suits and counter suits in Chancery. These cases involved the lease (for 'three lives and one and twenty years') on Sollies Orchard which was in the hands of Thomas Bound junior. Sollies Orchard was one of a number of properties involved in the marriage settlement when the elder Thomas Bound had married Mary Higgins in 1646, and was bequeathed to Mary King. It appears that Giles King and his wife, Mary, had launched a suit[151] against Thomas Bound claiming the lease of Sollies Orchard was theirs; this case was heard before a Master in Chancery who found in favour of the plaintiffs. Unfortunately, Thomas Bound died before the proceedings had been concluded and consequently Giles King and his wife had to issue a Bill of Revivor[152] against Thomas Bound's widow, Katherine, who had already launched a counter suit in Chancery against the complainants (the documents to this case have not been

150 A Chancery writ issued against defaulting debtors in Statute Merchant and Statute Staple.
151 This would be C 5/511/6: *King v Bound*.
152 C 5/511/7: *King v Bound*.

traced). Katherine Bound had inherited her late husband's estate and in the Bill of Revivor the plaintiffs declared that Thomas Bound had died intestate which was obviously a completely false allegation. The outcome of these cases has not been established but Sollies Orchard was later purchased by Humphey Soley (this could be the same property mentioned in the Index to Worcestershire Fines (1649-1714) when, in 1679, Phillip Bound sold some land or property to Humphrey Soley).

The *Statute of Merchants* (13 Edw. I (1285)) had its origins in the *Statute of Acton Burnell* of 1283 (11 Edw. I) which allowed creditors to enrol debts before a clerk in six towns of England, (London, Bristol, Lincoln, York, Shrewsbury and Winchester) and provided a remedy in the event of default on the part of the debtor whereby the sheriff could seize and sell his goods. The 1283 statute contained the proviso that where the debtor had 'no moveable goods whereupon the debt may be levied, then his body be taken where it may be found, and kept in prison until he have made agreement, or his friends for him; and if he have not wherewith he may sustain himself in prison, the Creditor shall find him bread and water, to the end that he not die in prison for default of sustenance, the which costs the debtor shall recompense him with his debt before he be let out of prison'. The objective of the imprisonment was more in the interest of the creditors, to keep the debtor safe in custody (and hopefully alive) until he cleared his debts, rather than as a punishment for his circumstances. Many sheriffs and officials refused to implement this statute, which proved unworkable and in 1285 it was superseded by the *Statute of Merchants*. This statute extended the scope of the earlier *Statute of Acton Burnell* and allowed creditors to enrol debts before officials (the mayor, chief warden or clerks) in other English towns but in cases of default the creditor could now immediately have the debtor seized and imprisoned. If the debtor refused or was unable to pay the debt the creditor could then obtain a writ for the seizure and sale of the debtor's goods and property to the value of the debt.

Further statutes were passed in an attempt to resolve the continuing problem of insolvent debtors. The first that referred to bankrupts was that of 1542 in the reign of Henry VIII entitled *'An Acte Against Such Persones as doo make Bankrupte'*, (34 & 35 Hen. VIII, c.4).

> 'Where divers and soondrye persons craftelye obteyning into theyre handes greate substance of other mennes goods doo sodenlie flee to partes unknowne or kepe theyre houses, not mynding to paie or restore to any theyre creditoures theyre debtes and dueties, but at theyre owne willes and pleasures consume the substaunce obteyned by credyte of other men, for theyre owne pleasures and delicate lyving, againste all reasonce, quytie [equity] and good conscience'.

This statute was specifically directed against debtors who fled their obligations and gave the Lord Chancellor the authority to take action against such persons by 'imprysonment of theyre bodies or otherwyse, as allso with theyre lands tenements fees annuities and offices …'. It empowered the authorities to seize the debtor's money, goods and merchandise and to reimburse his creditors but more significantly, the debtor was neither discharged nor given exemption in respect of future profits or earnings. Imprisonment did not favour the debtor who thenceforth would not have the opportunity to work and trade, thus enabling him to pay off his debts.

Mary Ellery's Complaint

In 1679 Katherine Symes and her daughter, Katherine Bound, became embroiled in another dispute concerning land and property and were two of the parties cited in a Bill of Complaint originated by Mary Ellery, a widow, of Upton-upon-Severn in another case in Chancery, Ellery v. Symes.[153]

This case had its origins in a transfer of various properties and parcels of land 'situate' in Upton-upon-Severn belonging to John Young of Hanley Castle. In 1633 Young had leased three cottages and about forty-five acres of land, including three acres called Parson's Field, to Roger Lowe of Bromsgrove.[154] The land was held on a ninety-nine year lease at the yearly ground rent of 'four pounds eleven shillings and four pence, two couples of sufficient hens and one pound of white sugar'. There was a windmill sited on the estate (in the appropriately named *Wyndmill Field*) which was excluded from the lease. The various premises were sublet to tenants and Parson's Field was at that time in use for the cultivation of hops. In 1637 Lowe assigned the lease of Parson's Field together with one 'messuage or tenement' to a Daniel Rawlinson at the yearly ground rent of 'five shillings and a sugar loaf'. The land was sublet at the rate of twenty shillings per annum and the property at ten pounds per annum. Then, in 1640, Daniel Rawlinson assigned the land and property in trust 'for the better support of his daughter Mary, the wife of Lawrence Hackett, and two of their daughters, Mary and Martha'. The two trustees were John Webley from Hanley Castle and William Webley from Much Marcle in Herefordshire. After the decease of his daughter, Mary, the rental income was to pass, in turn, to each of his granddaughters. The younger Mary Hackett (who was the Oratrix in the Bill of Complaint) had married William Ellery of Chipping Sodbury in Gloucestershire. By 1676 all the parties to the assignment were deceased with the exception of Mary Ellery. Daniel Webley of Hanley Castle, a relative of the trustees, had been appointed executor of the estates of the late John and William Webley.

In the Bill of Complaint Mary Ellery related that her husband, William, who 'having occasion for moneys desired to borrow the sum of thirty pounds of William

---

153 TNA C 6/234/13, (Bill of Complaint and Answers) and C 22/245/35, (Depositions).

154 During the cholera outbreak of 1832 that caused many deaths in Upton-upon-Severn it was 'decided to forbid internments in the churchyards and an area in Parson's Field about half a mile outside the town was used as a burial plot – see Emily Lawson, *The Nation in The Parish*, p.173.

Bound of Upton-upon-Severn', agreed to sign over his interest in Parson's Field as security for the loan. The Bill further related that William Bound lent fifteen pounds to William Ellery with a promise of a further fifteen pounds, the lease to be conveyed to Katherine Symes of Upton in trust for William Bound as security. Mary Ellery claimed that William Bound never paid the second instalment of fifteen pounds and that William Bound, Katherine Symes and 'William' Webley (there is an error in the document here and the latter should read 'Daniel Webley') had combined together to defraud her of the property. In her Bill of Complaint she referred to them as '*the Confederates*'. The Answers from the defendants were, as to be expected, rather different from Mary Ellery's account of the events leading to her Complaint. The most notable discrepancy was the name <u>William Bound</u> when the person involved was actually <u>Thomas Bound</u> of Upton-upon-Severn, the husband of Katherine Bound (Mary Ellery was confusing the names of two of the individuals involved). Mary had been somewhat economical with the truth regarding William Ellery's requirements for money. The defendants' Answer made his situation very clear: 'the said William Ellery beinge a prisoner for debt in the Gaole for the County of Gloucester and extremely wanting for money for his Deliverance out of the said prison' (the sum involved was actually thirty-one pounds). Thomas Bound agreed out of 'great kindness' to lend thirty-one pounds to Ellery despite being 'himself indebted and not very well in a purchasinge Condition'.

The depositions of the witnesses revealed the whole unhappy story. (On this occasion the Commissioners took the depositions at the house of John Bayly, an innholder at the sign of the Pyed Bull in Northgate Street in Gloucester.) William Ellery had been imprisoned for debt at the Castle in Gloucester and his wife Mary had prevailed upon Thomas Bound to lend them thirty pounds or thereabouts using their leasehold land in Upton-upon-Severn as security. On the 15th of June 1677 Mary Ellery and Thomas Bound together with John Towne (husband of Mary Best and brother-in-law to Thomas Bound) had all travelled to Gloucester and called at the house of Ferdinand Meighen, an 'Attorney at Lawe' in that city. Mary Ellery pleaded with Meighen to go with them to the gaol to speak with her husband William. To this Meighen agreed and the party, together with the attorney's young clerk James Elly, set forth to the Castle. On arrival at Ellery's prison cell the parties discussed the transaction. Mary Ellery was very agitated and desperate for a completion and 'did press and importune the said Thomas Bound to purchase' and 'did then declare that she had a minde to parte with the lands now in question for that shee had noe thoughts of comeinge ever again to live att Upton and did likewise declare that if they did not sell the premises att Upton there could be noe way to procure her husbands enlargement out of prison'. William Ellery told Meighen that if this was not done 'Mary his wife and children must perish'. Thomas Bound declared that he was 'not really wishing to purchase' but out of kindness

She did press and importune the said Thomas Bound to purchase.

eventually agreed and was to pay the sum of thirty-one pounds for Ellery's 'interest' in the land and the property. (He would have had some sympathy for the prisoner's plight having been imprisoned for debt himself.) There were three 'parties' to the transaction, Thomas Bound, Mary and William Ellery, and Daniel Webley, the trustee, who was not present. Bound agreed to pay sixteen pounds which was sufficient to secure the release of William Ellery from prison. The balance was to be paid when Webley had signed and sealed his part of the indenture. In the prison cell James Elly produced paper, parchment and writing materials and Meighen proceeded to draft the necessary documents whilst Elly 'Ingrossed the same'. (The attorney would have written out the conveyancing deeds on to paper whilst his clerk then carefully copied (i.e. engrossed) them onto parchment.) Whilst the documents were being prepared Mary Ellery was still in a most troubled state of mind and 'did earnestly presse and desire them both that the writinge might bee with all speed presented that same day' and continued to press upon Meighen and his clerk that the indenture 'might be sealed for that she feared other charges could be laid upon her husband'. The documents were duly signed, witnessed and sealed, and upon payment of the sixteen pounds the transaction was completed.

William Ellery was released from Gloucester gaol and returned to Upton-upon-Severn a free man and yet, alas, Mary's troubles were far from over. Within a few weeks Thomas Bound 'departed this life without payment of the residue of the money' and to compound their problems Daniel Webley had neglected to execute and enseal his part of the indenture. Katherine Symes and Katherine Bound then had to bring another action in Chancery to compel Webley to complete his part of the deed of transfer. Mary Ellery's version differed and she claimed that the 'Confederates' had 'procured' Daniel Webley to 'assign over the said legal estate in the premises' to themselves. William Ellery had then approached one of the sub-tenants, a William Bound, in order to borrow a further thirty pounds to tender to Katherine Symes for the redemption of the 'loan' on the premises although Katherine Symes refused to accept this money (it is not clear if Ellery ever received the balance of the money that had been promised by Thomas Bound). At this point in the Complaint Mary Ellery's account is very confused and the two stories become even more contradictory. Within twelve months of his release from gaol her husband, William Ellery, had died and on 5th May 1678 he was buried in Old Sodbury, Gloucestershire.

Mary Ellery was now a poor widow having to support her children and Symes and Bound had taken possession of the land in Parson's Field (and were receiving the rent) but had not taken possession of the property that was still in the hands of Mary Ellery. Consequently they brought an 'Action of Trespass and Ejectment' in the Court of Common Pleas against Mary Ellery to recover the building. This 'Action' then prompted the Bill of Complaint that was instigated by Mary Ellery in 1679. In common with many litigants the defendants, Symes and Bound, sought to impede the progress of her Bill through Chancery and 'for delay have prayed a Commission to take their answers in the Country'.

As a consequence of this procrastination and their counter-suit in the Court of Common Pleas the court issued a decree against the defendants: 'it is therefore ordered that an Injunction bee awarded for stay of the Defendants proceedings att Lawe against the plaintiff'. There is no evidence of a conclusion in this cause and like so many other cases it slowly ground to a halt in Chancery without any final decree. The fundamental issue in this Chancery case was the question of the nature of the property transaction which Mary Ellery claimed to be a mortgage that was redeemable on repayment of the capital, but the evidence of several of the witnesses indicated that it was an absolute sale without any clause for redemption. It is doubtful whether Mary ever reclaimed her inheritance. She had lost her husband and the land that her grandfather had bestowed for her 'better support'. One can only imagine to what depths the lives of Mary Ellery and her young family then descended.

An entry in the Upton-upon-Severn parish register provided a postscript:

> *1679: Surman a bastard son of Mary Ellery of Sodbury in Gloucestershire begotten as shee affirms by John Surman baptised 7th April.*

The rector had described the above Mary Ellery as being '*of Sodbury*' and not '*of Upton-upon-Severn*'. This would have the effect of placing the mother and child as chargeable on the parish of Sodbury and not Upton-upon-Severn, thereby relieving his hard pressed parishioners of any financial responsibility. Surman Ellery's life was brief. On the 31st October 1680 Mary Ellery stood in the churchyard at Upton-upon-Severn and watched a small coffin lowered into the earth.

William Ellery must have incurred the displeasure of his creditors in Gloucestershire and was imprisoned by the Justices of that county. Unfortunately there are no extant records for Gloucester gaol for the time of Ellery's imprisonment to establish his circumstances. Existing records date mainly from the eighteenth century when a new building was constructed but conditions in the seventeenth century would have been little different from Worcester goal which was likewise located in a Castle. If the debtor could not satisfy his creditors then his situation remained unresolved and many died in prison leaving their dependants to seek charity from the parish. In 1621 Merrell Alcocke, a Worcestershire widow, petitioned the Justices of the Peace 'praying for an allowance for herself and child as her husband Roger Alcocke had lately died in Gaol where he was imprisoned for debt'. Conditions were so awful as to defy description. Debtors were held with felons and other such criminals, and were usually kept in irons. The allowance for food was 'only bare subsistence, even if it was that'.

Many prisons in the seventeenth century were commercial ventures, operated to make a profit for the keeper as several incidents at Worcester gaol in the early seventeenth century vividly demonstrate. Following the death of the Worcester prison keeper, his widow, a Mrs Moore, succeeded to the post and subsequently, in 1616, she became involved in several disputes both with the authorities and the prisoners. In a petition to the Court of Quarter Sessions she claimed 'that her husband took the County Gaol at a very great and extreme rent, and gave credit to many poor prisoners, hoping for satisfaction at their enlargement [release]. Since her husband's death divers prisoners have not only run into debt to her but have made false accusations against her'. She then asked the court to make 'some order for the good of the Petitioner'. The petitions from those imprisoned for debt gave a very different account of their treatment. One petition claimed that she 'hath in a malicious manner putt manie others in amongst them …. in that cruell manner which hath never been used heretofore to anie debtor..'. She kept the civil prisoners (i.e. debtors) in the same cells as the felons and 'charged one prisoner 4d for lodging with another, although it was the prisoners own bed she charged him, in addition, 2d for a bedstead'. Mrs Moore was also purchasing ale at twelve shillings a hogshead from the brewer and selling it to the prisoners at thirty-two shillings a hogshead. In addition to this profiteering from the ale she was placing a charge upon the bread brought in for the prisoners and fining them. In another petition from the debtors they appealed to the Justices to 'be separated from the felons who had beaten and robbed them'. It was also claimed that she kept the debtors in double irons. Mrs Moore was finally brought before the Sessions to account for her actions and the Grand Jury declared her guilty of extortion.[155]

The Stuart authorities eventually became concerned about the numbers of debtors filling the prisons and in 1670 a further statute was passed: 'An Act for the relief and release of poor distressed prisoners for debt' which was in some part motivated by the after-effects of the great fire of London. This catastrophe had the result that 'very many persons now detained in prison are miserably impoverished, either by reason of the late unhappy times, the sad and dreadful fire, their own misfortunes, or otherwise …'. The same act addressed the manifold abuses of prisoners by their gaolers: 'it shall not be lawful for such officers to convey the said person to any tavern, alehouse, or other public victualling or drinking house, without the free and voluntary consent of the said person, so as to charge such prisoner with any sum of money for any wine, beer, ale victuals, tobacco…' etc. This act of imposed benevolence would have compounded the unfortunate debtor's financial distress. Another section of the act dealt with the common practice of gaolers keeping debtors confined in irons with the felons with the result that the 'prisoners for debt are disturbed and hindered in the night-time from their natural rest, by reason of their fetters and irons, and are otherwise much offended and troubled by their lewd and profane language and discourses, with most horrid cursing and swearing, (much accustomed to such persons)…'. (Act, 22 & 23 Charles II. c. 20, 1670.) This

155 Willis Bund, *Worcs. Calendar of the Quarter Sessions Papers*, p.clvii and pp.224–226.

was the underworld into which the unfortunate William Ellery had descended in Gloucester Castle.

Katherine Symes (formerly Best) died in 1692 and her daughter, Katherine Bound, in 1703. Katherine Bound left all her lands and property[156], including her half share of the King's Arms, to her nephew, Thomas Towne, eldest son of her sister, Mary:

> 'Item I give and bequeath (as farr as in one lyes) unto the said Thomas Towne and to his heirs and Assigns for ever All that my part and proportion of all the Messuages Lands and Tenements scituate and lyeing in the Burrough or Towne of Upton upon Sevearne aforesaid which descended and came unto my selfe and my Sister Towne as Coheirs of John Best my late father .....'

This will was also a deed or conveyance *devising* property to the new owner and carried a seal as well as Katherine Bound's signature. It is significant that she referred to Upton-upon-Severn as a Borough; there was no specific mention of Sollies Orchard, which had probably been sold by this date. Katherine Bound's inventory suggests that at the time of her death she was living in a property elsewhere in the High Street for her inventory refers to 'the forestreete roome over the shop' (the shop being in the possession of someone else as its contents are not mentioned). Mary Best had also moved a little further up the social order and married John Towne, described as 'gentleman', at St Swithin's church in Worcester. (The spelling and use of the surname 'Town' is inconsistent, sometimes John and Mary Town sign themselves 'Town' and sometimes 'Towne'. In some documents the name is spelt 'Towns'. Hereinafter wherever possible the name will be spelt 'Towne'.) The younger John Best had been the beneficiary of the estate of his uncle, Thomas Portman, a yeoman of Upton-upon-Severn, who died in 1648. There can be little doubt that he was the same Thomas Portman of Twyning who, in 1637, travelled to Bristol with the elder John Best and also deposed as a witness in the subsequent Chancery Case. In his will Thomas Portman (of Upton-upon-Severn) directed that his body be buried in the parish church of Twyning. Portman's freehold land in Upton-upon-Severn had been held in trust for twenty-one years to provide an income for the four young children of his brother-in-law, William Roberts, before coming to John Best junior in about 1668.

One patron of the inn at this time may have been Celia Fiennes, famous for her travels throughout England, who passed through Upton-upon-Severn during two of her journeys of about 1696 and 1701. Although she referred to the 'good Innes' on the road into Hereford and Wales she does not mention whether or not she rested in the town during her travels:

---

156 This also included the property bequeathed to her by the will of Thomas Bound the younger.

'Thence to Morton Hindmost in Glocestershire to a Relations house, My Uncle Rich'd Fiennes's widdow, a little neate stone built town, good Innes for ye travellers being ye road from London to Worcester and Herrifford and wales. Thence over Broadway hill to Parshur in all 30 mile by 12 of ye Clock, thence to Upton, where we pass on a large bridge over ye fine River the Severn wch runs from Worcester and to Glocester, Shrewsbury and to Bristol where it runns into the sea – in some places its very broad,' On returning from Herefordshire she continued that: 'From Newhouse I Came over Maubern Hills which are Like the Alps and have had much wet, the roads deep and difficult, to Upton in Worcester 10 mile, where I pass the Severn on a stone bridge – here it is not broad. Thence Pursha 5 mile, thence Esham 4 and Weston 4, in Glocestershire to my Cos'n Fiennes'.

In about 1701 the King's Arms changed its name once more, an event precipitated by a mole in the park at Hampton Court. King William III was out riding in his royal park, his horse stumbled over a molehill, the king fell and his injuries are said to have resulted in his untimely death. Following the accession to the throne of Queen Anne the old sign was taken down and replaced, for the inn was then described as 'lately called or known by the Name of the Queens Arms'.

John and Mary Towne had two sons, Thomas and John; the former had little benefit from his aunt's bequest for he died intestate in 1707 at the age of about thirty years; letters of administration were granted to his mother, Mary Towne, (her husband, the elder John Towne, had died before 1703). Mary Towne, together with her younger son, John, then became owners of the building. Samuel Gatfield, a tallow chandler, who was by this date already established and trading in the High Street premises, was one of the apprizers of Thomas Towne's effects:

Thomas Towne's Inventory, 15th September 1707
The Inventory of the Goods and Chattles of Thomas Towne, gentleman, 1707.

A true and perfect Inventory of all the goods and
Chattles of Thomas Towne Gent. Deceased late of the
parish of Upton upon Seavern in the Countie of
Worcester taken and apprized this fifteenth day
of September Anno Dom. 1707 by us John Halward
Samuel Gatfield & Jasper palfree

	£ : s : d
Imprimis All his wearing apparrell and money in his purse	12 : 0 : 0
Item All his plate with desparate debts	11 : 0 : 0
Item one Feather Bedd and all appertenances	6 : 0 : 0
Item Lining [linen] of all sorts	2 : 10 : 0
Item Brass and pewter in all	4 : 0 : 0

A true and perfect Inventory of all the goods and
Chattles of Thomas Town, Gent: Deceased late of the
~~parish~~ of Upton, upon Severn, in the countie of
Worcester taken and apprised this fifteenth day
of September Anno Dom 1707 by us John Halward
Samuell Gatfeild & Jasper palfree

		£	s	d
Imp	All his wearing apparrell and money in his purse	12	0	0
It	All his plate with despirate debts	ii	0	0
It	one ffather Bedd and all appertenances	6	0	0
It	Lining of all sorts	2	10	0
It	Brass and pewter in all	4	0	0
It	one Jack two spitts & other Iron ware	1	0	0
It	one couch 4 coushings	0	5	0
It	three old table Boards & half a doz: of Joynstooles	0	11	0
It	seven old Chaires	0	3	0
It	two looking glasses	0	4	4
It	one Bacon cratch	0	1	6
It	coupery ware of all sorts	0	7	10
It	old Books	0	4	9
It	old lumber and things unremembred	0	6	8
		38	14	1

John Halward
Samuell Gatfeild } Apprie:
Jasper palfree

Item one Jack two spitts & other Iron Ware	1 : 0 : 0
Item one Couch 4 Cousings	0 : 5 : 0
Item Fower old Table Boards & half a duzen of Joynstooles	0 : 11 : 0
Item seven old Chairs	0 : 3 : 0
Item two looking glasses	0 : 4 : 4
Item one Bacon Cratch	0 : 1 : 6
Item Coupery ware of all sorts	0 : 7 : 10
Item old Books	0 : 4 : 9
Item old lumber and things unremembered	0 : 6 : 8
	--------------
	38 : 14 : 1

John Halward   }
Samuel Gatfield   } Apprizers
Jasper Palfree   }

This was a modest collection of possessions for a young country gentleman. There is no suggestion of any occupation, no mention of trade, agriculture or livestock; he was a gentleman of independent means, having inherited land and property from his aunt, Katherine Bound. No description of the accommodation is given but the list of items would barely furnish two rooms. He was quite possibly occupying chambers provided for him in the extensive accommodation within the inn. 'Old Books' valued at 4s-9d would suggest that he had had some formal education.

All was not harmonious in the household of his brother, the younger John Towne, who appears to have contracted a most unfortunate marriage, probably more for the interests of his purse than his heart. In his will, written in 1710, presumably motivated by a serious domestic breakdown, he appointed his mother Mary as executrix and there was one most meaningful bequest to his perfidious wife:

> 'Imprimis I give and Bequeath to Mary Treacherous Dalby My wife the sum of one shilling to Be payed by my Executrix Twelve months after my Decease .... And I doo hereby Constitute make and appoynt my Executrix to Be Bringer up of my Child and to Coach her in the Feare Of God and to Be att her Disposall ....'

The bequest of 'one shilling' confirmed that John Towne had not forgotten to include his wife but had disinherited her intentionally – 'cut off with a shilling'. We are not told what misdemeanour his wife was guilty of, but the sentiments expressed in the will suggest that she was most probably in default of the Seventh Commandment. (John Towne died in May 1717 and the will was proved in 1718.)

After the 1636 conveyance of the building (from the Flooks to John Best) there is a long break in the deeds until 1710 when Mary Towne and her son John Towne sold approximately one half of the building to Samuel Gatfield. Mary Towne was now a poor widow, experiencing some financial hardship and 'she being behind hand in the world had occasion to sell the two messuages purchased by John Best and so settled in Joynture on her mother'.[157] The property had by then passed down through three generations by inheritance, and apart from Katherine Bound's will, there are no conveyancing documents for this period. Prior to purchasing the building Samuel Gatfield had, for some time, been trading in the premises as tenant to Mary Towne and there is a mention of a *Salles Shop* within the 1710 documents (at this date the term 'shop' could equally refer to a 'work-shop' or a 'sales-shop'). This confirmed the existence of a sales shop in the building prior to the date of the sale. Mary Towne kept some part of the building for her own use for the conveyance excluded 'All that one chamber or small Roome over the pantry there which is now in the possession of the said Samuel Gatfield and is not intended to be hereby conveyed'. The other moiety or portion of the building was retained for a few years by Mary Towne but had been mortgaged to a Thomas Hodge for the sum of sixty pounds. This part still continued as an inn – then in the 'occupation or possession' of Samuel Phillips, a tailor by trade, who was, presumably, the innkeeper but there is no documentary evidence on this point. The name changed back to the *King's Arme's* in 1714 when George I came to the throne following the death of Queen Anne. In 1717 Mary Towne and her son John sold the remaining freehold to Samuel Phillips for one hundred and five pounds.[158] It is not known how long the other moiety continued as an inn, but certainly it was no later than 1759.

For any commercial enterprise location was (and still is to this day) of paramount importance for success and whilst this building was later referred to as 'most advantageously situated for Trade, in an eligible part of the High-street', it had failed to prosper as an inn. Paradoxically its demise coincided with the advent of the stagecoach. Regular stagecoach services were extending out from London and other major cities during the seventeenth century, coming to Chipping Norton in Oxfordshire and Worcester by 1654 and to Bristol by 1657. Improvements in travel demanded the provision of different facilities. Carriers as well as coaching services proliferated during the seventeenth century putting greater demands on innkeepers who were obliged to provide better accommodation for the convenience of their clientele, including more extensive stabling and in some instances warehousing. Longer sites with room for stables and with access to a 'back lane' were especially suitable as this permitted carts and coaches to enter and leave the premises without turning or reversing – difficult manoeuvres with a team of several horses.[159] The

157 TNA C 11/993/18, *Answer of Mary Towne*, 1720.

158 TNA C11/993/18 – *Plea and Answer of Samuel Phillips*, 1720.

159 Alan Everitt, *Landscape and Community of England*, 1985, p.162.

Queen's Arms, or King's Arms as it then became once more, situated on the west side of the High Street, was at a great disadvantage in that space to the rear was limited and there was no exit on to a 'back lane'. Whilst the inn could have comfortably accommodated small carts with perhaps one or two horses, stagecoaches, drawn by four or even six horses required more space and extensive stabling. By comparison the White Lion Inn on the opposite side of the High Street was not so restricted in its development and obviously continued to prosper. In 1766 it was to be let and an advertisement in the Gloucester Journal revealed the facilities it had at its disposal:

To be Let,

And entered upon immediately, at an easy Rent,
THAT noted and well-accustomed Inn called the WHITE LION, situated near the Market-place in Upton upon Severn, in the County of Worcester, together with a large Quantity of new-built Stall Stabling, and other convenient Stabling, new built, for Coach and Chaise Horses; also a compleat Bowling-green, and large Garden inclusive, about four Acres of rich Pasture Ground adjoining to the said Inn, and more Pasture Ground to be let therewith, if required. – The Chaises, Furniture, &c. to be sold to the Tenant. – For further Particulars enquire of Mr. William Hurst, at the said Inn, who is going to retire from public Business.

(*Gloucester Journal*, February 3, 1766.)

It is almost certain that this lack of adequate turning area and room for expansion at the rear of the King's Arms resulted in a further decline in trade which followed on from the disruption of the Civil War, eventually leading to its demise as an inn.

6.

The Candle-maker

THE ancient ritual of 'Livery and Seizin' was duly enacted once again in September 1710.[160] Approximately half of the original premises including the stables was sold 'for and in consideration of the sum of Seventy pounds of good and lawful money of Great Brittain to be paid by the said Samuel Gatfield to the said Mary Towns and John Towns or one of them at such days or times and by such Proporcions as is hereinafter Agreed'. Even in the early eighteenth century there was still some feudal obligation imposed upon the owner of the building for an annual payment was due: 'To hold to the said Samuel Gatfield his heyres or Assigns for ever, free from all Incumberance Except the payment of Four pence Yearly for the time to come to the Lord of the Fee of the said premises'. Presumably in this instance it was to the lord of the manor, William Bromley. It was necessary at this time to grant a right of way to the stables and the rear of the building now occupied by Gatfield, a right of way which is still in existence to this day:

> 'In Consideration of One Guinea Money to be paid by the said Samuel Gatfield at the Execution of the said Conveyance the said Mary Towns and John Towns are to grant full liberty to the said Samuel Gatfield his heirs and assigns for ever to have a way through the Gates belonging to the other part of the said Messuage to Carry in Hay Coles or other Necessaryies at Convenient times and Seasons without any Contradiction And likewise to Carry out What he hath occassion to do...'

From this point onwards the history of the building concerns that part purchased by Samuel Gatfield on the north side of the plot. It was now a retail shop with living accommodation to the upper floors, a role which would continue for the next three

---

160 This transfer of title was also by Bargain and Sale with Feoffment, the deed was endorsed confirming that seizin had taken place before the witnesses – Abell Cooke, John Winbury, Samuell Philips and Richard Coucher.

hundred years. After later reconstruction this portion became the building that was described by Pevsner. Occasional references are made to the other half of the property where names of occupiers have come to light.

It is difficult to be precise as to when Samuel Gatfield first established himself in the building as a tallow chandler. It is almost certain that he was the same Samuel Gatfield, born in 1675 in the nearby village of Birtsmorton, the son of Joseph Gatfield who had a brother called Samuel. This elder Samuel Gatfield, who died in 1670, had also been a tallow chandler in Upton-upon-Severn and it is possible that he had rented several rooms within the inn including a 'sales shop' which faced on to the High Street. There can be little doubt that there was a family connection between these two tallow chandlers and after the early demise of the elder Samuel Gatfield it is quite possible that the business was continued by his wife, Jane, or even by his brother Joseph with the younger Samuel becoming their apprentice in about 1687, and eventually assuming ownership of the tallow chandlery. The elder Samuel Gatfield left both a will and an inventory. Whilst it cannot be confirmed that he was trading in the building the possibility cannot be precluded and it is useful to include his inventory as this gives an insight into a seventeenth century shop in Upton-upon-Severn. We do know for certain that his nephew, the younger Samuel Gatfield, was in occupation of part of the building by the beginning of the eighteenth century and the contents of this shop must have been very similar to those items appraised in the 1670 inventory.

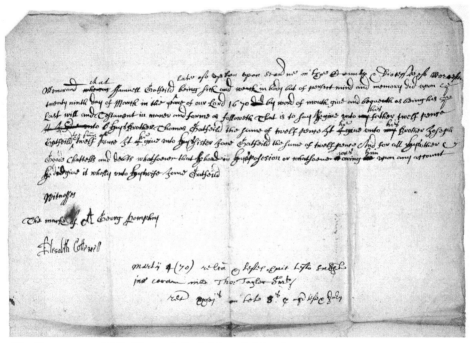

The Nuncupative Will of Samuel Gatfield, 29th March 1670.

The will of the elder Samuel Gatfield dated 29th March 1670 shown (shown opposite) is an interesting example of a nuncupative will. The unfortunate Mr Gatfield, who was just twenty-four years of age, appears to have expired before the ink was barely dry upon the parchment. The scribe had taken up his quill again and amended the will throughout, inserting 'late of Upton upon Severn.....', deleting the first person singular in the present tense and inserting the third person singular in the past tense. (A nuncupative will was one that had been uttered by word of mouth before credible witnesses, present at the testator's death-bed, who then had to write out the testator's intentions. Before the will could be proved the witnesses had to appear before the probate court and make sworn statements. In this example there were just two witnesses to the will but for the 'prevention of fraudulent practices' the Statute of Frauds enacted in 1677 changed this requirement to three witnesses.)

The inventory listed all the rooms of the property and the contents therein. The first room to be 'appraised' was the 'shope'.

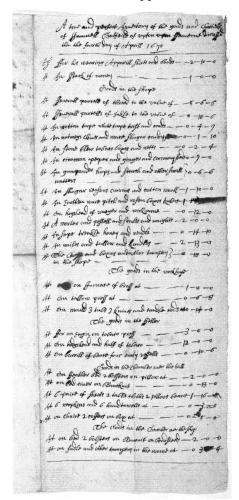
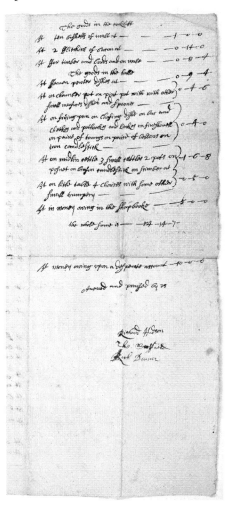

Transcription of Samuel Gatfield's Inventory, 1670
A true and perfect Inventory of the goods and Chattells
of Samuel Gatfield of Upton upon Seavern diceassed
the the [sic] fourth day of April 1670

	[£] [s] [d]
Imprimis For his wearing Apperill shirts and bands	2 – 10 – 0
Item In Stock of money	1 – 0 – 0
Goods in the shope	
Item Several parcells of thread to the value of	5 – 6 – 6
Item Several parcells of Inkle to the value of	0 – 18 – 6
Item In cotton tape white tape twist and cards	0 – 4 – 9
Item In nutmegs cloves and mace shugar candy	0 – 1 – 10
Item In stone blew tobaco boxes and netts	0 – 2 – 4
Item In cinamon peper and ginger and carroway seeds	0 – 9 – 0
Item In gunpowder hops and starch and other small } matters }	0 – 6 – 6
Item In shugar reasons currans and cotton wooll	1 – 10 – 0
Item In Earthen ware pitch and rosen boxes kulers	1 – ? ?
Item One hogshead of vinegar and wickyarne	0 – 12 – 0
Item A mortar and pestell and scales and waights	2 – 0 – 0
Item In sope treakle honey and readle	0 – 14 – 10
Item In nailes and tallow and kandles	2 – 13 – 0
Item The [Chests] and boxes and other trumpery } in the shope }	0 – 18 – 0
The goods in the workhouse	
Item one Furnace of brass at	1 – 0 – 0
Item One tallow press at	0 – 6 – 8
Item One mould 3 tubs 3 knives and candle rods at	0 – 14 – 0
The goods in the Sellar	
Item For one Engin one tobaco press	3 – 0 – 0
Item One hodgshead and half of tobaco	12 – 0 – 0
Item One barrill of beare four emty vessells	0 – 10 – 6
Goods in the Chamber over the hall	
Item One feather bed 2 bolsters one pillow at	2 – 0 – 0
Item One bed civer one blanckuit	0 – 13 – 0
Item 6 pairs of sheets 2 table cloths 2 pillows beares	1 – 16 – 0
Item 6 napkins and 6 handtowells at	0 – 3 – 0
Item one chaire 2 coffers one box at	0 – 5 – 0

The Goods in the Chamber over the Shop

Item one bed 2 bolsters one blancuit one beadsteed	2 – 0 – 0
Item one sadle and other trumpery in the roome at	0 – 3 – 4

The goods in the cockloft

Item ten bushels of malt at	1 – 0 – 0
Item 2 Flitchins of bacon at	0 – 14 – 0
Item For timber and bords and one male	0 – 8 – 4

The goods in the halle

Item Seven pewter dishes at	0 – 9 – 4
Item one chamber pot one pint pot with other small measures dishes and spoones	} 0 – 4 – 6
Item one frying pan one chafing dish one bar and cheekes and pothookes and linkes one fire shovell one pair of toungs one paire of bellows one iron candlestick...	} 0 – 4 – 0
Item one midlin cettle 3 small cettles 2 pots one posnot one brazen candlestick one skimber at	} 1 – 6 – 8
Item one litle table 4 chaires with some other small trumpery	} 0 – 5 – 0
Item in money owing in the shopbooke	5 – 0 – 0

the whole sum is _____	54 – 14 – 7
Item money owing upon a desperate account	10 – 0 – 0

Avowed and praised by us
Richard Hudson Thomas Gatfield Rich Dunne

(The 'desperate account' of £10 0s 0d money owing refers to be an irrecoverable debt. In 1670 this was a considerable sum of money. Samuel must have had difficulty in persuading one of his customers to settle his bill.)

The Workhouse

Samuel Gatfield's workhouse contained those few essential items for the production of tallow and tallow candles: a furnace, tallow press, moulds and candle rods. The manufacture of tallow candles dates back many centuries; in 1462 Edward IV granted a Royal Charter to the Worshipful Company of Tallow Chandlers who regulated the trade and price of tallow candles. At first this authority was limited to within the City of London but was later extended to other areas. The brass furnace in Gatfield's workhouse was used for rendering animal bones and flesh to produce tallow which would rise to the surface of the vessel and be skimmed off. The first skimming produced a finer quality white tallow whilst subsequent skimmings were yellow in colour and finally the animal remains were placed in the tallow press in order to extract the residual coarse tallow. There were then two methods of producing candles; either by suspending wicks from a rod (hence the 'candle rods') and repeatedly dipping them into the molten tallow, or by the use of moulds to produce better quality candles. The former method was of great antiquity but the use of moulds, which dates from the late fourteenth century, had the advantage of producing candles of a uniform size that were easier to fit into candle sockets. Candles were also produced from beeswax, an expensive option, only affordable by the more prosperous customers. The cheaper tallow candles, which always had the disadvantage of a most disagreeable smell, sufficed most of the population.

The Sales Shop
It is apparent from the list of items that were offered for sale in the 'shope' that Samuel Gatfield had diversified into other, perhaps much more profitable, merchandise. A variety of commodities including spices, sugar, treacle and honey, as well as *'reasons'* (raisins) and *'currans'* (currants) were for sale. Many of these articles were imported into Bristol from the continent and the East or West Indies before being dispatched up the river Severn by barge or trow to their various destinations. The most remarkable item in the inventory is the one and a half hogsheads of tobacco found in the cellar (by estimation about 1500lb, 680 kilograms or 24,000 ounces).[161] This quantity of tobacco would suggest that Samuel Gatfield had been involved in the wholesale trade supplying the alehouses in the vicinity with pipe tobacco – in the seventeenth century alehouse keepers often retailed tobacco to supplement their income.[162] (When Thomas Cocks of Crowle penned his letter to Sir Robert Berkeley in 1633 he referred to a beggar calling for a pot of ale and a pipe of tobacco.)

It has been said that Sir Francis Drake and Ralph Lane, the first governor of Virginia, are to be credited with the introduction of tobacco into England from the Americas in 1586. In 1607 the first plantations were established in Virginia, and by 1616 it had become the staple crop of the colonists. The habit of smoking tobacco in long churchwarden pipes soon became widespread amongst all levels and indeed all ages in society. The author of the Lechmere archive *'Hanley and the House of Lechemere'* remembered 'My father Edmund Lechmere dyed ye last of July 1650, hee being then 73 yeares of age & upwards, and is buried in Hanley Church in the very grave where my great grandfather was buried. Hee was a tall comely man, exceeding temperate in all things (but tobacco) and very kindly affectionate

---

161 Here the hogshead is of a different measure. Various sources give different measures for dry weight. A hogshead of tobacco was generally about 1000lb in weight. One and a half hogsheads of tobacco would be approximately 1500lb valued at £12 or 1.9 pence per pound.

162 see Peter Clark, *The English Alehouse*, p.85 & p.134.

to his children'. When Thomas Wilson died in 1669 his inventory listed 'One box, with tobacco' valued at six shillings. In spite of the popularity of this new 'fashion' there were already objections to its use and in 1601 Samuel Rowlands wrote:

But this same poyson, steeped India weede
In head, harte, lunges, do the soote and cobwebs breede
With that he gasp'd, and breath'd out such a smoke
That all the standers by were like to choke.

James I abhorred the habit of smoking tobacco and in 1604 wrote an essay titled '*A Counterblaste To Tobacco*' referring to 'the manifold abuses of this vile custom of tobacco taking'. In 1602 he raised the duty on imported tobacco by imposing a special impost of 6s 6d per pound, prior to this date the duty that had been introduced by Elizabeth I was only 2d per pound. Although tobacco was a valuable source of revenue for the Crown the duty was later reduced to 1s per pound and from 1620 all tobacco had to carry a government stamp.

It is possible that Samuel Gatfield had obtained his supplies of tobacco via the port of Bristol, the tobacco having been grown and processed in the new colony of Virginia where it was loaded on to sailing ships for the long and hazardous voyage across the Atlantic Ocean. At Bristol, the customs officials exacted the duty on the cargo before it was transferred to smaller vessels for conveyance along the river Severn to be unloaded at the towns upstream. However, a more probable explanation is that his tobacco had arrived in Upton-upon-Severn, conveyed by horse and cart, from the village of Kempsey just a few miles to the north along the Worcester road. The presence of the tobacco press and tobacco engine in the inventory suggests that Samuel Gatfield was involved in the illicit tobacco trade that was prevalent in England at that time for he possessed all the necessary equipment for processing the tobacco. The 'tobacco press' was used in the preparation of the fermented tobacco leaf which was compressed to squeeze out the liquor and reduce it to about one third of its original volume before being cut (shredded) by the 'tobacco engine'. It is unlikely that Samuel Gatfield would have had the 'engine' and the 'press' if he was importing tobacco from Virginia.

Tobacco plants had been introduced into Europe before 1530 and by the end of the century tobacco was being grown on a small scale in English gardens for medicinal use. It was first grown as a commercial venture in 1619 around Winchcombe in Gloucestershire; this soon caused much disquiet amongst the Virginia colonists, and the Virginia Company, fearing that the competition would harm the new colonies, urged the Government to take action. Consequently, in December of 1619 the Privy Council declared the growing of tobacco in England to be illegal. However, little was done to enforce the ban and cultivation soon spread into the Vale of Tewkesbury and to other Gloucestershire villages such as Kemerton and Conderton as well as nearby Overbury and Kempsey in Worcestershire. By 1627 cultivation had spread to thirty-nine places in Gloucestershire and seventeen in Worcestershire; eventually tobacco was being grown in twenty-two counties within England and Wales. The cultivation and production of tobacco was a 'highly speculative venture which, at its most successful could bring in superlative profits'[163] for its growers. The Vale of Tewkesbury and the neighbouring Vale of Evesham were particularly suited to the growing of tobacco and for a long period in the seventeenth century the commercial production of tobacco was of considerable socio-economic importance in the counties of Gloucestershire and Worcestershire. Its cultivation was highly labour intensive and provided local employment with much of the work being done by women and children. One acre of plantation required 10,000 plants which had to be planted in prepared seed-beds in February ready for transplanting in April or May. The crop required watering, weeding and pruning, all of which were laborious tasks, and in early autumn the leaves had to be individually picked by hand ready for processing. The finished tobacco was sold locally as well as in London and other towns in addition to being exported to Ireland. Landlords, cultivators and merchants were all involved in the production of tobacco. The local landowners were attracted by the high rents that they were being offered to allow cultivation. It has been said that 'No one in the later seventeenth century was so treacherous as to suggest that the Justices of the Peace were themselves growing tobacco, but it was certainly growing on their land. And the risks of the crop were still shared – indirectly by the landlords, who collected higher rents...'.[164] The justices were reluctant to implement the orders of Privy Council; in 1658 one soldier responsible for destroying the crop near Cheltenham complained: 'All the justices do refuse to give warrant for the peace and is rather a hindrance than always helpful'.[165] Further Acts concerning the prohibition of tobacco cultivation were passed in 1652 and 1653, and in 1654 a new directive from the Privy Council ordered the Acts to be enforced but all efforts to eradicate production met with stiff resistance particularly in Gloucestershire.[166]

One of the questions that the justices required the parish constables to answer regarding their parishes was that concerning the growing of tobacco. In the Quarter Sessions presentments for Worcestershire for 1591 to 1643 only eleven constables provided an answer to this question, always in the negative. The constable's presentments for Kempsey and Eckington do not give any response to this question of tobacco growing yet the crop was certainly being grown in these parishes by 1659. There is only one recognisance involving tobacco in this period

---

163 ©Thirsk, 1984, *The Rural Economy of England – Collected Essays,* Hambledon Continuum, an Imprint of Bloomsbury Publishing Plc., p.271.

164 Ibid. p.283.

165 Ibid. p.282.

166 Ibid. p.280.

and that was in October 1634 for the appearance of William Childes at Sessions to 'answer for the selling of tobacco by retail contrary to Proclamation'. There were no indictments at all for the cultivation of tobacco. J. W. Willis Bund, in the Calendar of the Worcestershire Quarter Sessions Papers, wrote that 'as far as can be judged from the replies no tobacco seems to have been grown in the county'. The constables were in an exceedingly difficult position; they must have been fully aware of any tobacco crops growing in their parish and would have been equally conscious of whose land it was being cultivated on. It must be concluded that in these circumstances the parish constables had adopted the cautious policy of 'see no evil, hear no evil, speak no evil'. Later records prove that tobacco was being grown in several parishes in Worcestershire and in 1659 seven growers came before the Quarter Sessions. The size of the fines imposed demonstrates that the Justices were determined to eradicate the illegal trade. The growers were: John Redding of Kempsey, Ralph Huntington of Upton Snodsbury, Edmond Baugh of Pensham, William and Thomas George of Eckington, Humphrey Taylor and Richard Goddard of Eckington. They were charged that 'they did plant sett growe and Cure Tobacco in seed plant and otherwise upon 400 poles or Rodds of ground and fields ... contrary to the Statute'. (A pole was an area of 30.25 square yards. Four hundred poles was 12,100 sq. yards or two and a half acres.) They were fined twenty shillings per pole – £400 (about £48,000 today).[167] The government faced a protracted battle lasting over seventy years before tobacco growing in England was finally eradicated.

With the introduction of tobacco came the use of snuff, and one form of snuff, 'wet snuff' was prepared by grinding the wet stalks of tobacco leaves before a process of fermentation. Various spices including cinnamon and cloves, and scents were used to 'flavour' the snuff. Samuel Gatfield had all the materials and equipment necessary for the preparation of wet snuff, a mortar and pestle for grinding the tobacco, scales and weights and a variety of spices.

Although 'sope' is listed in the inventory, and Samuel Gatfield had some of the materials for the production of soap (one of the main ingredients being tallow), there is no indication that he was manufacturing it. By 1636 the production of soap had been limited by monopoly and taxation, and although the Star Chamber had decreed that there should be no soap manufactured outside a one-mile limit of London and Bristol this state controlled monopoly was often ignored.

The contents of the above inventory reveal that, unlike previous inhabitants of the premises, the elder Samuel Gatfield was not dependant upon agriculture or animal husbandry to subsidise his living. He was able to support himself solely from his trading activities both as a tallow chandler and retailer in his 'sales shop' and had no necessity to farm the land for victuals.

167 WAAS, QS Midsummer 1659. 1/1/96/15-21.

Deed to Declare the Uses of a Fine, 20th March 1718, Mrs Towne to Samuel Gatfield.

By the beginning of the eighteenth century the younger Samuel Gatfield would have completed his long apprenticeship and set himself up as a tallow chandler. There is little doubt that he continued to retail the same commodities as his uncle before him and by 1710 he was sufficiently well established to be able to purchase the building from John and Mary Towne. Unfortunately, the new proprietor was destined to follow his predecessors and became entangled in the courts of law. Some eight years later, in 1718, the building was the subject of a further action in the Court of Common Pleas. Samuel Gatfield and Mary Towne were named, with other parties, in a '*Deed to Declare the Uses of a Fine*' the document associated with a *Fine sur cognizance de droit come ceo*. (In order to save legal costs several landowners frequently united to *levy a Fine* which would involve a number of unconnected properties. It then became important that their respective properties or lands should be defined, and this could be achieved by the '*Deed to Declare the Uses of a Fine*'.) By this legal process the Court of Common Pleas acknowledged Samuel Gatfield as the lawful owner of the building and enrolled his *Fine* in the court records. The specific reason why Gatfield pursued this action was not revealed by these documents and was not clarified until events that followed two years later:

The Irish Complaint

The clerks in Chancery had not forgotten this little town in rural Worcestershire. Their long goose quills were once again making elegant progress across sheets of parchment. In March of 1720 several inhabitants of Upton-upon-Severn were cited in yet another Bill of Complaint issued from the Court of Chancery. The plaintiffs were George Smith from Kinsale in Ireland and his wife, Elizabeth, who claimed to be the granddaughter of a previous owner of the High Street property. The various parties named as defendants to the Bill were Samuel Gatfield, Samuel Phillips, Richard Willoughby, Anne Commins and Mary Towne. Richard Willoughby was the owner of a separate property 'formerly an Inne and known by the sign of the Red Lyon wherein William Savage did dwell' situated in the Old Street in Upton-upon-Severn (this would have been the other building purchased in 1636 occupied by Thomas Powell).[168]

This suit in Chancery had its origins in events that had occurred many years before; in this instance across the Irish Sea and back to those events referred to as the 'Protestant Plantations' in Ireland which took place during a period dating from about 1568 to 1641.

Years of hostilities between England and Phillip II of Spain had, by 1585, finally descended into outright war and coastal settlements in southern Ireland assumed a strategic importance by providing garrisons to protect Munster and other provinces from possible invasion by the Spanish. Protestant settlers were 'planted' across the Irish Sea by the Tudor authorities in an attempt to colonise the country with people sympathetic to their administration. Several years later, in 1606, James I established the *Commission for the Remedy of Defective Titles*. This commission required all Irish landowners to prove good title to their estates. Where the title to land was found to be 'defective' the English authorities forced many Irish landowners to forfeit up to one third of their lands and granted these estates to English gentlemen, referred to as 'undertakers', who were responsible for subletting the land and farms on these estates. Notable undertakers included Sir Walter Raleigh and Richard Boyle, the first Earl of Cork. Many of these farms were only sublet to those settlers who had accepted the 'Oath of Supremacy' to the English crown. Government agents visited various counties in England recruiting suitable tenants, many of whom were the younger sons of tradesmen and yeomen who had little prospect of an inheritance of any lands from their parents. They were offered larger farms at much lower rents than they could possibly have aspired to in England. Thousands of protestant English and Welsh settlers arrived in Munster and County Cork during the first half of the seventeenth century and were granted land and property in the coastal towns including Cork and Kinsale. This influx resulted in the creation of so called 'Pocket Boroughs' controlled by the protestant majority and one of these settlers was a Robert Best who had arrived in Kinsale from Upton-upon-Severn.

Elizabeth Smith stated in her Bill of Complaint that she was the daughter of the late deceased Robert Best the younger, a chandler, of 'Kingsale' (Kinsale) in County Cork and granddaughter of the late Robert Best the elder, another chandler, of Upton-upon-Severn, who, together with his brother, John Best, (as she claimed) were joint purchasers of several properties in Upton-upon-Severn with the yearly value of fifty pounds. (These properties included the King's Arms and the Red

---

168 TNA C 11/1168/17 *Smith v Gatfield* and C 11/993/18 *Smith v. Town*.

Lyon.) She also claimed that John Best had predeceased her grandfather: 'and dyed some years since without issue upon whose decease the said premises came to and of right to the said Robert Best the elder'. The Bill continued, that following the death of her grandfather, these properties then came by inheritance to her father, Robert Best, who 'had no Notice of the death of his father and of the said premises being descended to him....'; and that he did not come over to England to 'enter upon and make his claim to the said premises' in Upton-upon-Severn (to 'enter' in this context means to make a formal entry into the property as an assertion of ownership). Elizabeth alleged that Samuel Gatfield, Samuel Phillips, Richard Willoughby, Anne Commins and Mary Towne or their 'Confederates' subsequently 'took advantage thereof and possessed themselves of the said Deeds and Conveyances and entered upon and took possession of the said messuages lands and premisses'. She also cast doubt on the authenticity of their title deeds: 'if the said Confederates have got any conveyance of the said premises the same were Fraudulently, Colourably[169] or Clandestinely made'. She further related that her father, Robert Best the younger, who had been living in Kinsale in Ireland had since died leaving her, Elizabeth Smith, as the sole heir of his estate: 'Leaving your Oratrix an infant of Tender years and who is still an infant under age'.

The five defendants all produced responses to this Bill. In the case of Samuel Gatfield, Richard Willoughby and Samuel Phillips the response was both a 'Plea' and an 'Answer'. The 'Plea' was an additional response to the 'Answer' and raised a point in law, which could have been that the subject of the Bill of Complaint was not a question of equity and consequently the case should be referred to one of the other courts – often an ecclesiastical court or a common law court – and not heard in the Court of Chancery.[170] The defendants described the location of their respective properties and recited their legal title to them.

The plaintiffs had made further accusations against the defendants who 'Comitt waste and Spoile on the said premises and Suffer the houses and buildings to be ruinous and run out of repair and to Decay'. The defendants strenuously denied these accusations. Samuel Gatfield described the High Street building as being 'very old and ruinous' when he first purchased it, 'but this defendant since his said purchase has new built a messuage or house and buildings upon the same and been at considerable charges thereabouts whereby he has advanced the value of the same'. Willoughby made a similar statement in his Answer stating that his building (the Red Lyon) was old and that he had 'advanced' the value of his property. In their Answers both Gatfield and Phillips referred to the *Fine sur cognizance de droit come ceo* dated 27th March 1718 in the Court of Common Pleas 'for the further confirmation of this Defendant's title'. The objective of this earlier *Fine* had been to strengthen the legal title to Gatfield's premises. Elizabeth and her husband

---

169 feigned or counterfeit.

170 Henry Horwitz, *Chancery Equity Records and Proceedings 1600-1800*, 2nd Edn (1998), pp.14-15.

must have arrived at Samuel Gatfield's shop in the High Street, in or before 1718, asserting their claim to ownership of the building. Consequently the defendant took counsels advice and proceeded with his action in the Court of Common Pleas to protect his property from gratuitous claimants.

But, as with the previous Chancery cases, wherein lies the truth from the testimony of the various parties to this dispute? The testimony of George and Elizabeth Smith is somewhat suspect. No details of the properties in dispute are given in their Bill. This information is only revealed in the Answers from the defendants. However, the most difficult item to reconcile is the given age of the plaintiff, Elizabeth, who stated that she 'has but lately attained her age of twenty-one years and was a '*Fame Covert*' (*feme covert*, i.e. a married woman) before she came of age' (she contradicted herself here, previously claiming to be under age). This claim implies that she was born about 1699. However by estimation, John Best, who purchased the property in 1636, was born about 1600 (certainly not much later than 1610) and his brother Robert would have been of a similar vintage. This gives a suspiciously long period of about one hundred years between the births of grandfather and granddaughter. Furthermore, Elizabeth claimed that John Best predeceased her grandfather and died without issue. The earliest title deeds to the King's Arms (assuming they are genuine), disclose that John Best did not die without issue and neither these deeds nor the Chancery Case of 1637 make any mention of a Robert Best.

In her 'Answer' Mary Towne described her genealogy in some detail, referring to the two wives of the late John Best and at least seven children from his two marriages. She was the only surviving issue of five children by his second wife, Katherine. (Ann Cummins was the only surviving daughter of another daughter, Ann, by John Best's first wife.) Mary Towne stated that she believed that Robert Best the elder, a shoemaker, '… dwelt in Upton-upon-Seavern but through Extravagant and Idle living he was forced to leave his country and went into some forraign Kingdom above Seaventy years ago and never since returned …'.

The testimony of both Samuel Gatfield and Richard Willoughby referred to the claims that Elizabeth made about her age. Willoughby asserted:

> 'And this defendant knows not that he [Robert Best] left the Plaintiff Elizabeth an infant. But believes she is not still soe or that she has not but lately attained her age of Twentyone years She being about or above fifty years of age as he believes.'

Fifty years or above was a much more credible age for Elizabeth Smith. This suggests that she was a cousin of Thomas and John Towne, the two sons of Mary Towne. Mary Towne's evidence was more detailed on this point:

'.... for by the view of her person itt is the Judgement of most persons who
have seen her she is near Sixty years of age but whoever she is these defendants
conceive the complainants have designs to perplex these defendants and put
them to a defensive suite & being persons of noe fixed being and their carriage
not great can Easily retreat back to their country and secure costs'. ('carriage'
referred to their manners or their social behaviour.)

The plaintiffs had one other insurmountable difficulty in establishing their case.
They were unable to produce any witnesses to support their claims: 'Witnesses who
would prove the truth of the premises, being either dead or gone into places remote
or beyond the Seas Unknown to your Orator and Oratrix'. All the defendants
denied any knowledge of Elizabeth Smith, her husband George or any connection
they may have had with their properties and requested the case be dismissed with
costs.

It is quite conceivable that Elizabeth was a descendant of Robert Best, once a
resident of Upton-upon-Severn who had removed himself to Kinsale in Ireland in
the early seventeenth century. Although many Irish records have perished some
records relating to Kinsale are still extant, including: 'The Courte Booke of ye Towne
of Kinsale wherein all matters of importance concerning the said towne are set downe and
Recorded and is begun the Twenty-first of March, anno Domini, 1653' (from The Council
Book of the Corporation of Kinsale from 1652 to 1800.) There are several references
to a Robert Best in the Kinsale Court Book. In July 1653 he was sworn in as one
of the town's burgesses and in 1661 his name appeared in the list of burgesses and
freemen of Kinsale who took the oath of supremacy. Later that year he was amongst
several persons licensed by the Corporation to retail wines.

In the 1659 Census of Ireland Robert Best was listed as living in High Fisherstreet
in Kinsale[171], and was mentioned in the Court of Claims on 18th July 1663 when
the court heard a case concerning Thomas Meagh who claimed a stone house and
garden in the parish of St Multotius, Kinsale, which was in the possession of Robert
Best (the outcome of the case is not recorded).[172]

There is an earlier reference to a Robert Best, dated 1642, in a Deposition of
Thomas Franklin where he refers to 'one Robert Best, a shoomaker, late of Kinsale,
English protestant...'. During the Irish rebellion in 1641 Franklin, a butcher, had
been robbed of 'one horse & sheepe' valued at one hundred and three pounds,
'hides to the value of one hundred pounds' and also of 'debts amounting to the sum
of one hundred and fortie pounds' due from various people including Robert Best

---

171 Séamus Pender ed., *A Census of Ireland circa 1659* (Irish Manuscript Commission, 2002), p.199.
172 Geraldine Tallon ed., *Court of Claims: Submissions and Evidence*, 1663 (Irish Manuscript Commission,
2006), p.226. (I am indebted to Dr. Micheál Ó Siochrú for these references).

(presumably these were 'bills of debt' or promissory notes).[173] The most satisfactory explanation for these references is that the elder Robert Best, a shoemaker, from Upton-upon-Severn had participated in the Irish 'plantations' and established himself and his family in county Cork in or before 1640. (It is quite conceivable that he was not the only person who was 'transplanted' from Upton-upon-Severn or Worcestershire at this time.) Interestingly, there are several other references to the surname Best in county Cork for there is further mention of a Robert Best within the Bisse documents in the deposition of one Mary Best, relict of a Leonard Best, which illustrates some of the hardships encountered by these 'settlers' during the rebellion:

> '... she being further examined deposeth that about Whitesuntide last her said husband having in company with him thirtie men when they left the Castle of Mitchelstowne in the com. [county] of Corke & all warders of the same purposeing to bring a prey from the rebells towards the releife of the said Castle, but the Enemy (the forces of the Lord of Cahir) laying ambushes for them murthered & killed this deponents said husband & Edw: Blissit Tho: Dan: Thomas Handcock John Watton George Horne Roger Laurence, Tho: Wats which parties left behinde them fourty fartherlesse Children betweene them not able to releive themselves. Robert Best late of Balaporine aforesaid this day was produced before us as a Wittnes & being Examined & sworne upon the holy Evangelist he deposeth that the Contents of this deposition is true in all particulars his cause of knowledge is that he lived in Bealaporine aforesaid whereby he knew the Estate of thother deponent & likewise was present when the said parties last mencioned were murthered in sort as the other examinant deposeth & further he deposeth not:
> Mary [mark] Bests marke
> Robert[R] Best his marke
> Jurat coram nob:
> 12 martij 1642
> Phil: Bisse
> Ric Williamson' [174]

---

173 Bisse Depositions, MS 822, fols 198r-198v County: Cork. Date: 22/10/1642. The 1641 Depositions (Trinity College Dublin, MSS 809-841) are witness testimonies mainly by Protestants, but also by some Catholics, from all social backgrounds, concerning their experiences of the 1641 Irish rebellion. The testimonies document the loss of goods, military activity, and the alleged crimes committed by the Irish insurgents, including assault, stripping, imprisonment and murder. This body of material is unparalleled anywhere in early modern Europe, and provides a unique source of information for the causes and events surrounding the 1641 rebellion and for the social, economic, cultural, religious, and political history of seventeenth-century Ireland, England and Scotland. – source: Trinity College Dublin.

174 Bisse Depositions: MS 821, fols 032r-032v & fols 047r-048v, County: Tipperary, Date: 12/3/1643.

The surname occurs again in Kinsale in 1692 when a Richard Best, possibly a shoemaker, came before the Grand Jury: "We present Barth. Ashwick, Richd Best and Tho. Roche for going aboard ship and making a market there with shoes and hats on the Sabbath day".[175]

George Smith is first mentioned in the Court Book in 1670 when he was appointed 'bellman' for the town of Kinsale. This appointment was extended in 1671:

> It*em*. George Smith was appointed bellman, and to go by night with his bell at 10, 12, 2, and 4 betwixt this and 16 April next, and from thence to 16 Oct., 1672, but twice a night, at 11 and 3; to have 6*li*. [£6] yearly. He is also appointed Beadle to keep out strange and sturdy beggars, and not to suffer idle persons to go about begging, being able to work for themselves; to keep the pigs out of the streets that annoy the inhabitants, and if any pigs be found after notice given by the bell, it shall be lawful to impound them, and not release them until he receive 12*d*. a piece from the owners, and for the second time to kill them, and take one half to himself and leave the other to the owner; also to keep the gutters in the streets open in case of great rain and floods, for prevention of injury to the inhabitants in their shops, cellars, and houses, for which he is to have 18*d*. a week.[176]

It is quite possible that Elizabeth Smith was who she claimed to be (i.e. the granddaughter of Robert Best of Upton-upon-Severn, who was a brother of John Best) but she had economised on her age in an attempt to gain some sympathetic consideration from the Master in Chancery. She was probably born before 1670 and was indeed about fifty or even sixty years of age as the defendants testified. In Kinsale she had married George Smith, a person of modest means. Perhaps Elizabeth had heard some tale from her father or grandfather concerning an inheritance left behind in England. Perhaps, like her grandfather Robert Best, she too had succumbed to a life of 'Extravagant and Idle living'. In their later years, when George could no longer catch the pigs, they had experienced some financial hardship in County Cork and, with high hopes of finding fortune, had set sail for England where they invented these claims to various properties in Upton-upon-Severn – in modern parlance they were 'trying it on'. The outcome of the case was not in favour of the plaintiffs, for their suit in Chancery did not proceed to any conclusion and the High Street building remained in the possession of Samuel Gatfield for another thirty years.

---

175 *The Council Book of the Corporation of Kinsale from 1652 to 1800: Annals of Kinsale*, p.lxii.

176 *The Courte Booke of ye Towne of Kinsale*, p.123.

There is a further, final, mention of the surname Best in the '*Annals of Kinsale*' when a Mary Best was presented to the Grand Jury in 1706: 'We present Mary Best, being a nuisance to the Corporation for several years past, and desire she be sent to Bridewell, and have 12d a week for her maintenance, a frize coat and waist coat, two smocks, two capps, one pair of shoes and stockings, to be supplied as she wants.'[177] ('Bridewell' refers to a prison for beggars and vagabonds.) It has so far not been established whether or not this Mary Best was a relative of Robert Best the elder – these Bests were a troublesome band of individuals – nuisances, litigious, extravagant and idle bodies with poor 'carriage'.

The title deeds show that Samuel Gatfield had continuing financial problems and on occasions he was obliged to raise further funds using the property as security. In 1739 he mortgaged the property for sixty pounds to Edward Nicholls, a maltster, of Tewkesbury and subsequently in 1741 Gatfield approached John Willoughby, a bricklayer or builder of Upton-upon-Severn, for financial assistance. The original mortgage was cleared by Willoughby but Gatfield still required additional capital: 'And whereas there is now justly due and owing to the said Edward Nichols the principle sum of Sixty pounds all interest being paid off and discharged And the said Samuel Gatfield hath occasion of the further Sum of twenty pounds which the said John Willoughby hath this day advanced and lent him on security of the said premises...'. John Willoughby was almost certainly related to Samuel Gatfield for the parish register of the nearby village of Welland shows the marriage of a Jane Gatfield to John Willoughby on 17th December 1699 (they had a son, another John, baptised in Upton upon Severn in 1707). Within three years Samuel was short of funds once more and had to raise a further forty pounds from John Willoughby.

Whilst these financial difficulties could have been attributed to poor management it is quite certain that other factors contributed to his problems – in particular the new excise duties introduced in 1710. At the beginning of the eighteenth century England was involved in expensive continental wars (the cost in 1709-10 being over £13 million), and to raise revenue, excise duty was imposed on a variety of household articles: soap, candles, hops, calicoes, dice and playing cards were all included (the duty on cards not being removed until 1960). Excise was a very unpopular levy because it was imposed on home produced goods [178]. Dr Samuel Johnson's dictionary of 1755 defined 'Excise' as 'a hateful tax levied upon commodities and adjudged not by the common judges of property, but by wretches hired by those to whom the excise is paid'. (The Attorney-General considered this description to be libellous but the authorities thought better of challenging it). Of these commodities, the first three were a significant part of Gatfield's business and candle making was his principle trade (tobacco still carried the import duty). The duty on candles, which were an indispensable part of everyday life, was extremely

---

177 *The Council Book of the Corporation of Kinsale from 1652 to 1800: Annals of Kinsale*, p.lxviii.
178 Graham Smith, *Something To Declare*, p.13.

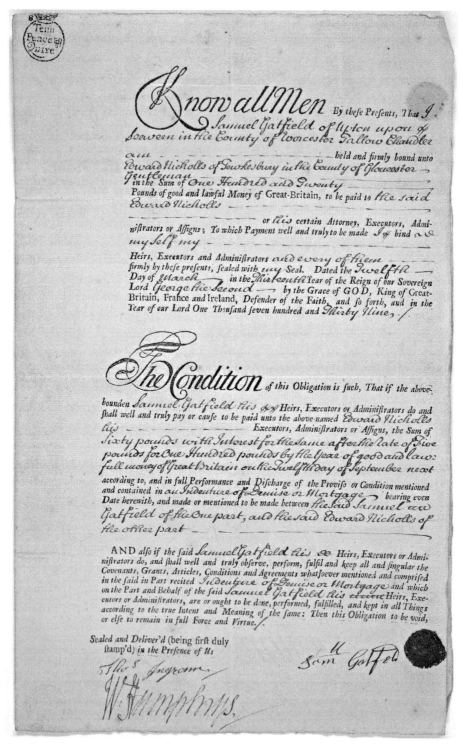

Bond to perform Covenants 12th March 1739 Mr Samuel Gatfield to Mr Edward Nicholls.

unpopular. When first introduced the duty on tallow candles was one halfpenny per pound, the more expensive wax candles (only affordable by the more affluent) bore 4d per pound. These duties were doubled the following year and placed a heavy burden on the poorer sections of society.

The introduction of the excise duty on the manufacture of candles doubtless made life doubly difficult for Samuel Gatfield. All chandlers or candle makers were required by the Excise Department to register their businesses. Regional excise officers were appointed to collect the duty and supervise the production of candles. Each excise officer had to appear before a justice of the peace and take an oath *'for the true and faithfull Execution of his Office on the duty laid on Candles'*.

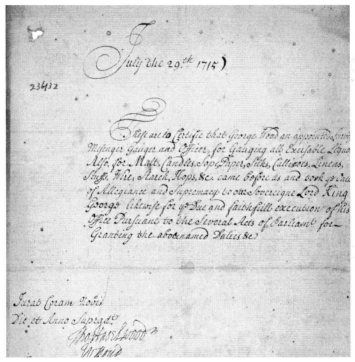

Excise Officer's Certificate, 1715.

The local officers compiled lists of chandlers which were sent to London (there were over 4000 manufacturers and about 6000 retailers of candles). This new 'candle tax' averaged over £135,000 per annum. The Excise officers had to be notified before work commenced and chandlers could not process tallow and manufacture candles without their supervision.

The duties of the Excise officers, or Gaugers as they were also known, stated that 'Every Chandler or Maker of Candles are to make true and particular Entries of their Workhouses, Storehouses, Utensils etc. every six Weeks' and 'the Officer is to require the Person who made it, to shew him every Melting-house Work house,

Ware-house, Store house, Shop, Room, or other Place, Copper, Kettle, Pot, Mould or other Vessel or Utensil expressed therein'; and 'the Officer must insert in his Entry Book, the Situation of all those places, and mark their Particulars in such manner, as may enable him, or the Supervisor, or any other, readily to find the same'. The Foot Officer was expected to visit every chandler (when at work) in his division at least once every six hours and 'never less than twice a day when silent; but oftener where any Fraud is suspected; and these visits must be as early in the Morning, and at late at Night as possible'.

Before the manufacturing of candles could commence the chandler or candle maker had to make and deliver to the Excise Officer a Declaration in writing containing:

1. A True Account of the Number of Sticks, of which making is intended to consist.
2. An Account of the Sizes, and true Number of Candles intended to be made on each Stick.
3. The particular Hour and Time of Day, or Night when such Course or making is intended to begin.

If the process of candle-making did not commence at the time declared or 'three Hours next after that time then the declaration is to be void'. If the candle maker intended to produce his candles from moulds instead of dipping then a similar Declaration had to be made and submitted stating how many moulds he intended to fill and how often 'he intends to draw the said moulds at such Making'. The local excise officer was required to attend within three hours of the declared commencement of work to discover if the candle maker had complied with his declaration. The excise officers had to check and weigh the candles after each production. Fraud was commonplace, some chandlers 'under-dipped' the candles prior to the weighing and then re-dipped them after the excise officer had departed. Other tallow chandlers used false weights or failed to declare the full quantity in an attempt to defraud the excise office. The officers were instructed to be on the lookout for 'unfair' practices. Where such deception was suspected they were instructed to 'frequently look through all Parts of the House, or other Place, that may be convenient for carrying on such a Fraud'.[179]

Whilst Samuel Gatfield was struggling with his financial problems and complying with the Excise rules, others in the town were making a very good living from their trade. One in particular was Thomas Clarrow (or Claroe) who owned the property next door to Samuel Gatfield. This building would undoubtedly have been a sizeable 'town-house', for in the early eighteenth century not all the High Street buildings were retail shops, many were the dwellings of merchants and

---

179 See Leadbetter, *The Royal Gauger or, Gauging made Perfectly Easy*, 3rd ed (1750) pp.340-344.

traders. Thomas Clarrow, described in his will of 1715 as a 'mariner', owned two Severn trows, property and several acres of land; the two trows the *'Thomas and Samuel'* and the *'Samuel and Sarah'* were named after his children. There are several references in local archives to Thomas Clarrow purchasing land in Upton-upon-Severn. He owned his property in the High Street together with a malt house, and eleven parcels of land.

By the beginning of 1749 Samuel Gatfield's financial problems had become critical and the title deeds revealed that he had defaulted on his debts to Willoughby:

> 'And Whereas the said Samuel Gatfield made default in payment of the said several sums of money to the said John Willoughby at the days and times in the above recited indentures limited or appointed for payment thereof neither are the said sums or any part of them yett paid nor all the interest for the forebearance thereof so that the estate or Interest of the said John Willoughby in the said premises for the remainder of the said term of one thousand years is become absolute in law and upon an account this day stated there appears to be owing or due unto the said John Willoughby for principle and interest the sum of One hundred and thirty five pounds......'

The property must have been valued at one hundred and forty pounds at this time for Willoughby paid Samuel Gatfield the sum of five pounds in final settlement of their affairs and although Gatfield had relinquished ownership of the building he remained in situ as tenant to Willoughby. The documents in this instance were complicated tripartite indentures between Gatfield, Willoughby, and a third party Nathaniel Jeynes, a maltster of Tewkesbury. Many people disliked the public ceremony of Livery of Seizin and a more private means of conveyance had developed by about 1600 known as the 'Lease and Release'. A 'Lease', for one year at a nominal rent, would be granted to the purchaser followed the next day by a 'Release' in which the vendor (and other persons with any interest in the property) would relinquish their rights to the property thereby *releasing* it to the purchaser who took full possession. In this instance the Release was to Nathaniel Jeynes who held the building as trustee for John Willoughby. The final paragraph of the Release required that Samuel Gatfield and his wife were to take a *Fine sur cognizance de droit come ceo* in the Court of Common Pleas; this would then transfer the full legal ownership to John Willoughby.

In the following year John Willoughby used the property as collateral for a loan. It was mortgaged to the impressively named Obadiah Arrowsmith, a Ledbury merchant, for one hundred pounds. It is most likely that he was raising capital to pay for extensive building works to the property for it was John Willoughby who must have been responsible for the 'nice mid-Georgian' frontage that had caught Nikolaus Pevsner's attention. During the eighteenth century several handsome

Artists impression of the original premises now divided into two properties.

merchants' houses were constructed in the Georgian style in Upton-upon-Severn. The High Street building was partly rebuilt with the addition of a second storey above the front sales area, the street frontage to the timber-framed building was removed and a fine new facing in red brick was erected complete with the Venetian window to the first floor. The shop windows to the ground floor would have been very similar to those shown in the drawings on these two pages. These windows were subsequently removed during alterations in the nineteenth century.

In 1752 Obadiah Arrowsmith 'having occasion for the said sum of one hundred pounds' requested repayment of the mortgage whereupon John Willoughby 'prevailed upon James Brooke the younger, clerk, of Hanley Castle to advance & lend him the same on security of the said Messuage or Tenement & premises'. Samuel Gatfield continued to occupy the building, as tenant to John Willoughby, until he died in 1754 at the ripe old age of seventy-nine.

John Willoughby, the builder, had a son, also called John, who was born in 1732 and who became a tallow chandler; it is most likely that he was apprenticed to Samuel Gatfield in about the year 1744. After the demise of Samuel Gatfield, the younger Willoughby is recorded as occupying the building, presumably continuing the trade of tallow chandler. The elder John Willoughby seems to be the same person who, a few years earlier, had been brought to the attention of the Quarter Sessions for removing the town gaol and was the cause of serious difficulties for the Parish Constable:

The High Street shop with its new Georgian frontage complete with Venetian window to the first floor.

'This 7th Day of July 1738 … : I Present John Willoughby & Adam Cooke for taking Down & carrying away the prison House or Gaol, belonging to the said town so that we are Destitute of a place to put a prisoner in till he can be brought to Justice this being all that I know of presentable in my Constablewick. – John Shipman, Constable'.[180]

By the middle of the eighteenth century the old parish church in Upton was in a ruinous state and at a public meeting held in December 1754, under the presidency of Mr. Bromley, it was decided that Mr. John Willoughby (the elder) was to be entrusted with the demolition and rebuilding of the parish church (the spire was to be removed but the supporting tower was to be retained). The contract for pulling down the remainder of the church and building 'a new church and chancel in the stead and place thereof' was for the sum of 'one thousand four hundred and sixty-nine pounds'.[181] A 'surveyor', Richard Squire, was appointed and regularly inspected the works. Squire seemed pleased with Willoughby's progress, and reported his findings to the churchwardens.

The name John Willoughby appeared on a list of jurors in a Presentment of the Town & Parish of Upton at a Court Leet & Court Barron held 24th October 1758. (This was possibly the younger John Willoughby who at this time was occupying the High Street premises, his father having moved to Baughton in the nearby parish of Hill Croome where he had purchased an extensive property from Margaret and Ellen Cotterel.) The jurors had to deal with the problem of stacks of coal and timber being left near the waterfront. 'We present all Coal Owners that fills the Quay with Coales & Slack to stand hindering other business or loading Goods to stand longer than law directs on the Penalty of paying One pound Nineteen shillings for every offence, We present all Persons that lodges timber in the Horse Fair longer than one Month at one Pound nineteen shillings each, the above penalties to be collected and given to the poor of Upton'.

John Willoughby junior continued to occupy the High Street shop for a time, and then, for some unexplained reason, he decided to join the army and was posted abroad. No record of his military career has come to light but at this period British troops were active in several campaigns across the world, in North America and India as well as in Europe.

John Willoughby the elder died in 1762 and went to his grave without knowing the fate of his eldest son, John. When his will was published in January 1762 his son was still in the army and several of the bequests made provision for the eventuality that his son *should not return alive* to England. John Willoughby died a wealthy man, owning properties in Ripple, Baughton and several in Upton-upon-Severn

---

180 WAAS Quarter Sessions, 1/1/315/35.
181 Emily Lawson, *The Nation in the Parish*, p.117.

including the lease of the School House in Old Street and a Lime Kiln situated 'below Upton Bridge'. The younger John Willoughby did live to tell the tale of his overseas adventures with the army and returned to Upton-upon-Severn where he resumed his former trade as a tallow chandler, presumably in another building. The elder Willoughby had sold the High Street property in 1759 to John Cottrell of Upton-upon-Severn for the sum of two hundred pounds, the outstanding mortgage of one hundred and thirteen pounds owing to Mr Brook being cleared, including principle and interest. By this date William Bishop, a cooper, was in possession of the other half of the original building and William Hudson, a glover, was in business in the dwelling on the North side.

John Cottrell, a barber, came from another long established Upton family; a John Cotterel has already been mentioned as the parish constable in 1634 (the spelling of Cottrell varied considerably). Cottrell's occupation was rather brief and uneventful. In the same year that he acquired the High Street shop John Cottrell and a John Wells appeared in the Church Wardens accounts and on April 17th 'were regularly chosen and appointed church wardens for the year by us' signed by the vestry. Later that year John Cottrell entered into a mortgage agreement with his fellow churchwarden John Wells for the sum of one hundred pounds using the building as security.

By the middle of the eighteenth century the fashion for wearing wigs or perukes was well established in Worcestershire towns and villages including Upton-upon-Severn. John Cottrell, barber, was also described as a peruke maker. Perhaps he had followed the example of Mr Powell of Newport Street in Worcester and travelled to London to learn the latest arts of hair fashion:

P O W E L L,
PERUKE-MAKER, HAIR-CUTTER, and DRESSER,
At the STAR, in NEWPORT-STREET, WORCESTER,
Begs Leave to acquaint the PUBLICK, That

HE undertakes to dress Ladies' and Gentlemen's Hair in the most elegant Manner, either in English or French Taste, --- As he is just returned from London, and is fully acquainted with all the various Methods of Hair-dressing now in Use, he doubts not of giving the utmost Satisfaction to all who shall be pleased to favour him with Employment, and trusts to his Skill for the Continuance of their Favours – He also makes all Sorts of Wigs, Plaits, Locks, &c. &c. in the newest Fashions, and as compleat as they are made in London.

He makes French Fillets for Gentlemen and Ladies, the finest Sort of Pomatum for the Hair, and strait or crooked Tortoise-Shell Combs for Ladies Use.

(*Berrow's Worcester Journal* – Thursday, 3rd May, 1764 – Powell was also trading in an inn.)

The Village Barber *by Henry William Bunbury, 1772.*

The fashion for wearing periwigs or perukes is said to date back to the restoration of the monarchy in 1660. Samuel Pepys made several references to them in his diary. The wearing of the periwig was not without its drawbacks as he vividly informed us in 1665: 'September 3rd: Up; and put on my coloured silk suit very fine, and my new periwig, bought a good while since but durst not wear because the plague was in Westminster when I bought it: and it is a wonder what will be the fashion after the plague is done as to periwiggs, for nobody will dare buy any haire for fear of the infection, that it had been cut off the heads of people dead of the plague.' He continued in a similar tone in 1667: 'March 27th: ... I did go to the Swan, and there sent for Jervas, my old periwig maker, and he did bring me a periwig, but it was full of nits, so I was troubled to see it (it being his old fault), and did send him to make it clean'. We can only imagine the origins of the hair Mr Cottrell utilised for his perukes, but it was possibly a very early example of recycling in Upton-upon-Severn!

John Cottrell's tenure of the building lasted barely ten years and a Miss Mary Batchelor was tenant, when in 1769, it was sold once again. Of Mary Batchelor little information has come to light. John Cottrell moved away and took a position as a salt officer in Droitwich where the production of salt was an important industry. Excise officers were appointed with the specific responsibility for collecting the duty on salt production. This was a career that attracted the sons of wealthy merchants and tradesmen. The officers were comparatively well paid, although it was required that new recruits should be able to provide security ranging from £200 to £2000. This obligation effectively barred entrants without recourse to financial support.[182] The title deeds show that a Mrs Brydges was the occupant of the other part of the original building at this date, but there is no evidence to suggest that it was commercial premises. William Hudson was still in business making his gloves in the building to the north side. The next purchaser was Samuel Sandelands, another barber from Upton-upon-Severn who paid two hundred and sixty pounds for the building.

---

182 Smith, *Something To Declare*, p.33.

7.

Be not made a beggar by banqueting upon borrowing

(Ecclesiasticus, 18:33)

DEBT, bankruptcy, insolvency and then imprisonment were regular features of life in early modern England, touching all levels of society. As trade and commerce increased at the end of the medieval period it came to be recognised that 'Trade cannot be carried on without mutual credit on both sides: the contracting of debt is therefore here not only justifiable, but necessary. And if by accidental calamities, as, by the loss of a ship in a tempest, the failure of brother traders, or by the non-payment of persons out of trade, a merchant or trader becomes incapable of discharging his own debts, it is his misfortune and not his fault. To the misfortunes, therefore, of debtors, the law has given a compassionate remedy, but denied it to their faults; since, at the same time that it provides for the security of commerce, by enacting that every considerable trader may be declared a bankrupt, for the benefit of his creditors as well as himself, it has also (to discourage extravagance) declared that no one shall be capable of being made a bankrupt, but only a trader; nor capable of receiving the full benefit of the statutes, but only an industrious trader'.[183] Thus it followed that imprisonment of honest traders, who through no fault of their own, had fallen into debt was not an equitable or satisfactory way of dealing with their situation. From the sixteenth century onwards the law gradually evolved to accommodate two kinds of defaulting debtor – the bankrupt and the insolvent. In 1570 a further Bankruptcy Act came onto the statute book (13 Eliz., c. 7) which was the first statute to actually define a bankrupt and who may become bankrupt and thereby differentiated bankruptcy from insolvency. This was an important development in the law concerning default of debt for whereas the insolvent was faced with the terrible prospect of debtor's

---

183 William Blackstone, *Commentaries on the Laws of England*, Bk. II, ch. xxxi, p.474.

prison the bankrupt was relieved of such penal servitude. The preamble of the 1570 Act detailed the continuing problems faced in dealing with bankrupts:

> '... those kind of persons have and do still increase into great and excessive numbers, and are like more to do, if some better provision be not be made for the Repression of them; and for a plain declaration to be made and set forth who is and ought to be taken and deeme for bankrupt...'.

This statute gave the Lord Chancellor the power to appoint commissioners to detain bankrupts, to seize their assets and to subject them to an examination of their affairs. The bankruptcy commissioners were also given more power to deal with fraudulent transfers. Blackstone explained the attitude to insolvent debtors: 'But still they are cautious of encouraging prodigality and extravagance by this indulgence to debtors; and therefore they allow the benefit of the laws of bankruptcy to none but actual traders; since that set of men are, generally speaking, the only persons liable to accidental losses, and to an inability of paying their debts, without any fault of their own. If persons in other situations of life run in debt without the power of payment, they must take the consequences of their own indiscretion, even though they meet with sudden accidents that may reduce their fortunes: ...'. [184]

Blackstone cited the all-important definition of 'qualifying trades' under the statutes: 'it hath been held, that buying only, or selling only, will not qualify a man to be a bankrupt; but it must be both buying and selling, and also getting a livelyhood by it. As, by exercising the calling of a merchant, a grocer, a mercer, or, in one general word, a chapman, who is one that buys and sells any thing. But no handicraft occupation (where nothing is bought and sold, and therefore an extensive credit, for the stock in trade, is not necessary to be had) will make a man a regular bankrupt; as that of a husbandman, a gardener, and the like, who are paid for their work and labour. Also an inn-keeper cannot, as such, be a bankrupt: for his gain or livelyhood does not arise from buying and selling in the way of merchandize, but greatly from the use of his rooms and furniture, his attendance, and the like: and though he may buy corn and victuals, to sell again at a profit, yet that no more makes him a trader, than a schoolmaster or other person is, that keeps a boarding house...'. [185]

The law came to recognise two states of default; firstly, that involving bankruptcy, concerning debtors engaged in trade or commerce who became eligible to be declared bankrupt and secondly, insolvency, where any default could be due to the profligacy of the debtor. People in professional occupations, farmers, landowners, servants and labourers etc. could not qualify to become bankrupt although many lied and were often described under the general title 'dealer and chapman'.

---

184 Ibid. pp.473-4.
185 Ibid. p.476.

In the seventeenth century the unremitting actions of debtors against their creditors led to further legislation. The preamble to '*An Act for the Better Relief of the Creditors Against Such as Shall Become Bankrupt,*' (1 James I, c.15, (1604)) stated: 'For that Fraud and Deceit as new diseases daily increase amongst such as live by buying and selling, to the hindrance of Traffic and mutual Commerce, and to the general Heart of the Realm, by such as wickedly and wilfully become Bankrupt...'. In the same Act the commissioners were given greater powers to investigate fraud and could imprison, without bail, any person refusing to give evidence to the commission, whilst the penalty for perjury was severe in the extreme: 'And that if upon his, her or their Examination, it shall appear that he, she or they have committed any wilful or corrupt perjury tending to the hurt or damage of the Creditors of the said Bankrupt to the value of Ten Pounds ... the Party so offending shall or may thereof be indicted ... and being lawfully convicted thereof, shall stand upon the Pillory in some public place by the space of Two hours, and have one of his ears nailed to the Pillory and cut off.' An Act of 1623 ruled that persons in the trade or profession of scrivener were 'subject and liable' to the statutes of bankruptcy (21 James I, c.19) and further legislation gave bankers, brokers and factors the benefit of the bankruptcy statutes.

The problems of fraudulent debtors continued to concentrate the minds of the legislators and a subsequent Act was passed in 1705 entitled '*An Act to Prevent Frauds Frequently Committed by Bankrupts*' (4 & 5 Anne, c.17). This Act was the first to make any provision for discharge of the debtors remaining debts. It also allowed the bankrupt to retain five percent of the 'Neat Product' of all the estate that was recovered, provided that his creditors had received more than eight shillings in the pound as a dividend. There were certain exclusions to this statute. In those cases where the debtor had lost in one day the sum of five pounds or one hundred pounds within the space of twelve months preceding him becoming bankrupt, 'in playing at or with Cards, Dice, Tables, Tennis. Bowls, Shovel-Board, or in or by Cock-Fightings, Horse-Races, Dog-Matches, or Foot-Races or other Pastimes ... ', he was denied the benefit of the bankruptcy act. As Blackstone had observed in the eighteenth century, English law, whilst severe in its approach to fraud, did come to adopt a more humanitarian attitude to debtors: 'at present the laws of bankruptcy are considered as laws calculated for the benefit of trade, and founded on the principles of humanity as well as justice; and to that end they confer some privileges, not only on the creditors, but also on the bankrupt or debtor himself".[186]

Whilst allowing for discharge from debts the 1705 Act also introduced the death penalty for fraudulent bankrupts: 'That if such Person or Persons so voluntarily surrendering him, her or themselves shall afterwards neglect or omit to discover and deliver his, her or their Estates and Effects shall be taken and adjudged to be a fraudulent Bankrupt within the true Intent and Meaning of this Act and thereof

---

186 William Blackstone, *Commentaries on the Laws of England*, Bk. II, p.473.

being lawfully convicted shall suffer as a Felon, without Benefit of Clergy.' The failure of a bankrupt to make a full disclosure of his assets was a serious crime. Between 1705 and 1813 several men were convicted as fraudulent bankrupts, some were pardoned but four were hung. The first, in 1712, was Richard Towne, a tallow chandler from London, who attempted to remove himself, his goods and his money to Holland but bad weather forced his boat back on to the English shore where he was captured and sent for trial. He was followed by Alexander Thompson, an embroiderer, who went to the gallows in 1756, and in 1761 the public hanging of John Perrott, a cloth merchant, at Smithfield caused quite a sensation in London. The last fraudulent bankrupt to suffer capital punishment was John Senior, a clothier from the village of Alverthorpe near Wakefield in Yorkshire, who was hung in 1813. Senior was probably no different from many other bankrupts and failed to disclose all his assets. The charge, at York Assizes, was that he 'did feloniously conceal and embezzle five bags of wool, thirteen pieces of cashmere, a web of cloth and other property, being more than the value of twenty pounds, with intent to defraud his creditors'. (It was a felony to conceal effects amounting to more than twenty pounds, exclusive of the necessary wearing apparel of the bankrupt and his family.) His total debts had amounted to £1181. His crime was compounded by the fact that he had re-commenced business as a clothier but traded under his brother's name. After all the evidence was submitted the Judge addressed the jury as to which questions in the case they should consider. The jury, after barely a few moments of consideration, pronounced the prisoner '*Guilty*'. 'Mr. Justice Le Blanc passed sentence of death upon the prisoner, and intimated that he could hold out to him no hopes of mercy'. [187]

Procedure in Bankruptcy

When creditors were unable to obtain satisfactory settlement from a debtor they could petition the Lord Chancellor for a commission of bankruptcy. The petitioners were bound by a security of two hundred pounds 'to make the party amends in case they do not prove him a bankrupt'. The Chancellor then appointed 'discreet' persons as Commissioners of Bankrupts who were required to establish proof of the debtor having committed some act of bankruptcy as well as being a trader within the meaning of the statutes. If the case was so proved then a notice of bankruptcy was published in the London Gazette together with details of three meetings. According to Blackstone, the creditors nominated assignees at the first of these meetings, the second meeting dealt with any further business and at the third meeting the bankrupt would surrender himself to, and thereafter conform to, the directions of the Commissioners for Bankrupts. (Some notices in the Gazette give a divergence from this procedure as the assignees were chosen at the second of these meetings.) The bankrupt would be examined by the commissioners and was 'bound upon pain

187 *The Hull Packet,* 6th April 1813.

of death' to make a full disclosure of his estate. All the personal estate and effects of the bankrupt were vested in the assignees of the commissioners who, once they had in hand all such effects as they could find, were obliged to 'reduce them to ready money' for distribution to the creditors as a dividend. It was possible for the bankrupt to be entitled to a reasonable allowance out of his estate, the value of which depended upon the amount of dividend paid out to his creditors. The higher the dividend the greater the allowance. The bankrupt could then finally be discharged and hopefully return to his trade or profession.

Insolvency

Whilst the bankrupt avoided the rigours of imprisonment the insolvent debtor was not so fortunate and many languished in prison, often for years, awaiting an upturn in their fortunes. Following the 1670 statute (*An Act for the relief and release of poor distressed prisoners for debt*), which did provide some relief for distressed prisoners, further statutes were enacted. These enabled insolvent debtors who complied with certain conditions to apply to the Quarter Sessions for release from prison, but it must be added that this was partly motivated by the desire to reduce overcrowding in prisons. In 1808 an Act was passed which allowed debtors who had been imprisoned for twelve calendar months to be discharged provided the debt did not exceed twenty pounds (48 George III, c. 123). The prisoner was allowed 'the necessary wearing apparel and bedding' for himself and his family and necessary tools for his trade or occupation, but not exceeding the value of ten pounds.

Towards the final years of the eighteenth century this was the status quo regarding debtors and insolvents, a subject with which Charles Dickens was well acquainted and which occupied much of his writing. Some of the earlier occupants of this property in Upton-upon-Severn had fallen into debt and were unable to meet their obligations; in the early seventeenth century the profligate Francis Hall had escaped the clutches of his creditor by drowning in the river Severn, albeit accidentally, and in the following century Samuel Gatfield had had to surrender the property to his mortgagee. Thomas Bound and William Ellery both fell foul of the law and were imprisoned by their creditors; in Ellery's case it ultimately led to his wife forfeiting her grandfather's legacy. Thomas Bound was more fortunate and did recover some of his land and property. Several of the individuals to be encountered next in this history during the late eighteenth and early nineteenth centuries followed in the footsteps of Thomas Bound and William Ellery; they too had an aptitude for falling into debt. Some became insolvent and endured the rigours of debtor's prison whilst others had the relative advantage of the bankruptcy laws. However, once discharged of their debts it is quite remarkable how soon some of them resurrected their lives and prospered again in their trades or professions.

8.

An Estate Too Far

S AMUEL Sandelands, the barber, came from another family long established in Upton-upon-Severn. There are references to Sandelands (Sandilands or Sandlands) from the sixteenth century onwards. A court roll of 1507 mentions a John Sandelands, in 1552 a John Sandlans was churchwarden and in 1587 a Francis Sandlands was one of the Edward Hall Charity trustees. Mrs Lawson referred to 'yeomen Cotterill and Sandilands, men whose ancestors had occupied the same lands for many generations'. In 1622 Richard and Alice Sandlands had perished, together with Francis Hall, in the tragic accident on the River Severn. Samuel Sandelands was quite possibly a descendant of Francis Hall alias Oliver whose daughter Elizabeth (a deponent in John Best's Chancery Case in 1638) had married William Sandelands. It would seem that some members of the family had followed the same trade for several generations for George Sandlands, a barber, is mentioned in the Quarter Sessions records for 1619.

Samuel Sandelands was born in 1741 and married Elizabeth Jelf, the daughter of Thomas Jelf from Queenhill, a small village lying just to the south of Upton-upon-Severn. Thomas Jelf was the same person as described in a Quarter Sessions indictment for Easter 1750 as 'being an evil disposed person of a wilful and insolent disposition'. Jelf was accused of stealing sixty-two live carp, valued at forty shillings, by draft net from two ponds belonging to the Earl of Coventry at Severn Stoke. He pleaded that he should not answer the indictment citing *The Indemnity Act* of 1747: 'Thomas Jelf in his own proper person comes and says that our Sovereign Lord the King should not be answered to the Bill ... because he says that by an Act of Parliament Entitled *An Act for the King's most gracious generall and free pardon* made in the twentieth year of his present Majesties reigne, it is Enacted that all and every his Majesties Subjects shall by the Authority of the said Act [be] acquitted pardoned released and discharged ... from all manner of Trespasses and other Misdemeanours not thereinafter excepted or foreprized which had been made done or committed before the fifteenth day of June one thousand seven hundred and forty seven'. The Court of Assize could not argue against Thomas Jelf's defence. His 'misdemeanour' was committed on the 23rd April 1747 and the indictment was annotated: 'Discharged by Act of Grace'.[188] Several Indemnity Acts were passed in the eighteenth century giving legal relief to religious nonconformists who were barred from holding various public offices in accordance with the Corporation Act of 1661 and the Test Act of 1673. The Indemnity Act of 1747 was intended to absolve Hanoverian supporters from infringements of the law following the suppression of the Jacobite uprisings of 1745. There were numerous exceptions to this Indemnity Act including piracy, 'voluntary murthers', 'wilful burning of houses', robberies of churches, 'carnal ravishments of women' etc, etc., and not forgetting 'persons of the clan McGregour' who were particularly singled out. (In the Jacobite rising of 1745, the Macgregors were at the forefront of the fighting at the battle of Prestonpans which resulted in a defeat for the Hanoverian army. The broad swords and billhooks of the highlanders resulted in horrific injuries to the English forces.) Poaching, it seems, was not excepted hence Thomas Jelf's discharge.

Thomas Jelf's brother, James, also from Queenhill, died in November 1772 leaving substantial bequests in his will. A total of six hundred and fifty pounds was left to several nephews and nieces. There was a bequest of one hundred pounds to Samuel Sandelands' wife, Elizabeth, and two hundred pounds to his great-niece and goddaughter Elizabeth Jelf Sandelands (Samuel's eldest daughter). The various sums of money were held in trust by Samuel Sandelands until the children came of age. Samuel was appointed executor and he was the beneficiary of the remainder of James Jelf's estate. In that same year Samuel Sandelands had a disagreement with his neighbour, a Mr Webb, concerning a boundary wall. The issue was eventually resolved and articles of agreement were drawn up, presumably to the satisfaction of both parties:

> **'Whereas** divers Disputes and Contentions have arisen between the said Thomas Webb and Samuel Sandelands touching the right and ownership of a wall on the North Side of the Dwelling House of the said Samuel Sandelands and adjoining the same and which divides the Yard behind the Dwelling House of the said Samuel Sandelands and the Yard behind the Dwelling House of the said Thomas Webb now in the possession of Mr Hudson as tenant thereof upon which said wall the Ancestors of the said Thomas Webb lodged a building. **And Whereas** the said Samuel Sandelands intended to remove the said Building from the said Wall or to prosecute his action against the said Thomas Webb unless he removed the same for the prosecution whereof and of the Expense attending any litigation touching the Claim of the respective parties to the said wall they have come to an Agreement .... as follows (that is to say) that the

---

188 Indictment: WAAS 101 BA1 359/35. Answer: WAAS 101 BA1 359/58.

said Thomas Webb shall release all his right and pretentions of right of or to the said Wall or any part thereof and shall pay to the said Samuel Sandelands his heirs or Assigns the Sum of Two pence a year on Christmas day in every year for so long time as the said Building or any part thereof shall remain on the said Wall by Way of Acknowledgement'.

(The payment of two pence per year on Christmas Day has, unfortunately, fallen into abeyance.)

Samuel was an active member of the local community and held various offices. He was a member of the church vestry and was appointed churchwarden in 1775, and in 1781 he was one of the assignees selected at the bankruptcy of Joseph Wear, a mercer of Upton-upon-Severn.

> ALL Persons who stand indebted to the Estate and Effects of JOSEPH WEAR, of Upton-upon-Severn, in the County of Worcester, Mercer, a Bankrupt, are desired immediately to pay the same to Mr James Skey and Mr. Samuel Sandelands, the Assignees; or to Mr. Dunn, Attorney at Law, the Solicitor of the Commisions, otherwise they will be sued without further notice.
>
> (*Berrow's Worcester Journal*, Thursday, 25th January, 1781.)

Within a few years Samuel Sandelands had decided upon a change of trade and entered the linen drapery business, an astute move into a much more lucrative occupation. (This move may well have occurred following the death of his wife's mother, Susannah Jelf, who left her daughter a substantial bequest of nine hundred pounds.) Linen drapers were to be found in every town and city in England – by 1817 no less than thirty-three linen drapers had established themselves in Oxford Street in London. Drapers supplied an extensive range of fabrics including linen of various sorts, cotton fabrics, ruff dowlas, wolsey, broad lawn, cambrick, muslin, silk and calico as well as ribbons, trimmings and threads. There were few manufactured textile articles available at this time and all elements of society patronised the drapers shop to acquire fabric to make their own clothes as well as sheets, pillowcases, bed covers, curtains and other household requisites. Eventually Samuel went into partnership with a Mr Thomas Husband, another linen and woollen draper in the town. The partners faced the perpetual problem of shoplifting, for some years later Berrow's Journal reported a theft of ribbon from the drapers shop in Upton-upon-Severn:

> Last week was committed to our Castle, by William Wrenford, Esq; William Boswell and Charles Scamp, for stealing five rolls of

Ribboning out of the shop of Messrs. Sandiland and Husband, of
Upton, in this county.

(*Berrow's Worcester Journal*, 14th July 1791.)

Samuel Sandelands lived with his wife and their four children in the extensive
accommodation above the High Street shop and it is conceivable that he enrolled
his young son, Thomas, as a pupil in the school recently established in Upton-upon-
Severn by Mr G. Roberts for the 'Education of Young Gentlemen':

Education and Board, AT the large and commodious House (formerly
the Rev. Mr. STEEL's SCHOOL), in the healthy and pleasant Town
of Upton-upon-Severn, in Worcestershire, YOUNG GENTLEMEN will
be educated and boarded by G. ROBERTS, who has been Assistant
at several Schools, and lately at that large and eminent Academy
at Barr, in Staffordshire, where he has taken the greatest Pains and
Attention to collect the most approved Method of instructing Youth,
as well as a proper and select Mode of conducting a School. And
as he does not propose to teach more than he is capable of himself,
he hopes the candid Public will allow that he will be the better
able to give a personal and due Attention to the more useful and
necessary Parts of the Education of Youths who may be designed for
Trades, Merchants, Compting-House, &c. &c. - His Design at present,
is therefore only to teach the Rudiments of the English Language;
Writing and Arithmetic in all its various Branches; Book-keeping
by single and double Entry; the useful Branches of the Mathematics;
and some other Parts of useful Learning: And begs Leave to assure
his Friends and the Public in general, that not only the greatest
Pains and Attention will be taken to their making a rapid Progress
and attaining to a Perfection in the same, but also a strict Regard
will be had to their Morals, Deportment, and Recreations, with a
constant Eye to their Accommodation, Diet, and tender Manner of
Treatment; and as his whole Study and Ambition will be to merit
the Favours and Patronage of his Friends and the Public, he hopes
his Plan, upon Trial, will gain their Approbation.

Proper Masters will attend (if desired) to teach Dancing,
Drawing, &c. - He opens School at Lady-Day next. Terms,
Thirteen Guineas a Year, and One Guinea Entrance.
N.B. Gentlemen's Estates accurately surveyed, and neatly mapped, at
such intervals as may not interfere with other Business.

(*Berrow's Worcester Journal*, Thursday, 9th March, 1780.)

If John Best or the elder Samuel Gatfield had returned to visit Upton-upon-Severn at this time there would still have been a familiar appearance to the town; the trows and barges plying the river Severn, the inns and alehouses open for business as usual, the tallow chandlers producing candles, numerous shoemakers, the tanner, the coopers and other familiar trades all at work. But by now Upton-upon-Severn had expanded considerably and had developed, as described by the Universal British Directory of 1791, into a 'market town' with 'a harbour for barges, and a charity-school for sixteen girls. The church has a square tower and five bells; also a clock. The body of the church is very neat, built in 1758. Here is a stone bridge with six arches, over the Severn'. Many of the buildings would have changed, the biggest transformation being the 'neat' parish church rebuilt by John Willoughby. Several buildings, including Sandelands' drapery shop, had acquired Georgian frontages with newly glazed windows displaying their extensive wares. William Jackson at the Talbot Inn was now the postmaster: 'The post goes regularly every day to Worcester, at ten in the morning; returns at six in the evening. – A mail-chaise to Worcester Tuesday and Saturday, at ten in the morning; returns the same afternoon'. The excise office, overseen by Samuel Bamford, was in the Cross Keys (the collection of excise duties must have been of some importance for the Directory listed four excise officers). A totally new addition since the seventeenth century would have been the two banks in the town, Skey, Brockhurst, and Co. and the aptly named, Leechman, Wall, and Co. ('banking hours from ten till one, and from three till five'). The former was a joint venture between two local brewers, James Skey and Thomas Brockhurst, but the bank did not thrive and the partnership was terminated in 1814. Larger businesses arrived when three cider merchants established themselves in the town. There were now four bakers, five butchers, five grocers and four ironmongers. Trades and crafts had diversified since the seventeenth century and now included a watchmaker, a cabinet maker, a cork cutter (cutting cork to provide stoppers for bottles, floats for fishing nets etc.), a stay maker and several hatters. The manufacture of 'Upton' chairs was another local craft. The medical profession was well represented with four 'surgeons' and two midwives. The retailing and compounding of medicines was also established at this time with at least one apothecary in business, and finally, there were four attorneys for those having recourse to legal matters.

Samuel Sandelands was by now a wealthy man, a respected tradesman and pillar of the local church. Upton-upon-Severn must have been a bustling town and his drapery business appears to have flourished. He owned numerous properties in Upton and in Queenhill, both freehold and leasehold, together with copyhold land in Ripple that was held of the manor of Ripple for three lives. His Upton-upon-Severn properties included the 'Star and Horseshoe' adjacent to the churchyard, the 'Wheatsheaf' (another public house) in Church Street and two coal yards. He also owned two properties in Dunn's Lane which were rented to the parish, possibly to provide accommodation for the poor of the town. The High Street building had been considerably extended and a large three-storey malt-house, together with a kiln for drying malt, had been constructed to the rear of the premises. Samuel Sandelands eventually retired from the business about the turn of the century and moved to the small village of Severn Stoke together with his wife Elizabeth and two youngest daughters who were still unmarried. His eldest daughter, Elizabeth, had married George Rogers, an attorney, from Bristol. In 1803 Sandelands purchased several parcels of land and property in Hanley Castle from John Bullock of Walton Cardiff for £3,100 (Subject to a mortgage for the sum of £2,000). This small estate was sold two years later to Anthony Lechmere of the Rydd in Hanley Castle for £3,300.[189]

In 1806 he drew up his will appointing his son, Thomas Jelf Sandelands, and James Skey as trustees of all his freehold, leasehold and copyhold estate. The income from these properties was bequeathed to his wife for her life and in the event of her re-marriage or decease the benefit of the properties then came to his children. If his wife were to remarry then the rental income ceased but she was to receive an annuity of fifty pounds per annum. Samuel was quite precise in his instructions regarding his wife's bequest: '*I do hereby expressly declare that the said Rents and profits of my said Estate and the said Annuity upon the Event of my Wife's marrying again so as aforesaid are given to her upon the express condition that my said wife do accept such provision in Lieu bar and full Satisfaction of and for her claim Estate or Interest of in or to the Legacy of Nine hundred pounds given by the will of her late Mother*'. After any such marriage his youngest daughter, Amelia Mary, would have received the benefit of the rental income from the High Street retail premises and the new malt-house. His son, Thomas, was bequeathed all his copyhold land at Ripple and the two unmarried daughters each received five hundred pounds. At some time during his tenure of the building Samuel Sandelands had acquired the benefit of a pew on the north side of the gallery of the parish church. The use of the pew was mentioned in the bequest to his daughter Amelia, and subsequently the pew was included in the freehold and appeared in all the title deeds to the High Street building until the consecration of the new church in 1879.[190] He also appears to have had some connection with the charity endowed by George King who gave one hundred and fifty pounds towards the establishment of a Charity School in Upton-upon-Severn. Samuel Sandelands died in 1806 and his daughter, Amelia, outlived him by just two years, dying in 1808, barely thirty years of age.

---

189 WAAS 705:134 BA1531/87/1/1&2, 5th and 6th April 1803 and 705:134 BA1531/87/1/6, 21st December 1805. These parcels of land appear to have comprised the Sink Farm estate in Hanley Castle.

190 The church pews in Upton are shown in Pamela Hurle, *Upton: Portrait of a Severnside Town*, Plate 26.

The Remarkable Rise and Fall of Thomas Jelf Sandelands (and several others)

Samuel's only son, Thomas, was born in 1777 and spent his formative years living in the spacious accommodation above his father's drapery business in the High Street. Thomas determined not to follow his father into the drapery trade and instead chose a professional career. In time he would prove to be the antithesis of his father – a respectable and successful businessman who had left a sizeable estate. Following his school education Thomas went on to study law and eventually qualified as an attorney. (He was listed in Pigot's 1830 Directory of Gloucestershire practising as an attorney in Tewkesbury High Street.) He also became a 'money scrivener' (someone who received money to place it out at interest or supplied money to those who wanted to raise loans on security, and received a commission on the transactions). In addition to these professional and monetary activities there is evidence that he had dealings in the 'West India trade'. By the age of twenty eight Thomas Jelf Sandelands had become a respected member of the legal profession and in 1805 was appointed Master Extraordinary as the front page of the London Gazette then reported:

> Whitehall August 3, 1805.
>
> The Lord Chancellor has appointed Thomas Jelf
> Sandelands, of Tewkesbury, in the County of Gloucester,
> Gent, to be a Master Extraordinary in the High Court of
> Chancery.
>
> *(The London Gazette, 30th July, 1805, p.985)*

(A Master Extraordinary was an official, usually a solicitor, appointed by the Court of Chancery in various counties in England for taking affidavits and recognizances etc. from parties to cases that would otherwise have been taken before the Masters in Chancery thereby saving the suitors and witnesses the time and expense of travelling to London.)

Thomas Jelf Sandelands later became entangled in a long series of Chancery cases and eventually issued Bills of Complaint against various parties who had been involved with the administration of his wife's considerable inheritance from her maternal grandfather. The prelude to this suit in Chancery is most remarkable and intriguing.

In 1807 Thomas married Maria Charlotte Greene (otherwise Maria Charlotte Goddard) at the fashionable St. George's Church, Hanover Square in London. Notice of the marriage appeared in *The Athenaeum*, a renowned literary and artistic review printed in the nineteenth century. Maria Charlotte was the only surviving child of the late deceased Lieutenant Thomas Goddard of *HMS Prince George* (a ninety gun ship of the line) and had inherited her father's sizeable estate. The marriage settlement comprised the sum of £5700 5s 4d in three percent consolidated bank annuities – a not inconsiderable sum of money (about £380,000 today). This settlement was in the hands of two trustees, John Hooke Greene (uncle to Maria Charlotte) and Richard Sandilands (cousin to Thomas Jelf Sandilands). (For some reason his name was now regularly spelt 'Sandilands' not 'Sandelands'.) One of the witnesses to the marriage was Maria Charlotte's aunt, Eliza Maria Greene Goddard. Thomas Goddard had died in 1796 when his daughter, Maria Charlotte, was only eight years of age and his estate had been put into the hands of three trustees: Walter Boyd, a merchant banker, of Broad Street in the City of London, John Hooke Greene of Fulham in the County of Middlesex and Osborne Standart (or Standert) of the Navy Office. Boyd and Greene had also been appointed legal guardians of Maria Charlotte until she came of age. The origins of her 'otherwise' name took a considerable time to resolve. There was some elusive connection between these two families, Greene and Goddard, and the answer was to be found with Maria Charlotte's paternal grandmother Elizabeth Greene (née Hooke) in Volume VI of '*Trials for Adultery: or, the History of Divorces. Being Select Trials at Doctors Commons, for Adultery, Fornication, Cruelty, Impotence, &c. From the Year 1760, to the Present Time*'. (Printed for S. Bladon, London, 1779-1780.) Doctors' Commons was a place where ecclesiastical lawyers conducted their business, situated near St Paul's churchyard in London, as described by Charles Dickens several decades later:

> 'Walking, without any definite object, through St. Paul's Churchyard, a little while ago, we happened to turn down a street entitled 'Paul's-chain,' and keeping straight forward for a few hundred yards, found ourself, as a natural consequence, in Doctors' Commons. Now Doctors' Commons being familiar by name to everybody, as the place where they grant marriage-licences to love-sick couples, and divorces to unfaithful ones; register the wills of people who have any property to leave, and punish hasty gentlemen who call ladies by unpleasant names, we no sooner discovered that we were really within its precincts, than we felt a laudable desire to become better acquainted therewith; and as the first object of our curiosity was the Court, whose decrees can even unloose the bonds of matrimony, we procured a direction to it; and bent our steps thither without delay.' (Charles Dickens, *Sketches by Boz – Doctors Commons*.)

JOHN GREENE
AGAINST
ELIZABETH GREENE
LIBEL given in the 12th of December 1772[191]

---

191 Libel in this context refers to a written declaration or charges of the plaintiff in a cause before the Ecclesiastical Courts.

The depositions of the witnesses in this case gave a lurid account of the proceedings. In the year 1756 the Reverend John Greene had married Elizabeth Hooke in Norwich and together they had produced four children; John Hooke Greene, born 1757; Eliza Maria and Charlotte Margaret both born in November 1760, followed in 1761 by Harriette Ann. In 1761 the Reverend Greene had been presented by the Earl of Buckinghamshire to the rectories of Hunworth and Stody in Norfolk. The family subsequently moved, in about 1765, to Lynn Regis (Kings Lynn) in Norfolk where they rented a house and 'one Thomas Goddard of Lynn Regis went to lodge and board with the said John and Elizabeth'. At the trial Elizabeth Magnant deposed that she knew the Reverend Greene 'by means of him frequenting the deponent's father's house in the city of Norwich, which was a public inn, known by the sign of the Dolphin'. The deponent succeeded her father as innkeeper at the Dolphin and she further deposed that 'it was generally reported by their neighbours and acquaintances that the said Elizabeth and Thomas Goddard carried on a criminal intercourse with each other, and committed the crime of adultery together'. In 1771 matters came to a head and there was a quarrel between the three parties. The Reverend Greene, having discovered their extra-marital activities, 'withdrew himself from bed, board and mutual co-habitation with his wife, Elizabeth'. Mrs Greene then packed her bags, departed the marital home and set forth for London with her lodger. Once arrived in the metropolis, Thomas Goddard went in search of suitable lodgings and enquired at the house of John Fennymore in Suffolk Street in the parish of St. Martin in the Fields. In his evidence to the court Fennymore testified that:

> 'he seemed to approve of the lodgings, and told the deponent he would give him an answer in half an hour; and he also said, that he was just arrived in town off a journey: that his things were at the Golden Cross Inn, at Charing Cross, and that the lady was then at the Cardigan Tavern, Charing Cross: that he went away, and in about a quarter of an hour afterwards returned with the lady in a coach, and they looked at the lodgings together; and the lady approving of them, the said Mr. Goddard immediately agreed with the deponent for such lodgings....'

Fennymore's wife was then called to give evidence.

In her deposition Ann Fennymore left little room for doubt about the activities of her new lodgers:

> 'and the deponent, soon after they were got into bed, went into the bedchamber to them with a lamp, which was to be kept burning all night and saw the said Goddard, and the said lady together, naked and alone; and the deponent tucked up the bed-clothes, as they lay in bed together....' and she further deposed: 'that

they continued such lodgings for about ten days, and constantly and regularly, night after night, lay together, naked and alone, in one and the same bed …'

The evidence given by the nineteen-year-old maid, Sarah Sutton, confirmed Mrs Fennymore's account:

'... the deponent constantly attended the said Mr Goddard and such lady, who behaved to each other as man and wife in every respect; and constantly and regularly night after night, lay together naked and alone in one and the same bed and had, as the deponent supposes, carnal knowledge of each other ....'

This was an infamous affair for Georgian England and there was a remarkable similarity in the wording of the evidence of these two deponents. The testimony of some witnesses in eighteenth century divorce proceedings was questionable for, as in this instance, they may have been instructed what to say by the lawyers representing the parties involved. (Canon law required two witnesses to such acts of infidelity and accepted circumstantial evidence that adultery had taken place.) Collusion between the parties was commonplace to ensure a smooth passage for the case through the courts.

In the face of all the irrefutable evidence (including the maid's supposition) the Ecclesiastical Court duly granted the Reverend Greene a divorce from his wayward wife, Elizabeth. It must be remembered that in the eighteenth century it was extremely difficult for a woman to divorce her husband. The couple appear to have made little effort to disguise their relationship. In fact they had ensured there were several witnesses to their amorous activities and consequently the unfortunate Reverend Greene had little difficulty in obtaining a divorce:

SENTENCE

'Upon hearing the depositions of the witnesses in this cause, a final decree or sentence was given to the following effect, viz. that Elizabeth Greene, after the solemnization and consummation of the marriage, altogether mindful of her conjugal vow, &c. did, in the years and months libellate, commit the crime of adultery with a strange man, calling himself Thomas Goddard, and did violate her conjugal duty: it is therefore pronounced and decreed, that the said Reverend John Greene, clerk, ought by law, to be divorced and separated from, bed, board and mutual cohabitation with the said Elizabeth Greene, his wife, &c. and they are divorced and separated accordingly'.

Night after night, lay together, naked and alone, in one and the same bed.

In these circumstances, where the Reverend Greene had successfully sued for divorce on the grounds of his wife's adultery, the court would not have allowed Elizabeth any alimony and consequently she could have been left penniless. Added to this, because she had eloped with her lover, by ancient custom of medieval law she would have lost her right to dower (a common law right to one third of her husbands property for her life), although she would have retained the right to any marriage settlement or any property held in trust for her benefit. The choice of London as a destination when Elizabeth departed the marital home with her lodger was not a random decision taken in the heat of the moment. Litigants who had taken up residence in London for twenty-one days were allowed, by a legal loophole, to bring their cases before the Consistory Court of London. This gave litigants the distinct advantage of having more practised proctors (lawyers), cases were heard much more quickly and before an experienced judge. (The Reverend Greene had also moved from Norfolk to St Giles in the Fields, Middlesex.)

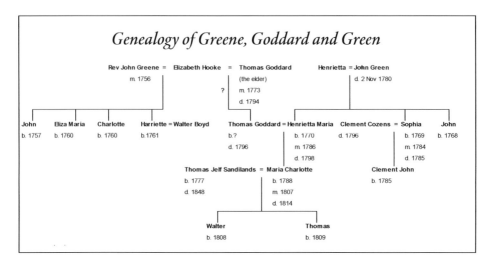

Genealogy of Greene, Goddard and Green

Nevertheless the chains of matrimony were still not completely unfettered. In the eighteenth century 'divorce' could have two meanings; under canon law it meant a *divorticum a mensa et thoro* literally a divorce 'from bed and board'. The parties were required to give bonds of one hundred pounds not to re-marry whilst the other spouse was still alive. If one of the parties did desire to re-marry the only course of action available to them was to obtain a *divorticum a vinculo* – a full legal divorce granted by a private Act of Parliament. This was an expensive option costing several hundred pounds and only available to persons of wealth. Legal actions in the late sixteenth century, during the reign of Elizabeth, had prohibited divorce with remarriage – the only option then was to obtain a *divorticum a mensa et thoro* in the ecclesiastical court. However, various private Acts introduced through Parliament, starting with the famous Roos case of 1690, paved the way for a full divorce – a *divorticum a vinculo.* The Roos case was an enabling Act which would allow Lord Roos to remarry and was not an Act specifically to obtain a divorce. Subsequent Acts allowing divorce were passed in the early eighteenth century but only to childless husbands who had obtained a *divorticum a mensa et thoro* and where inheritance was being threatened by the illegitimate offspring of an adulterous wife. Eventually the precedent for a full legal divorce by a private act of Parliament was established.[192] Before 1858 there were only three hundred and eighteen such Acts granted by Parliament of which just four of the petitioners were women. In 1773 John Greene successfully promoted an Act of Parliament to obtain a divorce from his wife Elizabeth, thereby leaving himself free to re-marry – '*An Act to Dissolve the Marriage of John Greene, Clerk, with Elizabeth Greene his now Wife, and to enable him to marry again, and for other Purposes therein mentioned*' (13 George III c. 91).

---

192 For a detailed explanation see Laurence Stone, *Road to Divorce England 1530-1987,* who provides an enlightening and entertaining account on this subject.

For the husband it was essential to safeguard any interest he held in land or property and the bastardization of any spurious issue of his wife negated any unwanted claims on his estate. This state of affairs regarding divorce remained in place until the Matrimonial Causes Act of 1857 which reformed divorce law, the full title being '*An Act to amend the Law relating to Divorce and Matrimonial Causes in England.* The Act came into force on the 1st January 1858. In the eighteenth century it was usual in Parliamentary divorces for the husband to keep his wife's marriage portion but to allow her an annuity according to the value of her portion and her status in life.[193]

There was another child born to Elizabeth Greene, named Thomas Goddard, who was destined to become father-in-law to Thomas Jelf Sandelands. The paternity of the younger Thomas Goddard is most uncertain, the elder Thomas Goddard referred to him in his will as his 'son-in-law' (i.e. in this context his stepson, or he could have been adopted by Thomas Goddard the elder to legalise any inheritance). However, John Hooke Greene referred to him as being his 'brother by half-blood', and if this was correct then he would have been the 'issue' of Elizabeth Greene and presumably Thomas Goddard the elder (as someone once observed, 'maternity is a matter of fact, paternity is a matter of opinion'). The elder Thomas Goddard seems to have been a wealthy man. He was one of the leading proponents of the Polygraphic Society that was established in the late eighteenth century to make facsimiles of oil paintings which were sold at a fraction of the price of the original works of art. The technique of Polygraphs, or Pollaplasiasmos as it was originally called, was a chemical and mechanical process for copying works of art, invented by Joseph Booth, a portrait-painter. It was claimed that by this 'secret process' copies of the 'best masters, either old or modern, were so closely imitated as to render those pictures scarcely distinguishable from the originals themselves, even when hung in the same room'. [194]

On the 12th May 1773, two days after the Reverend John Greene's Act of Parliament received its royal assent, Thomas Goddard made his wedding vows in the parish church of St George's, Bloomsbury, with Elizabeth Hooke a 'spinster' of that parish. At least two of her four children (by now in their teenage years) evidently went to live with their mother and her new husband, Thomas Goddard, and adopted the surname Goddard.

Her son, John Hooke Greene, also had some connection with the Polygraphic Society. He eventually left England and became the Collector of Customs at the Cape of Good Hope. The eldest daughter never married and took the name Eliza Maria Greene Goddard (she being a witness at the marriage of Thomas Jelf Sandilands and Maria Charlotte). We may never know the reason why Elizabeth Greene took a lover, but the fact that two of her daughters chose to live with her

---

193 Ibid. p.345.

194 Richard Alfred Davenport, *Sketches of Imposture: Deception and Credulity,* London 1837, p.226.

and not their father could be some reflection of the character of the Reverend John Greene.

Thomas Goddard the younger married Henrietta Maria Green who, most confusingly, was the daughter of another John Green (but without the final 'e'), an officer in the Honourable Company of East India Merchants. He appears in the company records in 1758 listed as 'Lieutenant Fireworker' for the Bengal Artillery and was promoted to Captain-Lieutenant in 1761. After the battle of Udhua Nullah in 1763 he 'was promoted the following day by Major Adams for good service on that occasion' to the rank of captain. The battle of Udhua Nullah occurred at the time of a colonial dispute with the Nawab, Mir Kasim. After being defeated in the battle, the Nawab was roused to exasperation and wrote to Major Adams: 'If you are resolved to proceed in this business, know for certainty that I will cut off the heads of Mr. Ellis and the rest of your chiefs and send them to you' (Mr Ellis was the chief of the East India Company factory at Patna).

The Nawab carried out his threat on the evening of October 6th 1763 – about sixty Englishmen were murdered. One year later an entry in the East India Company records for the 12th November 1764 noted: 'Captain John Green of the artillery has been obliged to resign the service on account of his bad health …. and that he has been of remarkable use to the Company and they experience the loss of a very deserving and skilful officer'. He sailed back to England in an East India Company ship called the 'Devonshire'. The evidence suggests that he married his wife, Henrietta, whilst recuperating in England, although this marriage has not yet been traced. Certainly their three children, Sophia, John and Henrietta Maria, were born at this time.

By 1770 John Green had recovered his health and made arrangements for his return to India. He gave power of attorney over his affairs to his wife, Henrietta, and to a Thomas Sanderson, a coal merchant of 'Petty France in the City and Liberty of Westminster'.

Having returned to Calcutta he resumed his position with the East India Company and was promoted to the rank of Major in 1771. Major Green was appointed Inspector of Military Stores at Fort St. George at a salary of four hundred pounds per annum and also enjoyed the pay and allowances of Major of Artillery. After four years of separation Mrs Green decided to join her husband in Calcutta and likewise made arrangements for her affairs by granting power of attorney to Thomas Sanderson and to Arthur Scaife, an 'eminent' armourer, founder and brazier, of Grace Church Street, London. (Readers of *Pride and Prejudice* will be familiar with Gracechurch Street. This was the address of Mr and Mrs Gardiner, uncle and aunt of Miss Elizabeth Bennet, where they lived in some comfort but '*within view of his own warehouse*'. This was an address for 'tradesmen' – '*Mr Darcy may perhaps have heard of such a place as Gracechurch Street, but he would hardly think a month's ablution enough to cleanse him from its impurities…*'.) Henrietta Green set sail for India early in 1774 and during the long voyage wrote a short letter to a friend in England[195] :

> *Dear Sir*   *Lat 34 15 South*
>
> *I have the pleasure to acquaint you that we are all well and within Sight of the Cape of good hope but Whether we Shall go in there is out of my power to Say, but am in hopes we shall have had a good passage thus far being all pretty well, one Accident only a Man Lost Which depresed my Spirits very much. Oh Sir what a tryal the Absince of my friends ys? but hope a few years will return me to them with my Dear Husband. I must once more repeat my thanks for all the favours Confered on me by you and Capt Oliphant which permit me to Asure I shall never forget pray make my respects to him and to Mrs Puttam and tell her I would write a few Lines but no time. When did you see Mr & Mrs May my Loving Respects to them will rite the first Opportunity. I nead not remind you of the promise to Asist Mr Sanderson as I am Sure you will in every thing in your power, for he is a Worthy man & an Honest one, my love to your Children, remember mine. I recommend them and Lucy to your favours. I hope Sam is come out I Shall Write from the Cape if we go in have not time to Say more but to Asure that I am your*
> > *Sincere and Obliged*
> > *friend, Henrietta Green*

(The recipient of this letter was probably Arthur Scaife – 'Latitude 34 15 South' is due west of Cape Town.)

Several of John Green's letters[196] to friends in England have survived. This correspondence mainly concerned his financial arrangements – sending Bills of Exchange back to England to provide money to support his wife and young family, but the letters were enlivened by various items of news and comments describing colonial life in India. In one letter to Sanderson dated 11th January 1775 he describes the fate of a Mr Haynes:

> '*The poor lad was cast away coming from Madrass, and for five weeks suffered many hardships, stripped of every thing as soon as landed, even to his shirt, and deprived of provisions, laying all the time under trees in the open air which at this season is very cold, he got an ague and fever, on coming up the river within one hundred miles of Calcutta, died in the night in a fitt – there is no will found...*'

---

195 C 105/29: *West v Greene, Correspondence, Calcutta.*
196 Ibid.

John Green wrote again to Thomas Sanderson on the 16th September 1776 and from the tone and content it is apparent that his wife, Henrietta, had died within a short time of her arrival in India. He concluded his letter 'Indeed there is little if any Social happiness in this country, pleasure there is none, the Labour, Heat and fatigue a man undergoes to get a few pounds to enable him to return home again is not to be conceived'. In March 1777 he despatched another letter 'By the hand of Colonel Cumming' who was returning to England with his wife. In this letter John Green mentioned Mrs Cumming who 'had a very sincere regard for Mrs Green, who never mentions her unhappy fate without tears in her eyes'.[197]

Fraud and corruption were rife in the East India Company in the eighteenth century and enormous fortunes were being made. In one remarkable letter dated 21st November 1777 despatched by John Green to Arthur Scaife in England concerning transferring money to England he wrote that:

> *'I am also to inform you there is no remittance to be made through the Company – they it is true have Ordered 150,000£ to be taken up in the Country nearly two thirds of this the Directors have taken for themselves & friends and the Rest is between the Governor General and Council, Judges &c There are no other remittances than the following either to purchase Gold or Diamonds and insure them or purchase piece goods and send them to Cairo and get Bills for the money there or send them home in Specie'.*[198]

The Governor General was Warren Hastings, who, in 1773, had been appointed the first Governor General of India; £150,000 was an enormous sum of money in 1777. The letter concluded with the news that 'Major Hopman was killed in Duel the 4th of this month'.

On the 15th September 1779 John Green was promoted to Lieutenant-Colonel in the Bengal Artillery. By this date he was also a contractor, supplying various 'articles' to the East India Company.[199] He died just one year later in Fort William, Calcutta, and was described as 'a highly respected officer'. It was later claimed that he had died intestate, an 'omission' that would impinge upon the lives of many people including Thomas Jelf Sandilands. His personal effects and property were substantial.

It was stated in a later Chancery Case that 'John Green, the elder, was in his lifetime and at the time of his decease possessed of or entitled to a very considerable

---

197 This letter took over eight months to arrive at its destination. It was dated 27th March 1777 and marked as being received in London on 4th December 1777. Other letters took a similar length of time. Colonel Cumming was probably Sir John Cumming.

198 The 'Country' refers to Bengal; 'piece goods' were fabrics and cloths such as calico woven in standard lengths and manufactured in India and other oriental countries; 'specie' = cash.

199 See *Reports from the House of Commons Vol VI, East Indies – 1783*, (1806) p.472: 'January 1779 – Amount paid to Lieutenant Colonel Green – 16,321 rupees.' (this was about £1,700).

personal Estate in India and which after his decease was very considerably increased by his personal representatives in India herein after named by the completion of certain contracts which he the said John Green the Elder had entered into before his decease … '.[200] This estate amounted to at least £28,000 (more than £3 million in today's money) and possibly double that figure; the administration of his estate eventually led to several cases in the Court of Chancery. In classic Dickensian style these cases ground slowly through the courts for nearly thirty years; many of the parties involved died whilst Chancery was pondering the evidence, and even the heirs of some of the parties died whilst the cases stalled. John Green's estate in India was put into administration and the Indian court appointed three residents of Calcutta, William Greene, Esquire, William Golding, Esquire, and David Cuming, as administrators – all of whom were described as his 'friends'. (William Greene does not appear to be related to John Green and is very probably allied to a family of Irish gentry and landowners by that name). It was later claimed that after settling the debts of the deceased the administrators 'retained a very considerable part of the said Intestate's effects in their own hands and lent out the same at Interest to their friends and connections in India and made great profits thereby'.[201]

John Green had died a widower leaving his three young children, all minors, as orphans. In England, on 23rd October 1781, Lucy Sanderson, widow of Thomas Sanderson who had recently died, made a declaration, sworn before the probate court in London, stating that she was the 'Executrix or Guardian lawfully assigned to Henrietta Maria Green, John Green and Sophia Green, minors, the natural and lawfull and only Children of the said deceased'. She was appointed Administratrix of the deceased's estate 'for the Use and Benefit of the said Minors during their Minority …'. She declared that 'the said deceased's Effects lay at Fort William in the East Indies the Particulars whereof she cannot set forth but believes according to what Information she can procure that the same may amount in Value to the Sum of two Thousand Pounds or thereabouts'.[202] Clearly there was a considerable discrepancy in the declared value of John Green's estate. There was another, perhaps far more important, discrepancy at this time. All the ensuing Chancery cases describe the late John Green as dying 'intestate' in Calcutta. However, in a letter dated 2nd May 1781 written by William Greene in Calcutta and addressed to Thomas Sanderson in London, Greene clearly informs Sanderson that 'In looking over my poor Friends papers I found a Will of which No 3 is a Copy'.[203] The existence of John Green's will is never mentioned again in these records. It is

200 TNA C 13/186/5 *Sandilands v Gaisford et al.* – Bill of Complaint.

201 Ibid. Bill of Complaint.

202 TNA PROB 31/697/526 Exhibit: 1781/526. John Green esq. widower of Fort William, East Indies, Lieutenant Colonel in the service of the East India Company at Fort William, East Indies, who died abroad. Probate inventory, or declaration, of the estate of the same, deceased.

203 TNA, C 105/29, *West v Green*.

possible that Sanderson never saw this letter and the enclosed copy of the will for he died in September 1781.

The recipient would most certainly have been his wife, Lucy Sanderson. William Greene's letter also mentioned Warren Hastings:

> *'I have the Pleasure to tell you that the Colonel's Estate will turn out above £15,000 the Sum I in my former letters Acquainted you I judged it might come to; in two or three days I hope to be able to pay into the Company's Cash here one hundred and fifty Thousand Current Rupees Valuing these rupees at two shillings amounts to the Sum of £15,000 Sterling. W. Hastings has been very good to the Children of our poor Friend, a Short time before his Death he received an Order from the Council to make up a great number of Guns and Carriages, he completed very few of them But Mr Hastings has allowed the Administrators to Continue making them up, this has considerably added to the Estate and if I am allowed to finish the whole (and which I believe I shall) will enlarge the estate much more; it is needless for me to Say anything to you concerning the Education of the Children I am Sure you and Mrs Sanderson will have them brought up in a manner Suitable to their Handsome Fortune'.*

The reference to guns and carriages would explain John Green's connection with Arthur Scaife, 'armourer and brasier' of London. Within two years of John Green's decease Arthur Scaife was in financial difficulties, perhaps he had lost both his contact and contract to supply armaments to Bengal, and by 1783 he had been declared bankrupt. The administrators of John Green's estate in Calcutta appointed Thomas Allan, Esquire, of Berners Street, as their London agent and several large sums of money were eventually remitted to Allan from India.[204]

The ensuing events suggest that relations between Lucy Sanderson and her three young wards were less than congenial. Within three years the eldest daughter, Sophia Green, had eloped with Clement John Cozens, another one-time resident of Calcutta. The deposition of Joseph Pasley, a witness in a forthcoming Chancery case, provided details of the marriage which took place on the 21st April 1784 'he this deponant did by the name of Thomas Brown perform the Marriage Ceremony between the parties'. The wedding took place 'at the House of James Black at Springfield in the parish of Gretna in the County of Dumfries in North Britain.' Sophia was just fourteen years old. Joseph Pasley (alias Thomas Brown) was a person of some considerable fame and notoriety, variously described as a blacksmith

---

204 Thomas Allan of Berners Street is mentioned in connection with a trust fund for the Theatre Royal, Drury Lane. (London Metropolitan Archives: Declaration of Trust, ACC/0720/001, 4 Sept. 1775).

and the 'High Priest' of Gretna Green, charging ten, twenty or even fifty pounds for performing marriage ceremonies according to his judgement of the size of their purses. He had had several occupations, tobacconist, then fisherman before turning to the 'more lucrative occupation of performing one of the ecclesiastical functions'. James Black was innkeeper at the sign of the Scotch Arms, Springfield.[205] ('Brown' and 'Black' seem to be suitably anonymous surnames.) The marriage lasted barely twelve months for Sophia Cozens died in June 1785 leaving behind Clement John and their infant son, another Clement John, as her heirs. 'Being minded and desirous to make some provision for his child' Clement Cozens established a trust in favour of his infant son appointing James Cooper of Grays Inn and Samuel Cooper, Gent. as trustees.

In 1786 the other daughter, Henrietta Maria, at the age of about sixteen married Thomas Goddard junior, the presumed son of Thomas Goddard (the lodger) and Elizabeth Greene (née Hooke). Young Henrietta Maria arrived with considerable personal debts – she was 'indebted to Divers persons in several sums of Money amounting in the whole to about eight hundred pounds or thereabouts'. In todays money this would be in excess of £87,000. Henrietta Maria must have lived in some style, the only intimation of which comes from an entry for 1785 in the Schedule attached to the impending Chancery case: 'March 12th: Paid to her Mantua maker on her Account – £3 9s'. (A mantua was a loose dress or gown worn by ladies of fashion and £3 9s was about £370 today). Thomas Goddard wished to pay off the debts incurred by his prospective bride and to facilitate these disbursements a trust, involving one third of the late John Green's estate, was established in 1787 for the benefit of Henrietta Maria and her new husband. It was agreed by Thomas Goddard and Henrietta Maria that they would transfer her one third portion of John Green's estate (including any monies still outstanding) to the trustees, Thomas Goddard the elder and Charles Herries (the latter appears to be a merchant banker and father of John Charles Herries – a leading politician and Chancellor of the Exchequer in the nineteenth century).[206] For Thomas Goddard to take a wife who had such considerable debts was a hazardous course of action. Once married the bride's entire estate and property became incorporated into that of her new husband for which he then took full responsibility, and this, of course, would have included his wife's debts. Wives were not personally liable for their debts; if their creditors could not be satisfied then it was the husband who would face insolvency and the certainty of debtors' prison.

---

205 TNA C 12/2426/16, *Cozens v Sanderson*. The depositions of witnesses in this Chancery case were taken at an inn – at the house of Joseph Saulder, innkeeper at Sark Foot in the Parish of Kirkandrews upon Esk in Cumberland.

206 Herries & Co. were merchants trading in Jeffrey's Square, St Mary Axe. Charles Herries was also a Colonel of the Light Horse Volunteers of London and Westminster and is buried in the nave of Westminster Abbey. His brother was Sir Robert Herries another eminent banker.

The estate of the late John Green remained in the hands of the various administrators with the beneficiaries still anticipating their legacies. In an attempt to resolve this impasse Clement Cozens instigated a cause in Chancery in 1787 citing numerous individuals and claimants involved with John Green's estate.[207] The defendants named in his Bill were: Lucy Sanderson, William Greene, Thomas Allan, Thomas Goddard the younger and Henrietta Maria his wife, Thomas Goddard the elder, Charles Herries, John Green the younger, Samuel Cooper, James Cooper and finally his own infant son, Clement John Cozens the younger. This may have been a collusive suit and the twofold objective was to obtain a judgement from the Master in Chancery to establish the true value of the estate and then an instruction to the administrators as to how it should be divided amongst the beneficiaries. The case was further complicated by the fact that the late John Green had previously been appointed administrator of the estate of Francis Cozens, (the father of Clement John, the elder) who had died in Calcutta in 1763. (He seems to be the same Francis Cozens who was one of the few people to have survived the siege of Calcutta in 1756 and who took part in the conflict at Mussulipatam against the French in 1763 after which he was promoted to lieutenant.) This other estate was partly unadministered and still in the hands of John Green when he died.

Another, even greater, complication in this affair was the will of one Christopher Oliphant, 'late of the Parish of Saint Andrew, Holborn in the County of Middlesex Gentleman deceased' who had appointed Arthur Scaife and a relative, John Oliphant, as his executors. He had also given power of attorney to a Captain William Swallow to collect his debts in the East Indies. Swallow subsequently died and had appointed a Robert McFarlane as his executor; McFarlane declined this appointment and Lieutenant-Colonel John Green obligingly agreed to be the administrator of Swallow's estate in India. A portion of this estate, which included the debts owed to Christopher Oliphant, was still in Green's possession when he died and accordingly came into the hands of his administrators, either Lucy Sanderson, or Messrs Green, Golding and Cuming in India. In the meantime, John Oliphant had died and the bankers, Robert Mayne & Co., had gone into bankruptcy apparently holding funds due to Arthur Scaife, who had also been declared bankrupt. The assignees of Arthur Scaife had then submitted a Bill in Chancery in an attempt to recoup the monies due 'from the said John Green to the said Arthur Scaife as one of the Residuary legatees and Executors named in the will of the said Christopher Oliphant'.[208]

The Answers given by several of the defendants to Cozens' Bill suggest that Lucy Sanderson was a major cause of the difficulties in the administration of John Green's estate. In her Answer she claimed that she had spent considerable sums of money for the maintenance and education of the three children of John Green. However William Greene had a different perception of events:

207 TNA C 12/2149/16 *Cozens v. Greene*, and C 12/2426/16, *Cozens v. Sanderson*.
208 TNA C 12/1391/39, *West v Greene*.

'This defendant saith that he verily believes that the said Lucy Sanderson hath received considerably more of the effects of John Green deceased or of the effects procured for the benefit of his estate than she hath paid on Account of such estate but that she refused or is unable to give an satisfactory account thereof.'[209]

Thomas Allan answered in a similar manner:

'he verily believes the said Lucy Sanderson hath received considerably more of the Effects of the said John Green deceased than she has paid on Account of such Estate but notwithstanding this Defendants repeated and strenuous Efforts he has not been able to obtain from the said Lucy Sanderson a satisfactory Account of what effects of the said Intestate she possessed herself of the same.'[210]

A note in the schedule of accounts shows that a few years earlier Thomas Allan had attempted to contact Lucy Sanderson – '21st May 1782, Paid a Person for her trouble in discovering Mrs Sanderson's Residence in Westminster ------ 5s'.[211]

In 1788 the case was eventually referred to a Master in Chancery with an order to investigate the matter and he established that the sum of £28,210 18s 6p had come into the hands of Thomas Allan, London agent of the administrators in Calcutta. Out of this money Thomas Allan 'had advanced several sums of money for the maintenance of the said Henrietta Maria Goddard which amounted to the sum of £1,707 11s 10p and that he had paid for the maintenance and education of the said John Green several sums amounting to £1,142 4s 2p'. The court eventually directed that the residue of the estate of the deceased should be divided between his three children i.e. Sophia, John and Henrietta Maria (or their rightful heirs). John Green the younger was still an 'infant' (i.e. under twenty one years of age).

From the documents relating to this case a picture emerges of a woman recently widowed and with an uncertain financial future who grasped an opportunity to avail herself of a small fortune. Lucy Sanderson appointed herself as guardian of the three orphaned children and executrix of their father's estate in England. The exact amount of the estate in England was not disclosed. Maybe the three children realised they were being deprived of their father's legacies and when the two young girls were of sufficient age they saw marriage as a means of escaping the clutches of Mrs Sanderson and retrieving their 'handsome fortune'. Once they were married any money or property to which they were entitled then came under the control of the new husband and not Lucy Sanderson. Sophia eloped to Gretna Green with Clement Cozens and Henrietta Maria left Lucy Sanderson and moved into lodgings

---

209 TNA C 12/2426/16, *Cozens v. Sanderson.*
210 TNA C 12/2149/16, *Cozens v. Greene.*
211 TNA C 12/2149/16, *Cozens v. Greene*, Schedule.

prior to her marriage to Thomas Goddard (the Schedule of Accounts lists several payments to a Mrs Fletcher for Henrietta's board). By this time the younger John Green must have likewise found his situation disagreeable and removed himself to Caen in France.

It is not clear if Clement Cozens ever received any money from his late wife's estate but by 1795 he had what today would be described as a 'cash flow problem'. Confined to a cell in the King's Bench prison for debt he drew up his will on the 18th October 1795. The instructions in the will are a poignant reminder of the hazards of eighteenth century jails. He directed his Executors 'to oppose any Will or Codicil which may appear hereafter be set up as made by me in this prison in which I shall leave any Legacy or Sum of Money to any person or persons whatsoever and particularly to any person or persons who may be or may have been a prisoner or prisoners with me in this place'. One week later though he did add a codicil:

> '25th October 1795. I give to my Brother in Law Thomas Goddard and Henrietta Maria his Wife, my Brother in Law John Green and Edward Cotton a prisoner in the King's Bench, Rings of the Value of one Guinea each. *Clement John Cozens Witness Saml. Cooper Junr'.*

Four guineas was probably the sum total of his worldly goods. He had previously petitioned under the '*Act for the Discharge of Certain Insolvent Debtors*' but unfortunately had not been released.[212] Clement Cozens was dead within twelve months of writing his will. His case had stalled in the mire of Chancery proceedings without any satisfactory outcome and the inheritance he anticipated from his late wife must have finally eluded him. The younger Clement Cozens eventually joined the 80th Regiment of Foot, being promoted to lieutenant in 1804.

Many Acts of Parliament were intended to control the excesses of human folly. The habitual drunkard and the insolvent debtor were kindred spirits – nothing in moderation. Numerous statutes to control drunkenness in the seventeenth century have already been referred to and, whereas there was little sympathy for the intoxicated peasant squandering his last few groats in the alehouse, Parliament eventually took a more humanitarian approach to the plight of the imprisoned debtors; their situation being further improved by a statute of 1813 which established the Court for the Relief of Insolvent Debtors (53 George III. c. 102). This act specifically provided a remedy for the insolvent debtor and the means to re-establish himself in society. Any debtor who had been imprisoned for three months or more could petition the court for his release. A schedule of the prisoners debts and effects had to be attached to the petition and submitted, together with a sworn oath, to the commissioner and the debtor was released into the world once again.

---

212 *An Act to remedy certain Omissions in an Act, passed in the last Session of Parliament, intituled, 'An Act for the Discharge of certain Insolvent Debtors'.* (35 George III, c. 88. 1795).

Charles Dickens was well acquainted with the fate of the insolvent debtor, the 'Insolvent Court' and its commissioners. His father, John Dickens, indebted to his baker, was arrested in 1824 and committed to the Marshalsea Prison. The twelve year old Dickens never forgot the circumstances into which his family descended or the visits he made to his father in Marshalsea. His description of the Insolvent Court gives little merit to the building or its officers:

'In a lofty room, ill-lighted and worse ventilated, situate in Portugal Street, Lincoln's Inn Fields, there sit nearly the whole year round, one, two, three, or four gentlemen in wigs, as the case may be, with little writing-desks before them, constructed after the fashion of those used by the judges of the land, barring the French polish; a box of barristers on their right hand; an enclosure of insolvent debtors on their left; and an inclined plane of most especially dirty faces in their front. These gentlemen are the Commissioners of the Insolvent Court, and the place in which they sit, is the Insolvent Court itself.

It is, and has been, time out of mind, the remarkable fate of this court to be, somehow or other, held and understood, by the general consent of all the destitute shabby-genteel people in London, as their common resort, and place of daily refuge. It is always full. The steams of beer and spirits perpetually ascend to the ceiling, and, being condensed by the heat, roll down the walls like rain; there are more old suits of clothes in it at one time, than will be offered for sale in all Houndsditch in a twelvemonth; more unwashed skins and grizzly beards than all the pumps and shaving-shops between Tyburn and Whitechapel could render decent between sunrise and sunset. ... ... A casual visitor might suppose this place to be a temple dedicated to the Genius of Seediness. There is not a messenger or process-server attached to it, who wears a coat that was made for him; not a tolerably fresh, or wholesome-looking man in the whole establishment, except a little white-headed apple-faced tipstaff, and even he, like an ill-conditioned cherry preserved in brandy, seems to have artificially dried and withered up into a state of preservation to which he can lay no natural claim. The very barristers' wigs are ill-powdered, and their curls lack crispness.

But the attorneys, who sit at a large bare table below the commissioners, are, after all, the greatest curiosities. The professional establishment of the more opulent of these gentlemen, consists of a blue bag and a boy; generally a youth of the Jewish persuasion. They have no fixed offices, their legal business being transacted in the parlours of public-houses, or the yards of prisons, whither they repair in crowds, and canvass for customers after the manner of omnibus cads. They are of a greasy and mildewed appearance; and if they can be said to have any vices at all, perhaps drinking and cheating are the most conspicuous among them. ...'

(Charles Dickens, *The Pickwick Papers*, Chpt. XLIII. (1837))

Several more years were to elapse before another case concerning John Green's estate and the unadministered legacies commenced proceedings through the courts. No further records concerning Lucy Sanderson have come to light and so it is not possible to come to any definite conclusion about her activities.

By 1808 Thomas Jelf Sandilands had not only married well but had inherited part of his late father's estate. Maria Charlotte, his wife, had produced two sons, Walter Samuel Tollet Sandilands and Thomas John Maxwell Sandilands. It was said that 'he was in very good circumstances and was living upon his own property and that he was then carrying on a very extensive and lucrative business as an attorney'.[213] His star was in the ascendant and in 1810 the thirty-three year old attorney negotiated the purchase of a substantial estate of two hundred and thirty-eight acres in Aston -upon-Carrant in Gloucestershire from Wakeman Long, an attorney at law from Upton-upon-Severn. The purchase price was £17,700 (about £1,000,000 in today's money) to be paid in three instalments: '£3,000 on 1st August next, the sum of £1,000 on the 29th September next, and the residue on the 25th day of March next'. Sandilands appears to have been of an optimistic turn of mind for he had one slight difficulty with this proposed acquisition – he was not in possession of sufficient funds to complete the purchase and consequently he turned to relatives and his bankers for assistance. Initially, he had acquired £3,902 3s 7d from John Hooke Greene and his cousin, Richard Sandilands – the trustees of the settlement made prior to his marriage (this sum being the produce of £5,700 5s 4d 3% consolidated bank annuities then standing in their names). He was also obliged to arrange a loan of £2000 from Attwood, Spooner and Carden & Co., a firm of bankers with an office in Worcester. Sandilands eventually came to an agreement with Wakeman Long to arrange a mortgage to cover the outstanding balance of the purchase price.

Thomas Jelf Sandilands, it seems, had aspirations of elevating his social status towards the gentry although in the inflexible hierarchy of Regency England he would, to many people, still retain that lingering aroma of 'shop'. Nevertheless Thomas had risen to the rarefied air of the upper levels of Georgian society and he was acquainted with some distinguished figures in the worlds of high finance and politics. The most notable of these was Walter Boyd, a merchant banker, financier and Member of Parliament, who had set up a banking business in Paris as Boyd, Ker et Cie. Walter Boyd, trustee to Maria Charlotte's estate from her late father, had married Harriette Anne Goddard (otherwise Greene) the youngest daughter of John Greene and Elizabeth Hooke.[214] Following the death of Thomas Goddard the elder

---

213 TNA: C 13/336/19, *Sandilands v Greene.*

214 Various biographical sources state that he married Harriette Anne Goddard, citing her as daughter of Thomas Goddard but in fact she was only Goddard's step-daughter. Confusingly there were two Walter Boyd's associated with Boyd, Ker et Cie. Walter Boyd, junior, being a cousin of Walter Boyd who had established the Paris banking house in 1785 and had married Harriette Anne Goddard. It is highly unlikely that the Walter Boyd appointed as legal guardian of Maria Charlotte Goddard and associated with the Goddard family was Boyd junior.

in 1794, Walter Boyd had been appointed to replace him as a trustee of the trust fund established in 1787 from John Green's estate for the benefit of Henrietta Maria and Thomas Goddard the younger. The violent events of the French Revolution led to the hasty departure of Walter Boyd from France and the premises of Boyd, Ker et Cie in Paris were sealed by the revolutionaries in October 1793. Their chief clerk and cashier, Antoine Gregoire Geneste, was charged with high treason and went to the guillotine on 18th April 1794. Walter Boyd re-established himself in England with help from Paul Benfield, an unscrupulous individual who had made a fortune in India. Together they opened the banking firm of Boyd, Benfield, & Co. in London, where Boyd was responsible for contracting large government loans to the value of over £30 million. Spain, Austria, Prussia and Great Britain were all at war with France and he was responsible for negotiating large loans for the Emperor of Austria to finance his military campaigns. In 1797, following a coup d'etat in France, the Paris property of Boyd, Ker et Cie was confiscated by the new regime, and in 1798 Boyd, Benfield, & Co went into liquidation; this failure also ruined Charles Herries who was left penniless. Boyd himself was declared bankrupt in March 1800 and returned to France in 1802 after the Peace of Amiens, but in 1803, when war was declared between England and France, many British subjects were interned as hostages and Boyd was held, together with his wife and son. Eliza Maria Greene Goddard (aunt to Thomas Sandilands' wife Maria Charlotte) was also in Paris at about this time; she may have been detained by the authorities, or perhaps she was making a very hazardous journey to visit her sister, Harriette Anne. Just before she returned home in 1806 she drew up her will, obviously concerned for her safety in a country that was at war with England; the preamble started 'being in perfect health and in my sound mind but Considering the uncertainty of life and the accidents to which I may be exposed on my Journey to England which I am about to undertake do make this my last Will and Testament'. [215] Walter Boyd was released in 1814 and eventually recovered his banking establishment and property in Paris which was valued at about £1.5 million.

The tide of fortune started to turn against the draper's son from Worcestershire. By now Thomas Jelf Sandilands owned land and property in the parishes of Ashchurch, Tewkesbury and Twyning in Gloucestershire and in the parish of Ripple in Worcestershire. In October 1814 the bank was requesting repayment of his outstanding mortgage amounting to £2333 14s including interest due and the mortgage to Wakeman Long had still not been redeemed. The following month his wife, only twenty-six years of age, died leaving Thomas alone to bring up his two young sons. Both his wife's parents, Henrietta Maria and Thomas Goddard the younger, had predeceased her, leaving Thomas Jelf Sandilands as the heir to his late wife's estate – the residue of the one-third portion of the late Lieutenant-

---

215 TNA PROB 11/1513/186. One of the witnesses was Robert D. Boyd – Walter Boyd's nephew, Robert Dundas Boyd.

Colonel Green's estate. Perhaps, when he purchased the Aston-upon-Carrant estate, he had extended his borrowing in anticipation of his wife's inheritance of a part of the 'handsome fortune' left by the late John Green. However, circumstances dictated that very soon he would be forced to sell two parcels of his land to satisfy his creditors.

By the end of 1814 Sandilands' creditors were still pressing for settlement of their accounts and it was at this time that he instigated proceedings in Chancery in an attempt to recover the monies he considered he was entitled to as heir to the late John Green's estate.[216] There were two other 'Orators' to this Bill – Walter Boyd of Broad Street, London and Charles Herries of St Mary Axe, in London, (The financially distressed Walter Boyd was being vigorously pursued by his numerous creditors, both in England and in France.) The defendants to this Bill were David Cuming, Samuel Cooper and Lucy Sanderson. The Orators in this cause alleged that the administrators of John Green's estate had not distributed the residue of the money to the rightful heirs or their representatives. Of the original administrators appointed in India, William Golding had died insolvent in Calcutta, William Greene had moved to County Tipperary in Ireland (and was well beyond the jurisdiction of the Court of Chancery) and David Cuming could not be located. Added to this Thomas Allan had refused to supply his accounts concerning the estate to the Orators. The course of events dictated that the plaintiffs were obliged to draw up and issue a second Bill in Chancery; this new Bill provided an account of events concerning the first Bill issued:

> '... and your Orators further shew that the said David Cuming left the East Indies after the decease of the said Intestate and returned to England in or about the year 1790 and on his arrival in this Country he assumed the management of such parts of the estate of the said John Green deceased as had been remitted to this Country and the said David Cuming resided in England in a retired manner and different places and your Orators were unable to discover his place or Residence until the year 1814 when your Orators Discovered that the said David Cuming was resident in the Village of Christleton near the City of Chester and they thereupon prepared their bill in this honourable Court to compel the said David Cuming to account for the personal estate and effects of which the said intestate was possessed at time of his Decease which had come to the hands of the said David Cuming'. [217]

Having been 'discovered' in Christleton David Cuming then removed himself to Islington in London. However, before the plaintiffs could serve a subpoena

---

216 TNA C 13/189/68 *Sandilands v Cuming*.

217 TNA C 13/186/5, *Sandilands v Gaisford et al.* Bill of Complaint.

compelling the defendant to answer to the court, the uncooperative Mr Cuming promptly 'departed this life' leaving his entire estate to his sister Jane Gaisford of 'number 23 Highbury Place, Islington'. The plaintiffs then had to draw up and issue the second Bill against the new defendants who were Jane Gaisford, the Bank of England, Samuel Cooper and Lucy Sanderson. (The latter was later removed as a defendant, although the reason is not known.) The Bank of England held funds and securities belonging to Cuming. Apart from the £28,210 18s 6d that had come into the hands of the London agent (Thomas Allan), the Orators alleged that sums of money amounting to one hundred and twenty thousand rupees (£12,000) had been lent, at interest, to various individuals in India; these were namely Charles Crofts (in all probability a 'confidential' friend of Warren Hastings), Edward Hay (in all probability the secretary of the 'Secret Committee' of the Honourable East India Company) and also William Greene himself. Furthermore they alleged that a substantial amount of money, amounting to over £16,500, had been in the possession of David Cuming (and now his heir). Most of this sum was in securities held by the Bank of England but £3,500 had been lent to Sir Charles Rouse Boughton, baronet.

This second Bill of Complaint seems to have made little progress through Chancery and there is no evidence to suggest that Sandilands ever recovered his late wife's inheritance. In 1815 Wakeman Long requested settlement of his account, this being £7,944 of the purchase money for the Aston-upon-Carrant estate that was still outstanding. By April of 1816, Sandilands' financial situation was precarious. In desperation he approached his cousin, the Reverend Richard Sandilands, for additional security against the outstanding interest on his mortgage (Richard Sandilands was the author of a religious work: 'A Sermon preached, for the benefit of the Charity School instituted at Upton upon Severn: in the year 1787'). The Reverend Sandilands agreed to assist and duly executed a bond dated 25th April 1816 'in the penal sum of £500' as surety for his cousin. This financial guarantee was not enough to save the situation and Thomas Jelf Sandilands continued his remorseless slide into debt. Within twelve months his position was beyond salvation. Wakeman Long had died in February 1817 without receiving his money and Sandilands must have been painfully aware of the fate that awaited him; being in a professional occupation he did not qualify to be declared bankrupt, an option that was only open to persons involved in 'trade', instead he was faced with the dreadful prospect of the Insolvency Court and the certainty of imprisonment. Fortunately for Sandilands the creditor who petitioned for bankruptcy described him as a money scrivener, an occupation classified as 'trade'. A 'commission of bankruptcy' was issued on 1st March 1817 and once again Thomas Sandilands featured in the London Gazette, only on this occasion for rather less auspicious reasons:

W hereas a Commission of Bankrupt is awarded and issued forth against Thomas Jelf Sandilands, of Twyning, in the County of Gloucester, Money-Scrivener, and he being declared a Bankrupt is hereby required to surrender himself to the Commissioners in the said Commission named, or the major part of them, on the 17th of April instant, at Five of the Clock in the Afternoon, on the 18th of the same month, and on the 13th day of May next, at Twelve of the Clock at Noon, at the Swan Inn, in Tewkesbury, in the said County of Gloucester, and make a full Discovery and Disclosure of his Estate and Effects; when and where the Creditors are to come prepared to prove their Debts, and at the Second Sitting to chuse Assignees, and at the Last Sitting the said Bankrupt is required to finish his Examination, and the Creditors are to assent to or dissent from the allowance of his Certificate. All persons indebted to the said Bankrupt, or that have any of his Effects, are not to pay or deliver the same but to whom the Commissioners shall appoint, but give notice to Mr. Anthony Watts, 10, Symond's-Inn, London, or to Mr. Samuel Beale, of Upton-upon-Severn, Worcester-shire, Solicitor of the said Commission.

(*London Gazette,* 1st April 1817, p.827.)

The final meeting regarding Sandilands' Certificate was adjourned until August 1817. The bankruptcy proceedings then became somewhat complicated. The description of his 'trade' given in the commission of bankruptcy led to a further court action, which was not held until August 1819 at Gloucester Assizes, because the creditor was unable to produce evidence before the Bankruptcy Court that Sandilands was actually a money scrivener. Sandilands claimed the action should fail on this count but the court disagreed with this argument and the bankruptcy proceedings duly continued.[218] This financial chaos had left the unfortunate Reverend Sandilands in an exceedingly difficult position. (It was later claimed that the Reverend Richard Sandilands had entered into a bond with John Hooke Greene 'in the penalty of £10,000 or thereabouts to indemnify him against all loss

---

218 'Gloucester, *coram* Holroyd, J. Wednesday, August 25th, 1819. Smith *v.* Sandilands. This was an issue directed by the Vice-Chancellor to try the validity of a commission of bankruptcy, which had issued against the defendant, and was dated the 1st of March, 1817. On the production of the commission it appeared that the defendant was described in it as a money scrivener only: but the plaintiff, being unable to prove a trading as a money scrivener, proposed to shew that the defendant had been in partnership with a West India merchant, and that he had traded to that settlement ...'. (Niel Gow, *Reports of Cases argued and ruled at Nisi Prius in the Court of Common Pleas, 1818-1820.* London 1828).

or damage he may sustain in consequence of his having caused the sum of £5700 3% consols to be sold'). Having provided a surety for Thomas Sandilands' outstanding debts with Attwood, Spooner and Carden & Co., which still amounted to £1,789 18s 4d together with interest of £241 7s 9d, he had some liability to settle with the bank. In May 1818 the Reverend Sandilands was obliged to sign a Warrant of Attorney to confess judgement and agreed with the bank to put them in possession of the rectory of Turnaston in Herefordshire of which he was rector and all the Tithes thereof. He was also required to assign to the bank his title to various freehold lands in the Herefordshire parishes of Michaelchurch, Exley and Craswell. At this point, having fallen from grace, life in England had become intolerable for the dispossessed and by now insolvent Reverend and it appears that, without notifying his bishop, he set forth post-haste to Dover where he caught the first boat to Calais. He became minister of the English Church of St. Omer in French Flanders where he died intestate in 1836 at the age of seventy-seven. (The Turnaston rectory was reclaimed by the church in 1834 when the Bishop of Hereford issued an Order of Sequestration 'as a result of the continued unlicensed absence of the incumbent'.) His estate came to his son and heir the Reverend Thomas Samuel Butler Sandilands who applied for an Action of Ejectment against the bank in the Court of the Queen's Bench in an attempt to reclaim his father's freehold property. He maintained that as his father was now deceased the power of attorney was no longer valid. The bank countered this claim by bringing their own action in the Court of Chancery stating that in these circumstances the power of attorney was not revoked by the death of Richard Sandilands and was part of the security for the debt. The court found in favour of the bank and the defendant (the Rev T.S.B. Sandilands) agreed not to proceed with his action.

The freehold and leasehold estates and all the effects of Thomas Jelf Sandilands should now have been in the hands of the assignees who were responsible for disposing of the assets and paying the numerous creditors. However, four years later this situation was still unresolved and in 1823 two of the creditors submitted another Bill of Complaint into Chancery requesting the court to investigate the matter.[219] After four years of litigation through Chancery it was eventually ordered by a Masters decree dated 1827 that, in the interests of all the parties concerned, the estate should be put to auction. The Master in Chancery decided that the executors of Wakeman Long had first claim on the estate, the trustees of Maria Charlotte's marriage settlement had second claim and the bank came a poor third in the queue. The forthcoming auction of the estate was advertised in the Worcester Journal:

---

219 *Long v Thompson*, Bill of Complaint 1823 – there is no TNA reference for this case. It is referred to in C13/336/19 *Sandilands v Greene*, Bill of Complaint.

TO BE PEREMPTORILY SOLD

Pursuant to a Decree of the High Court of Chancery, made in a Cause, Long v. Thompson, with the approbation of James William Farrer, Esquire, one of the Masters of the said Court, at the Royal Hotel, in Cheltenham, in the County of Gloucester, on Thursday, the 10th day of January, 1828, at two o'clock in the afternoon, in 4 Lots;

CERTAIN VALUABLE FREEHOLD and LEASEHOLD FARMS and LANDS, containing in the whole upwards of TWO HUNDRED and ELEVEN ACRES of rich ARABLE and PASTURE LAND, situate and being in the Parish of Ashchurch, in the County of Gloucester, distant from Cheltenham six miles, and from Tewkesbury three miles.

(*Worcester Journal*, Thursday 27th December, 1827.)

For some reason, on 25th of September 1828, there was a second auction of freehold farms and lands amounting to one hundred and nineteen acres. This was possibly because not all of the lots had reached their reserve at the first auction; the second auction was mentioned in an Indenture of 1832 which stated that the highest bidder for Lots 1 and 2 was a Henry Paget who purchased the lots for £4,180 and £1,210 respectively. No records of the sale of Lots 3 and 4 have come to light but the proceeds of the sale 'produced less by a very considerable sum than the monies due to the said Executors of the said Wakeman Long in respect of the said Mortgage'.[220] It took another four years before various parties finalised the sale by an Indenture of Lease and Release dated March 1832,[221] there were fifteen signatories to this document.

The proceeds of the sale of this estate were insufficient to clear all of Thomas Sandilands' liabilities and what happened next is not completely clear, for, somehow, Sandilands was still in possession of several properties including his offices in Tewkesbury.[222] No records of the bankruptcy proceedings have been traced and it is not certain if he was completely cleared for he was still being vigorously pursued by his creditors. He was still 'indebted to various individuals in divers sums of money upon mortgage and other securities some of whom have become impatient for the payment of their demands and are pressing for their discharge through the different Courts of Law to the detriment and delay of his other creditors who are

---

220 TNA, C 13/336/19, *Sandilands v Greene*, Bill, 1834. Various documents giving differing figures but it appears that Wakeman Long was still owed over £9000.

221 GA D622/1 1832 23rd March The assignees of Mr Thos. Jelf Sandilands and others to Mr Henry Paget; Release.

222 Birmingham City Archives hold a draft copy of an indenture between Thomas Jelf Sandilands and Elizabeth Callow of Woolverton, Worcestershire, spinster, concerning premises in Tewkesbury dated 6 Dec 1831 (MS 3192/Acc1928-014/360320). Sandilands had mortgaged several properties to Elizabeth Callow for £650 and was requesting a further £100.

more patient and are equally entitled to payment'. He then came to an arrangement with a William Wall of Worcester and a William Law Phelps of Puckrup in the parish of Twyning for them to acquire his remaining assets upon trust to dispose of in order to satisfy these creditors. The assignment deed of these assets stated that Sandilands had 'already been put to great and grievous expenses in Law proceedings by some of his creditors to obtain payment of their respective demands and being desirous of preventing the further exhaustion and destruction of his property by similar measures hath resolved to convey and assign to the said William Wall and William Law Phelps **All** his real and personal Estate for the purposes hereinafter mentioned for the sum of Ten shillings of lawfull British money'. The real estate (Sandilands' offices and other property in Tewkesbury), was conveyed on 3rd June 1833. The assignees also acquired all his personal effects, chattels and money for the nominal sum of five shillings. Thomas Sandilands then possessed little more than the clothes he wore and a few shillings in loose change. Even at this date the ancient process of 'Livery of Seizin' was still being observed and Sandilands delivered to William Law Phelps a spoon 'in the name and as possession of all the Goods Chattels and Personal Estate within mentioned'.[223] (It was not until the *Real Property Act* of 1845 that transfer of property was allowed by deed alone; Livery of Seizin was finally abolished by the *Law of Property Act* passed in 1925.) Thomas Jelf Sandilands was by now virtually destitute, his creditors may have had him imprisoned for the London Gazette printed a further notice bringing down the curtain on his tale of financial ruin:

THE COURT FOR RELIEF OF INSOLVENT DEBTORS

The Matters of the PETITIONS and SCHEDULES of the PRISONERS hereinafter named (the same having been filed in the Court) are appointed to be heard as follows:

At the Court-House, at Gloucester, in the County of Gloucester, on the 12th day of July 1833, at Ten o'Clock in the Forenoon precisely.

Thomas Jelf Sandilands, formerly of Twyning, near Tewkesbury, then of High-Street, afterwards of Barton-Street, and late of High-Street, Tewkesbury aforesaid, all in Gloucestershire, Attorney at Law.

(*London Gazette* 21st June 1833, p.1220.)

---

223 GA Q/RID/4/39, 1833, Assignment of messuage in High Street, Tewkesbury.

The minutes of the case show that the prisoner, 'Thomas Jelf Sandilands, late of Tewkesbury, Attorney at Law, Insolvent Debtor', was brought before the court and 'Adjudged Entitled to the benefit of the Act and Ordered to be Discharged forthwith'. [224] (It is not clear why Sandilands was imprisoned. It is possible that the bankruptcy proceedings had not been concluded as a result of litigation in Chancery. It has been said that debtors who voluntarily submitted themselves to two months imprisonment could apply to the Court for Insolvent Debtors for release, the debtors property had to be transferred to assignees for payment of creditors – see Hugh Barty-King, *The Worst Poverty*, pp.119-120). Whatever the case he was released by the Court and Thomas Sandilands had finally put an end to the financial predicament which had occupied nineteen years of his life; the legacy he had anticipated from John Green had evaded him. He went on to continue practising as an attorney in Tewkesbury for several more years.

Nonetheless this was not the end of Chancery proceedings. Litigation concerning the marriage settlement for Maria Charlotte Green and Thomas Jelf Sandilands still rumbled through the courts of law. In 1834 their two sons, Walter Samuel Tollet Sandilands and Thomas John Maxwell Sandilands, instigated another action in Chancery against various parties including the trustees responsible for the £5,700 bank annuities held for the benefit of their mother.[225] The trustees named were John Hooke Greene and the Reverend Richard Sandilands, the latter being now insolvent and living in France beyond the jurisdiction of the court. In their Bill the plaintiffs claimed:

> '...that the conduct of the said John Hooke Greene and Richard Sandilands in advancing the produce of the said sum of £5700 5s 4d three pounds percent consolidated Bank annuities to the said Thomas Jelf Sandilands without taking any security for the same than the said Bond of the said Richard Sandilands and without procuring any other security than the said Agreement or alleged Agreement of the 31st January 1811 was a gross breach of trust and that the benefit of the said trust monies has become wholly lost to your Orators in consequence thereof and that the said sum of £5700 5s 4d 3% annuities ought to be replaced or the produce thereof repaid by the said Defendant John Hooke Greene and that the trust funds when so replaced should be vested in new Trustees upon the trusts of the said Indenture of Settlement.'

Whilst his two sons were engaged in pursuing their claim on their late mother's estate their father, Thomas, did not settle down to a quiet life in rural Gloucestershire for he was once again embroiled in controversy. The beginning of the nineteenth

---

224 GA Q/RID/2 12 July 1833. Minutes of proceedings in cases of insolvent debtors under Acts of 5 George IV, c. 61, and 7 George IV, c. 57.

225 TNA: C 13/336/19 *Sandilands v Greene*.

century was a period of political change in England as pressure was brought on government to reform the electoral system. In 1832 only about one person in every twenty-four had the right to vote. In that same year the Reform Act was passed by parliament and whilst this brought about some changes to the electoral system it was not enough to satisfy the 'Reform Movement'. Various political groups had formed with varying ideas regarding electoral reform and Thomas Sandilands was described as being a member of the 'Reform Party'. He was still in practice as an attorney in Tewkesbury and on the 20th July 1836 was briefly appointed Town Clerk for Tewkesbury Corporation. This was a contentious appointment as a result of which the Tewkesbury Town Council got themselves into a most extraordinary ravel. It was reported that within the space of five days three individuals had held the office of Town Clerk for Tewkesbury Corporation. This story was reported in the *Gloucester Journal* and taken up by the London and provincial papers. The *Standard London Newspaper* announced to its readers:

> "*Defeat of the Tewkesbury Liberals.* – A sad fracas has happened in this borough, owing to the resignation of the town clerk, … the council proceeded to the election of a new town-clerk. There were two candidates put in nomination, Lindsey Winterbotham, esq., the present mayor, and Mr. Thomas J. Sandilands; and on a poll, the latter was elected by a majority on nine votes to four. This has caused considerable excitement in the town, particularly as Mr. Winterbotham has for years been the leader of the movement party, whether on a question of a political, municipal or parochial nature. The mayor and his friends are so annoyed at the result, that they have intimated their intention of resigning their respective offices."

The *Gloucester Journal* then reported 'that owing to several unforeseen obstacles having presented themselves… connected with the appointment of Mr Sandilands to the office of town-clerk it was desirable to rescind the resolution to that effect…' (The newspaper reports did not reveal what the 'unforeseen obstacles' were, but the appointment of a former resident of Gloucester gaol and one-time bankrupt may have been too much for some of the eminent Tewkesbury burgesses to digest.) On the 25th July the town council elected Mr Joshua Thomas to the office of town clerk. The *Times* newspaper took up the story: 'It became necessary for the purposes of the reform party …… to remove Mr Sandilands from the office to which he had been so recently appointed. He was at first requested to resign, but this he refused to do; he was then offered the clerkship of the magistrates of the borough for his son; but even this was not enough to influence him, until he was informed by his friends that he would at any rate be very shortly ousted by the Conservatives, who were becoming the strongest party in the council. Being alarmed at this intimation, he at last yielded to the wishes of his friends… Mr Thomas was appointed to succeed him'.

Then, on the 6th of August, the *Gloucester Journal* reported: "We learn from good authority, that the offices of town clerk, and clerk of the peace of the borough of Tewkesbury, to which Mr Sandilands was elected on the 20th ult., have not been resigned by him – nor exchanged for any other – and that the attempt to deprive him of them will become the subject of discussion in the Court of King's Bench at its next sitting in November."

The legal particulars of this appointment were further complicated because some parties involved thought that Sandilands had also been appointed as Clerk of the Peace for the borough. The matter was not settled until it went to a hearing before judges on the Queen's Bench[226] and the proceedings of the case were reported in most of the national newspapers. (Queen Victoria came to the throne in June 1837 hence the change to 'Queen's Bench'.) The court confirmed the dismissal of Sandilands and Mr Thomas continued in office as town clerk. The episode did not reflect well upon the council members and caused some amusement amongst the justices of the Queen's Bench. This slight upon Tewkesbury council caused one member to write an anonymous letter to the local newspaper complaining about some of the errors in the detail of the case that had excited the '*chuckling grin of noodles*' at the expense of the parties involved.

Thomas Jelf Sandilands continued with his professional career and when the 1841 Census was taken he was listed as a solicitor residing at the Bulls Mouth Inn in the parish of St Annes & St Agnes in London (although he was still listed under 'Attorneys' in Pigot's 1844 directory for Tewkesbury). There is no evidence that he ever re-married and he died in 1848 in Finchley, Middlesex aged seventy-one years.

226 The Queen v. Thomas, 1837.

9.

Medicine, Murder and Manure

THE beginning of the nineteenth century saw a change in the tenure of the premises. After a long period of owner-occupiers trading on their own account there came a succession of tenant shopkeepers and merchants. Following the retirement of Samuel Sandelands the drapery business was continued for some years by Thomas Husband who went into partnership with a William Gould; together they traded as mercers, drapers and grocers. Thomas Husband was one of the three stewards appointed by the trustees of the Girls Charity School in Upton-upon-Severn which had been established in the early eighteenth century by bequests from the wills of Mr Richard Smith, a rector, and his wife, Ann. The school was for the 'proper education of at least twenty Poor Girls of this Parish'. Enquirers were informed that 'Mr Thomas Husband receives the Rents and keeps the Accompts of the Charity'. (The trustees had appointed stewards as they resided some distance away from Upton.) A further bequest to the school came in 1824 from Sarah Husband, one of the daughters of Thomas Husband.

William Gould – Mercer and Draper

With the retirement of Thomas Husband the partnership with William Gould was dissolved in July 1807 and an appropriate notice was placed in the London Gazette:

Upton-upon-Severn, July 31, 1807

Notice is hereby given, that the Partnership lately subsisting between Thomas Husband and William Gould, of Upton-upon-Severn, in the County of Worcester, Mercers, Drapers and Grocers, is dissolved by mutual Consent, the said Thomas Husband having retired from the Business, and which will continue to be carried on by the said William Gould alone, in all its Branches, in the same Shop in which the same hath for a long series of Years been conducted by the said Thomas Husband. The said Thomas Husband and William Gould embrace the present Opportunity of making their grateful Acknowledgements to their Friends and the Public, for past Favours; and the said Thomas Husband presumes to recommend the said William Gould to their future Countenance and Support, which the said William Gould begs Leave to assure them he shall endeavour to gain and preserve, by the most respectful Attention to the Execution of their Commands, and by furnishing the best Articles upon the most reasonable Terms.

Thos. Husband
William Gould

(London Gazette, 8th August 1807 p.1050.)

William Gould did not continue trading in Upton-upon-Severn for very long and soon relocated his drapery business to Stratford-upon-Avon. This was not a successful move and clearly he did not embrace the sentiments in the above notice for within three years he too had been declared bankrupt.[227] Thomas Husband continued to live in Upton until his death in December of 1807 and among the bequests in his will was one to the 'Trustees for the Worcester Infirmary the sum of Thirty pounds to be applied in aid of the said charity'. (A memorial to Thomas Husband was placed in the old parish church and moved to the new parish church of St Peter and St Paul in 1877.)

Mathews & Thacker – Ironmongers

In May 1809, three years after the death of Samuel Sandelands, the trustees of his estate sold the High Street property to William Mathews and his brother-in-law, Thomas Thacker, who were already in business in the shop as ironmongers. Their partnership was short-lived and on the 30th December 1813 it was dissolved by 'mutual consent' and a very brief notice appeared in the London Gazette. In June 1814 the property was sold to Thomas Thacker's father, Samuel Thacker, a bricklayer or builder from Upton, (although in his will, dated 1810, he described himself as 'gentleman'). Samuel Thacker who, 'not being at present provided to pay the whole purchase money' of eight hundred and fifty-five pounds, prevailed upon a Mr. John Ireland for a mortgage for six hundred pounds.[228] Samuel Thacker was a prosperous builder who owned numerous properties and land in Upton together with a lime kiln, the rents from which were to provide an income for his wife after his decease. In addition to his freehold estate he held a leasehold interest in a brickworks in 'Royal Meadow'. In March 1815 Samuel Thacker added a codicil to

---

227 *London Gazette*, 21st March 1812 p.551.

228 The name Thacker appears in a list of names in the inscription on one of the parish church bells: 'This bell was raised by subscription in 1837 by S. Harrison, S. Thacker ....'. VCH p.216.

his will. He must have taken exception to the behaviour of his son-in-law, William Mathews, and changed the bequest to his youngest daughter Ann:

'Whereas I have in my Last Will given the whole of my Property (after the decease of my Wife and subject to certain exceptions therein contained) to be equally divided amongst my Children, Thomas, Sarah, Elizabeth and Ann. Now I hereby revoke the said Gift and Bequest to my said daughter Ann and give and bequeath her part or share of my said property to my Executors named in my said Will Upon Trust that they or the Survivors or Survivor of them shall place the same out to Interest upon Government or Real Security and to pay the Interest from time to time as the same shall become due into the proper Hands of my said daughter Ann without its being in anywise subject to the Will or contract of her Husband William Mathews or any future husband... '.

Samuel's youngest daughter had apparently encountered some problems in her marriage to William Mathews and the codicil was intended to ensure that the bequest remained solely for her benefit. Two years later a terrible summer storm precipitated Samuel Thacker's demise:

1817 June 30. On Saturday se'nnight, Mr Thacker, builder, of Upton upon Severn, took shelter from the violence of the storm, at a toll-house near that town; he had not been in the house many minutes when, after making an observation on the awfulness of the storm, he suddenly expired. It is supposed that the extreme agitation he suffered on beholding the conflict of the elements, occasioned his death.

(*Gloucester Journal* 30th June 1817, p.3 col. 2.)

In his will Samuel Thacker had appointed trustees to administer his estate which, in November 1819, was put up for sale by auction at the White Lion Inn, in Upton-upon-Severn. The High Street building was Lot 8:

LOT 8 -- All that capital DWELLING-HOUSE substantially built, and most advantageously situated for Trade, in an eligible part of the High-street, heretofore in the occupation of Messrs Mathews and Thacker, Ironmongers, but now untenanted; together with the Ware-house, Stable and Yard behind the same; and also an excellent MALT-HOUSE, with Flat Kiln attached thereto, in the occupation of Mr. Joseph Charlwood; forming altogether most desirable Premises for any business requiring room. The House consists, on the basement floor, of good Cellaring; on the ground floor, of an excellent front Shop, 17 feet by 10, with a Counting-House adjoining, Parlour and

Kitchen; on the first floor, a neat Dining or Drawing Room, and three good Bed Chambers; and on the attic, three chambers.

(*Berrow's Worcester Journal*, 14th October 1819)

On the day of the auction the High Street premises did not achieve the reserve price and was withdrawn from the sale. A conveyance, dated three years later, revealed that the highest bid had been £605 and would not have cleared the outstanding mortgage of £630 still due to John Ireland. At the time of the auction the shop and living accommodation were unoccupied, although the malt-house was in the possession of Joseph Charlwood, a maltster who lived in Old Street. In 1822 the trustees reached an agreement with Mr Charles Cowley, a mercer of Upton, who purchased the building for £755. This sum cleared the outstanding mortgage and left £125 for the trustees to distribute to the beneficiaries. On the 27th August 1822 the new landlord, Charles Cowley, married Susannah Hudson in Upton-upon-Severn. The High Street property was part of a pre-nuptial marriage settlement between the groom and his new bride; this settlement effectively created an entail; Charles Cowley, his wife and any subsequent children, had the benefit of the rents. The building remained in the possession of the Cowley family until 1862 and up to that date the occupants were their tenants. [229]

After the partnership with his brother-in-law had been dissolved in 1814 Thomas Thacker continued the ironmongery business in the High Street property and lived there with his young family. He had married Mary Croft in Shrewsbury in 1812 and their son, Samuel Croft Thacker, was born in 1815. On the 23rd May 1816 the *Worcester Journal* advertised the auction of all his 'Valuable STOCK of Heavy and Light IRONMONGERY GOODS, Oils, Colours, Bags, Cords, Twines, Brushes, Japanned and Tin Wares, on the said Premises'. He then followed his father as a builder. When the property was put up for auction in 1819 Thomas Thacker was in occupation of the Red Cow public house in Old Street and some ten years later Pigot's 1830 Trade Directory listed him at the Black Swan in Queen Street (now Dunn's Lane). Thomas Thacker continued in the building trade and his wife, Mary Thacker, took responsibility for the running of the public houses; he died in 1836 at the age of fifty-six leaving his wife, Mary, a widow at the age of forty-one. She eventually became proprietor of the White Lion Hotel in Upton and was listed in Lascelles' 1851 trade directory:

Thacker Mary, White Lion, Family and Commercial Hotel and Posting House, horses, gigs, flys, mourning coaches, and hearse, bowling green and billiard table, High st.

---

229 The settlement was by a Lease and Release dated 23rd and 24th of August 1822. These indentures have not survived but are referred to in later documents. The two trustees were Thomas Bird the younger and William Barber.

The 1851 Census provided details of the occupants of the White Lion, listing Mary Thacker as head of the household living with her granddaughter, Mary Ann Thacker, and employing several servants. Trade must have been slack for the sole visitor was the local surgeon, Charles Sheward. This census return raises the question as to the whereabouts of six-year-old Mary Ann's parents. Her father was Samuel Croft Thacker who had been appointed an Excise officer in 1839 and, as a consequence of the policy of the Excise Department of frequently moving its officers, had been stationed in various parts of the British Isles. After training in Worcester he was posted to Hereford for two years and was then transferred to Liverpool.

Then came a move to Aberystwyth where he met and married his wife, Anne Jones. By 1848 he was in Carrickmacross, Ireland, where he worked for two or three years before returning to Liverpool. (In 1849 the Excise Department was absorbed into the newly formed Inland Revenue service.) In about 1853, after service in Liverpool, he was posted to Ironbridge or Broseley in Shropshire. However, in March 1856 Samuel Croft Thacker was on the move once more, only this time he had an appointment with Mr Justice Erle in the Nisi Prius Court at Cheshire Spring Assizes. The Chester Chronicle[230] reported the case in detail.

He had been cited as defendant in 'an action to recover the sum of £55, the balance of £99 due for malt supplied by the plaintiff, Mr Robert Buttress, between October 1854 and January 1855'. It was said that the defendant, whilst being employed as an excise officer in Broseley, was also connected with an inn at Shrewsbury called the London Apprentice. The Excise regulations forbade its officers from being the landlord of any public house, consequently, in order to accommodate these orders, the name of the defendant's mother, Mary Thacker, had been placed over the door to the inn. The Chester paper declared that 'the defence to the present action was that Mrs [Mary] Thacker, and not the defendant, was liable for the payment of the amount in question'.

Mary Thacker was the daughter of John and Eleanor Croft who had kept the London Apprentice in Shrewsbury. According to the evidence given, it was said that some years previously it was kept by a 'Miss' Croft (and presumably, after her decease it came into the hands of either Samuel Croft Thacker, who was at that time in Ireland, or Mary Thacker). The defendant claimed that the inn was then kept by his mother and that his wife had left Ireland 'to reside at the London Apprentice, owing to his mother's inability to manage the building on account of ill-health'. Mary Thacker, described as 'Old Mrs Thacker … a little infirm, but not bedridden', was called to give evidence. She said that 'at the time of Miss Croft's death she was keeping an hotel at Upton-on-Severn, and she sent Ann Thacker to manage the business at the London Apprentice until she could dispose of the hotel at Upton' (this would be the White Lion). Ann Thacker was summoned, and testified that

---

230 *The Chester Chronicle*, 5th April 1856.

'Mr Buttress called for some money when Mary Thacker was out, and as he was very saucy, she asked him whether he would take a two months' bill'. She then stated that she 'had often appended her mother-in-law's signature to bills'. This statement contradicted the plaintiff's evidence for he claimed that the bills were in the name of 'Mr Thacker'. The plaintiff told the court that he had been offered a bill for £20 at two months notice which, when paid into the National Provincial Bank, had been dishonoured. (A 'bill' means a 'Bill of Exchange' i.e. in this instance a post dated cheque.) It seems that Samuel Croft Thacker's wife and mother were struggling to make a living out of the London Apprentice, and whilst stationed in Ireland he was having to send money to support his young family in Shrewsbury. After his return to England his financial situation deteriorated, his debts mounted and he attempted to obtain a loan of one hundred pounds 'in order to meet the pressing demands of creditors'.

As is often the case, much of the evidence from the witnesses was contradictory; it is not clear who was actually running the inn; whose name was on the bills to be drawn on the bank or who was taking responsibility for payment of debts; the management of the inn seems to have been disorganised if not chaotic. Although Mary Thacker's name was above the door, the evidence suggests that her daughter-in-law, Anne Thacker, was managing the business. (The 1851 census for Shrewsbury gave Anne Thacker's occupation as 'Innkeeper'.) The lawyer acting for the defendant, argued that 'in all reasonable transactions credit would be given to that person whose name appeared as manager of the establishment to which the goods were supplied', and that the plaintiff was fully aware that Mrs Thacker's name was over the door.

The learned Judge, after hearing from several parties to the case, had obviously sided with the plaintiff. He then addressed the jury, and remarked that 'when a wife carried on dealings with her husband's knowledge, and contracted debts, the plain inference was that the husband had given authority for her to obtain credit, and if the jury were of the same opinion, a stop could be put to the case without further evidence'. The jury requested that the case continue and that they should hear all the evidence, but having listened to the remaining witnesses and after a short deliberation, they found in favour of the plaintiff, Mr Buttress, who was awarded costs. It is doubtful if he received any money from his court action for a notice in the London Gazette provided a postscript:

> WHEREAS a Petition of Samuel Croft Thacker, of Broseley, in the county of Salop, in lodgings with William Hall, Accountant, of Broseley, previously of Broseley aforesaid, previously in Housekeeping, of Eldon-place, Liverpool, in the county of Lancaster, before that of Carrickmacross, in the county of Monaghan, in Ireland, and formerly of Ardee, in the county of Louth, Ireland, Officer of Inland Revenue, an insolvent debtor, having been filed in the

County Court of Shropshire, at Madeley, and an interim order for protection from process having been given to the said Samuel Croft Thacker, under the provisions of the Statutes in that case made and provided, the said Samuel Croft Thacker is hereby required to appear before the said Court, on the 17th of May next, at ten in the forenoon precisely, for his first examination touching his debts, estate, and effects, and to be further dealt with according to the provisions of the said Statutes; and the choice of the creditors' assignees is to take place at the time so appointed. All persons indebted to the said Samuel Croft Thacker, or that have any of his effects, are not to pay or deliver the same but to Mr. George Potts, Clerk of the said Court, at his office, at Madeley, the Official Assignee of the estate and effects of the said insolvent.

(*London Gazette,* 25th April 1856 p.1573)

Thacker does not appear to have been imprisoned for his debts, although it wasn't until 1869 that the practice of jailing insolvent debtors ceased. These incidents appear to have incurred the displeasure of his superiors for Samuel Croft Thacker was suspended by the Inland Revenue Service. He was, however, eventually re-instated to his position as excise officer and moved to Lancashire where he continued in this occupation for many years until he retired. He died in Accrington in 1897, aged eighty.

John Day – Grocer and Druggist
The next trader in the premises following in the footsteps of Thomas Thacker was John Day, a businessman with an aptitude for overcoming adversity. He acquired the tenancy of the High Street building in about 1820 and a few years earlier, in 1813, had rather over-extended himself financially and the London Gazette revealed his rather desperate situation:

'By the order of the Court for Relief of Insolvent Debtors; the petition of John Day, late of Upton-upon-Severn, in the county of Worcester, druggist and grocer, now a prisoner for debt in the King's Bench prison; in the county of Surrey, will be heard at the Guildhall of the city of Westminster, on the 6th day of October next, at the hour of Nine in the Morning; and that a schedule, containing a list of all the creditors of the said prisoner, annexed to the said petition, is filed in the Office of the said Court, No. 59, Millbank-street, Westminster, to which any creditor may refer; and in case any creditor intends to oppose the discharge of the said prisoner, it is further ordered, that such creditor shall give notice in writing of such his intention, to be left at the Office of the said Court, two days at least before the said 6th day of October'.

JOHN DAY

(*London Gazette,* 12th September 1815 p.1873)

Although John Day was in 'trade', his debts must have been below the minimum criteria for bankruptcy, and consequently he was declared insolvent and imprisoned. Whilst the practice of taking inventories for the purpose of probate had ceased during the eighteenth century, it is fortunate for us (although perhaps not for Mr Day) that an auctioneer made a complete inventory of his goods and effects in connection with his insolvency. This inventory, taken in 1813, included the contents of his house as well as his sales shop and warehouse, and whilst he was not a tenant of this building until 1820, this inventory provides an accurate reflection of the contents of his druggist's shop when he had re-established himself in the same trade in the High Street building. The inventory of his sales shop lists an impressive number of items, both for the grocery trade and for his 'profession' as a 'druggist' (Listed in Appendix C).

Grocers have long been associated with the sale of drugs (here referring to those raw materials used in the preparation of medicines). The Grocers Company, one of the oldest Livery Companies of the city of London, was given, by a charter of Henry VI in 1447, 'ample jurisdiction and control, and the examination of drugs'. The same charter 'extended the company's control and oversight to druggists, apothecaries and confectioners'. They could enter shops within the city of London and impose fines for 'deceits', i.e. fraudulent articles. In 1617 the apothecaries formed a separate Livery Company, 'The Worshipful Society of Apothecaries'. Apothecaries mixed and compounded drugs for both physicians and the general public, whereas the 'druggist' was a dealer in 'drugs' of both vegetable and animal origin. 'Chemists' were dealers and manufacturers of chemicals although the difference between these various trades or professions was not always precise. The origin of the 'chemist & druggist' of the seventeenth and eighteenth centuries is not absolutely clear, some authorities give it as a merger of 'chemists' and 'druggists', whilst others give it as coming from the apothecaries. Very many so called 'chemist and druggists' were simply grocers who had adopted a 'professional' title. Exactly how much medical knowledge John Day had of this extensive range of drugs is questionable. Many self styled 'chemists and druggists' were 'illiterate general dealers quite unequal to the task of compounding medicines'. A report, prepared some years earlier in about 1794, stated: 'There was scarcely a village or hamlet without a druggist; adulteration and sophistication [falsification] seemed to be general, and the druggists of Manchester appeared to excel all others in such nefarious ingenuity'.[231]

John Day successfully extricated himself from his financial difficulties, was discharged by the Court for Insolvent Debtors and released from prison. By 1820 he was re-established as 'Druggist and Grocer' in the High Street in Upton-upon-Severn. Whatever his qualifications as 'chemist and druggist', John Day was not only engaged in retail but, as the advertisement for his 'Genuine Vegetable Cough Pills' indicates, he was also a manufacturing chemist. John Day promoted his

231 James Grier, *A History of Pharmacy*, (1937) p.113.

patent Pills over a wide area of the West Midlands, placing advertisements in the Worcester Journal, the Birmingham Gazette and the Hereford Journal; another of his remarkable health restoring products was 'Dr. Baillie's Antibilious Pills':

The following valuable MEDICINE is sold, by appointment of the Proprietor, by Beilby, Knott, and Beilby, T. and W. Wood, High-street ; R. Peart and B. Hudson ; Bull-street ; J. Cope, Druggist, High-street ; J. Haywood, Druggist, 31, New Street ; G. Souter, 5, Ann-street ; M. Banks. Market-place ; F. Westcott, and H. James, Drug-gists, Birmingham.

DR. BAILLIE's VEGETABLE COUGH PILLS,

for Colds, Coughs, Asthmas, Impeded Respiration, Incipient Consumption, and every Disorder originating in a derangement of Pulmonary Function.

The sanative influence of this valuable composition, which is prepared from the original recipe of the above eminent Physician, has been experienced by many individuals , who would, if required, voluntarily attest the same. This remedy, which is now offered unhesitatingly to a discerning public, contains no ingredient but what has a specific operation to ac-complish, and whose mode of action is medicinally compatible with those of its associated constituents. The generality of remedies for coughs, &c. possess opium as a characteristic compound, which, although it may immediately alleviate dis-tressing symptoms by its sedative power, and thus lull the patient into a state of confidence that is certainly beneficial to him, will at length awake him from this fancied security by producing consequences, which, if they do not immedi-ately terminate the existence of the wretched sufferer, render the remainder of it almost insupportable.

These Pills have not the least particle of opium nor any other deleterious article; they are perfectly mild and innocu-ous. In incipient cold or cough which is produced by a dis-turbance of the balance of circulation, they produce their beneficial results, by restoring and equalizing this balance up-on which health depends ; and where from neglect or other causes these diseases have become chronic, the patient will by taking a few doses be experimentally convinced of their medicinal worth. In cases of asthma and difficulty of breathing they act almost like a charm, emulging the mucous follicles of the lungs of that viscid phlegm which is the primary source of uneasiness. and by their specific action on the pulmonary structure eradicating that morbid irritability which continues to keep up the disease. And no less in incipient consumption than in the above-mentioned complaints are these Pills calcu-lated to afford marked and permanent relief ; many persons who have been labouring under its most aggravating attacks have, by a persevering continuance in their use, been recalled from those paths which would shortly have brought them to the confines of the grave, and been reinstated in the possession of that most invaluable of all sublunary treasures – HEALTH These Pills are prepared only by JOHN DAY, Chemist, Upton-upon-Severn, who possesses the original recipe ; by whom they are sold wholesale and retail, and likewise by the principal Medicine Vendors and Stationers in the kingdom, in boxes at 1s. 1½d. and 2s. 9d. each.

(Birmingham Gazette, 10 March 1828)

DR BAILLIE'S ANTIBILIOUS PILLS, Entirely Vegetable

Prepared from the Original Recipe of the late celebrated Dr. Baillie, Physician to his late and present Majesty.

THE well-known talents of this eminent medical luminary are sufficient to recommend to Public Notice any compound bearing his name as its inventor. But even were every consideration of this kind totally abstracted, the testimony and experience of numerous individuals would satisfactorily substantiate the efficacy of this inestimable composition.–The Proprietor of this Recipe has been in-duced thus to give publicity to these Pills, in consequence of the unexampled benefit that has been derived from them by those persons with whom he has been personally ac-quainted ; and he most positively avows, that they do not contain a Particle of either Mercury, Antimony, or Aloes, their constituents being procured solely from the Vegetable Kingdom. They are not offered to notice as a Catholicon or Universal Remedy (according to the mode too much in vogue in the present day, and which cannot be too strongly repre-hended) ; the diseases for which they are antidotes are chiefly limited to Bilious and Dyspeptic Affections ; for these they are unhesitatingly pronounced Remedies. –These Pills are perfectly mild in their manner of operating : –Primarily, That they act upon the Intestinal Canal, carrying off all re-dundant Bile, and whatever other Crudities it may contain, so that upon this account alone, they would be valuable as a FAMILY MEDICINE, but particularly to those suffering from Dyspepsia or Indigestion, in which complaint Habitual Costiveness is an essential concomitant. Secondarily, They exert a peculiar influence upon the Stomach of the Dyspep-tic, correcting that increased irritability which prevents its secretions from being prepared in a perfect state, from which cause the assimilation of the food is performed in a manner so imperfect, as scarcely to afford sufficient nutriment to the body. But with regard to those labouring under Bilious Disorders, effects the most desirable will by their use be speedily produced, as they subvert that morbid sensibility of the hepatic system, upon which these disorders princi-pally depend, and enable that important viscus to secrete the biliary fluid in an elaborate and healthy manner.

Sold, Wholesale and Retail, by JOHN DAY, Chemist and Druggist, Upton-upon-Severn ; and Retail, at Deighton's Library, by Wheeler, and Savigny and Green, Worcester ; Green, Droitwich ; and most respectable Medicine Vendors in the Kingdom, in Boxes, at 1s. 1½d. and 2s. 9d. By pur-chasing the larger size, a considerable saving is effected.

(Berrow's Worcester Journal, 19 July 1827)

The sales of patent medicines, or 'quack remedies' as they were often called, grew alarmingly during the eighteenth and nineteenth centuries. There were few human ailments, it was claimed with great exaggeration, that could not be cured by the administration of these 'efficacious' potions. These remedies were frequently concocted by unqualified entrepreneurs with little or no knowledge of the contents of their miracle cures; the medicinal properties of the ingredients were often untried or untested and some were even dangerous. Many European countries attempted to regulate the trade but Britain took a more *laissez faire* approach and, as always, saw an opportunity for raising revenue by taxation. In the budget of 1783 a medicine tax was introduced on proprietary medicines sold by unqualified practitioners – sales of medicines by qualified apothecaries and doctors were excluded. The seller was required to purchase an annual licence (twenty shillings in London but only five shillings elsewhere) and all patent medicines had to be wrapped in paper bearing a government stamp. The implementation of the 1783 tax proved to be totally unsatisfactory and a *Medicine Duty Act* was passed in 1785. The penalties for unlawful sales could be quite severe: ranging from a fine of five shillings for selling without a licence to punishment of death without benefit of clergy for forging any seal, stamp or mark with intent to defraud (the authorities took a very dim view of forgery). Government continued to pursue the sale of medicines as a useful source of revenue and in 1812 the *Medicines Stamp Act* arrived on the statute book. An adhesive stamp to the value of the tax to be paid had to be attached to all manufactured medicines. The tax imposed depended upon the price of the medicine. On medicines costing up to one shilling the tax was one and a half pence and three pence on medicines priced between one shilling and two shillings and six pence (California Syrup of Figs was taxed at three pence). The medicines tax was doubled during the First World War and the Medicine Tax Act was not abolished until the introduction of purchase tax in 1940.

Pigot's 1828 trade directory gives several entries for a John Day trading in the High Street, first of all under Post Office: 'John Day. Post Master. – Letters for LONDON, and the North and West of ENGLAND, are despatched by a mail cart from WORCESTER at a quarter past two, and arrive every morning at twelve'. The name also appears under 'Grocers and Tea Dealers' as *'John Day (& druggist)'*, under 'Bakers and Flour Dealers' and finally under 'Maltsters'. Whilst it is certain that this John Day was trading as a grocer, a chemist and druggist, and that he was also the post master, it is not clear whether or not he was in business as baker, flour dealer or maltster. John Day was in possession of the whole premises including the malt-house and he could have been responsible for the baking ovens that were constructed adjacent to the malt-house. The remnants of the brick arches of these ovens are still visible in the yard to the rear of the building. Day could have been employing tradesmen and a journeyman baker, or the malt-house and baking ovens could have been let to someone of the same name, possibly a relative. At this date he was the only druggist mentioned in the directory.

Regrettably John Day was not the most successful of businessmen and most disappointingly his 'Genuine Vegetable Cough Pills' did not make his fortune. Once again he featured in the London Gazette: 'and he being declared a Bankrupt is hereby required to surrender himself to the Commissioners in the said Commission named, or the major part of them, on the 21st and 22nd of October instant, and on the 18th of November next, at Eleven in the Forenoon on each day, at the George

Inn and Commercial Hotel, in the Town of Ledbury, in the County of Hereford, and make a full discovery and disclosure of his estate and effects ….'

(*London Gazette*, 7th October 1828, p.1836.)

On this occasion his debts must have been sufficiently large for him to be declared bankrupt and thereby he avoided the rigours of imprisonment. The assignees took possession of all his worldly goods and stock in trade to 'reduce them to ready money'. Notice of the forthcoming auction appeared in the Worcester Journal – everything to be sold 'without any reserve':

UPTON-UPON-SEVERN
To Chemists, Druggists, and the Public in general.
TO BE SOLD BY PUBLIC AUCTION,
BY MR BENTLEY,
Without any reserve,
All the entire STOCK in TRADE, SHOP FIXTURES,
a neat HOUSEHOLD FURNITURE, and
other Effects, belonging to Mr. JOHN DAY, Chemist and
Druggist of UPTON-UPON-SEVERN, in the County of
Worcester.
Days of Sale and other Particulars will appear in the next Journal.
(*Berrow's Worcester Journal* 23rd October 1828)

It is most curious that further 'Particulars' did not appear in the following issue of the *Worcester Journal*. Perhaps funds arrived in the nick of time to satisfy his creditors and thereby John Day avoided bankruptcy. Whatever the outcome once again this was only a temporary financial hiatus in his business affairs. The bankruptcy proceedings must have been suitably resolved and the creditors satisfied for within two years John Day was yet again trading as a 'chemist and druggist'. However, he was soon to be summoned to appear a third time before the courts of law. On this occasion it was concerning a far more serious offence.

In the early nineteenth century anyone with a modicum of knowledge and sufficient finance could set up in business as a chemist and druggist. There was little legislation covering the sale of medicines and no control at all over self styled 'chemists' who established themselves in this profession. Only the more affluent people could afford to consult a doctor, the National Health Service was many years away and the greater proportion of the populace turned to their local chemist and druggist for advice on treatment for their ailments. John Day was probably typical of many self-styled 'chymists' of that era, his principle trade was almost certainly grocer but he also sold and manufactured patent medicines. Many of these proprietary medicaments were of dubious efficacy and a large number contained significant amounts of opium, mercury, antimony and other noxious substances. Items such as opium and its derivatives, which today are classified as dangerous drugs, were sold to the public without control. Other pharmaceuticals, drugs and poisons including arsenic and strychnine were all available for sale over the counter. This lack of control and the general availability of such articles inevitably led to many deaths from poisoning, both accidental and deliberate, notably from arsenic and opium. In the United Kingdom between the years 1839 and 1849 a total of 239 people were tried for murder or attempted murder by the use of poison. The sale of such poisons was not subject to any control until 1851 and an article written, in 1842, illustrates that their widespread availability was a cause of much concern:

'In this country any chemist or druggist can furnish the means of self-destruction or murder for a few pence, and in too many instances have done so with the utmost indifference. The sale of a poison is regarded as a mere act of commercial intercourse; *tant pis* for the unfortunate victim of error or passion; he has the benefit of a coroner's inquest; the vendor of the poison receives a reprimand, and things resume their natural course – that is, arsenic and oxalic acid are retailed without compunction, and men are hurried from time to time into eternity.'[232]

Such alarming comments about self-destruction and murder are vividly illustrated by an incident that occurred in Upton-upon-Severn in 1830. This affair resulted in the indictment of William White and Francis Crockett for the 'wilful murder' of White's wife, 'by administering a poisonous drug, for the alleged purpose of producing an abortion'. Crockett had procured a quantity of corrosive sublimate (mercuric chloride) which it was claimed had been given to the ill-fated Jane White. Francis Crockett was brought to trial at Worcester Lent Assizes in March 1831. The provincial papers covered the trial in great detail:

CHARGE OF MURDER…. *Francis Crockett*, 57, a man wearing a carter's frock, was charged with the wilful murder of *Jane White* of Upton-upon-Severn, by administering rock mercury to her, mixed with water.

Mr. Godson, for the prosecution, said the deceased was the wife of William White, and it would appear that the prisoner dealt a little in the science of physic, occasionally giving his advice, and also drugs, to his poor neighbours. It might be that he knew the effects of the drugs he administered, but the great probability was, that he was not sufficiently acquainted with them. It would be proved that the deceased Mrs. White died on Friday, the 8th August; and it would also be shown that she had, on the Wednesday before, been attended

232 *Provincial Medical Journal and Retrospect of the Medical Sciences*, 1842, pp.35-6. (From Medical History, 1992, 36: 53-69).

by a surgeon, and that, on the Sunday morning previous to that, she must have taken something which deranged her constitution. The prisoner was sent for, and he gave her an emetic, which removed from her a great proportion of what she had been previously taking. The husband of the deceased had been charged with this offence; but as to him the Grand Jury had ignored the bill, thinking he had nothing to do with the death of his wife; but having been accused of her death it was thought better not to call him as a witness.

It would appear that it was thought that Mrs. White was *enceinte* [pregnant]; though, in fact, she was not in that situation; but, however, it might be that there had been no intention of doing Mrs. White any injury, but that what had been given her was with a wish to do her good, still that would leave the case as one of manslaughter, if the Jury should think the prisoner was ignorant of the effect of what he prescribed; for he should contend that a person administering drugs with the nature and operation of which he was unacquainted would be guilty of manslaughter if he thereby caused the death of any person to whom he so administered them.

Edward Evans was the first witness called. He said I am father of the deceased Mrs. White. I lived in the same cottage with her and her husband, in the parish of Upton-upon-Severn. The prisoner lived at the distance of about a mile and a quarter from our cottage. He used to work with the husband of the deceased; they had mown together most of the summer. The prisoner had from time to time come to our cottage. On the morning of the 1st August, which was a Sunday, I got up between five and six o'clock; the deceased was very sick, and her husband was holding her; I was directed by the husband, William White, to go to the prisoner; I accordingly went; I told my message to the prisoner; I got to his house between six and seven o'clock, and he came between nine and ten o'clock to our cottage. I saw him come in at our door, and go to a shelf and take a bason; he stirred something that was in the bason, but whether he put anything into the bason I cannot tell. He went upstairs; the deceased being then ill in bed. He came down stairs again and warmed the stuff at the fire, and stirred it. I asked him to have a rasher of bacon, but he would not. I then went to church. The deceased had told me that she was pregnant. The prisoner did not tell me what was in the bason. It appeared to me to be oatmeal.

Anne Briscoe said, I am a neighbour of the Whites; I was sent for on the Wednesday morning, before the death of the deceased. William White came for me, and when I went to their cottage I found the deceased very ill in bed. I went again on the Thursday, and she was then very ill. I, in consequence of a direction given to me by the deceased, took a deal pill box to Mr Sheward, the surgeon. I went to see the deceased on the Friday, and stayed all night.

Mr Sheward said, I am a surgeon. I attended Mrs. White on the 4th August; she was very ill, she complained of violent pain. I saw her again on the Thursday, which was the 5th; she said she thought she was *enceinte*. On the Friday she was considerably worse, and complained of more pain. She appeared to me to be nearly in a dying state; I stated to her that I thought there was no probability of her recovery. I was there halve hour.

Anne Briscoe recalled — On the Friday night I sat up with the deceased, who died about nine on the Saturday morning. She did not appear to get better during any part of Friday night. She said nothing about her danger; she spoke about a quarter of an hour before she died. About an hour before she died, she desired I would go to Mr. Sheward, and she said that if I would not, she would go and fetch him herself. I think she was then light-headed, but she was capable of rising up in her bed at that time. I had not observed her to be light-headed before that time.

Mr. Sheward re-called — When I saw the deceased on Friday, after I told her she would not recover, she was perfectly aware of her danger. I told her I had understood she had taken something; she said she had, and that d — d man had poisoned her. I asked what man, and she said Crockett. She said she hoped I would do what I could for her, for the sake of her family. I told her I thought there was no chance of her recovery.

Mr. Justice Bosanquet — This shows a degree of hope in her mind. To render a declaration of this kind admissible in evidence, the person making it must be under the impression of an almost immediate dissolution.

Mr. Godson — My Lord, although I cannot go further on the capital charge, it will be my duty to offer evidence with a view of establishing the minor charge.

Examination resumed — I had a bottle given me at the cottage of the deceased, which had contained corrosive sublimate. That is called rock mercury by the lower order of the people. I opened the body of the deceased six or eight hours after the death. There were inflammations and ulcerations of the stomach and intestines.

The interior part of the stomach was ulcerated. I found nothing in the stomach to cause this. The death was caused by inflammation, which had been produced by some poison. It was such an appearance as might have been caused by corrosive sublimate taken in water. On the same day I saw the prisoner at Mr. Goodman's, the surgeon. He said to Mr. Goodman and me that he had purchased cream of tartar, salts, and sugar of lead, at Mr. Day's. He was asked if he had purchased any corrosive sublimate, and he said he had purchased four penny-worth of rock mercury at Mr. Day's, and also an emetic on the Sunday previous.

Examined by the Learned Judge — Corrosive sublimate and most poisons are used in medicine.

Mr. Goodman said, I am a surgeon. I asked the prisoner what he had been buying, as was mentioned by the last witness. I was present at the opening of the body, and I concur in opinion with Mr. Sheward.

Mr. Justice Bosanquet — You don't bring the prisoner to the house till the time when the deceased was sick.

Mr. Godson — We show him purchasing the thing which is found in her bed-room, and then sent for to the house and administering an emetic.

Mr. Twinberrow said, I have analyzed the contents of a bottle. They were oxymuriate of mercury, more commonly called corrosive sublimate. I had a box sent to me that contained three parcels, in two of which were corrosive sublimate, and, in the third calomel. They contained about a drachm and a half each. If a person came to me for corrosive sublimate I should not sell it to him; but if I did, I should sell a drachm of it for a penny. Four pennyworth would be about half an ounce; but I think that from five to ten grains would be fatal.[233] The bottle and the box were identified by Mr. Goodman.

Mr. Day was called but not examined.

Mr. Justice Bosanquet — Really it would be much too dangerous for me to call this prisoner for his defence. The question is not of what this person died, but who it was that gave her that which caused her death. There is no proof that the prisoner saw her before she was ill, and there is no proof that he had given her anything. It might be that she died from the administering of corrosive sublimate, but still, though the prisoner bought some of that article, it was an article used in medicine, and whether he administered it, or whether it was administered by the husband, there is no evidence, as the statements made by the deceased were in such circumstances as to render them not admissible. Gentlemen of the Jury, you must acquit the prisoner.

Verdict — *not guilty.*

Mr. Justice Bosanquet — Prisoner, I hope you will be very cautious how you administer medicines, for if you administer these dangerous medicines without sufficient caution, and the person dies, you will be guilty of manslaughter, and if you administer them to procure an abortion, you will be guilty of a felony,

The prisoner — My Lord, I did not do this.

Mr. Justice Bosanquet — I say this as a caution to you and other people.

(From *Berrow's Worcester Journal* 17th March, 1831.)

If murder or manslaughter had been proved would John Day have been in any way culpable? The court never sought his evidence nor opinion in this case of alleged murder. To him, and most people in the early nineteenth century, the selling of 'four pennyworth of rock mercury' would have been no different to selling an ounce of Jamaica pepper or a bag of starch. Our predecessors had a very different attitude to the sale and use of drugs and poisons to that found today.

---

233 Twinberrow & Evans, were 'Chymsts and Druggists' of 53, Broad Street, Worcester.

FATAL FACILITY; OR, POISONS FOR THE ASKING.

Child. "PLEASE, MISTER, WILL YOU BE SO GOOD AS TO FILL THIS BOTTLE AGAIN WITH LODNUM, AND LET MOTHER HAVE ANOTHER POUND AND A HALF OF ARSENIC FOR THE RATS (!)"

Duly Qualified Chemist. "CERTAINLY, MA'AM. IS THERE ANY OTHER ARTICLE?"

Punch, *Vol. xvii, p.97 (1849).*

The following year would have seen a rush of customers to John Day's shop, all anxious to purchase some miracle cure to save themselves from 'King Cholera'. An epidemic of the dreaded disease arrived in Upton-upon-Severn in July of 1832. It had already ravaged the city of Bristol in April and soon reached Gloucester and Tewkesbury. 'Boatmen coming up Severn from these towns brought startling reports of the numbers taken ill, and their strange sufferings; and while some were doubting the danger, but more dreading it, cholera had really come and slain its first victim, a young man who was an ostler at one of the inns'.[234] When the disease had finally run its course in Upton-upon-Severn a total of fifty people had died, many of the victims were buried in Parson's Field.

Various patent medicines (of the quack variety) claimed to be able to provide a cure for cholera. One popular remedy was 'Morison's Universal Medicine', a 'cure' for numerous ailments, which was widely advertised accompanied by glowing testimonials as to its efficaciousness. One 'cathartic' testimonial came from Robert Ellis of Norwich addressed to a Mr Charlwood:

MORISON'S UNIVERSAL MEDICINES, a
CERTAIN PREVENTION and CURE of the
CHOLERA MORBUS. – The attention of the Public is
requested to the following (among other) proofs of the
efficacy of MORISON'S MEDICINE:

Mr Charlwood, – Sir, – Feeling satisfied that the life of my wife, Charlotte Ellis, has been saved by the prompt use of Morison's Pills. I send you the particulars, which I hope you will make as public as possible.

Last Sunday morning, about seven o'clock, my wife, who is 60 years of age, was seized with a violent retching but could get nothing up; severe internal and external pains, trembling in every joint of the frame, a violent heat in the bowels, almost unbearable. At this time Thos. Roper, a neighbour, knowing the good effects of Morison's Pills, which he had by him, dissolved about fifteen pills, No. 2, which he gave her in my presence – in about twenty minutes they brought such contents from her stomach, I never saw anything like it before; in about an hour he gave her ten more pills dissolved, which operated downward — after this she felt perfect ease. At seven o'clock in the evening she took seven more pills in their whole state, had a comfortable night's rest, and for fear of any return of the complaints, she continues to take a small dose daily, though I believe there is no fear of a return. In this short space of time she is recovered, and able to do for her family. Any person wishing further particulars, may have any information by calling on your agent, Mr Farrow, Magdalen street, or of myself.

(*The North Devon Journal*, Thursday, September 27, 1832.)

234 Emily Lawson, *The Nation in the Parish*, p.169.

Morison's produced two varieties of Pills, No.1 and No.2. The latter was shown to contain aloes, colocynth, gamboge and cream of tartar with a small amount of ginger – a remarkable combination of violent purgatives. But not all treatments with these Pills had such a happy ending. The hazards of such cures were shown in another charge of manslaughter, on this occasion at York Assizes where, in 1834, Joseph Webb, 'a most respectable looking man and proprietor of the London Coffee-house' in York, was charged with the manslaughter of Richard Richardson. Webb, a person with no medical training, gave Richardson, who was gravely ill with smallpox, a considerable dose of Morison's Pills which, it was claimed, had accelerated his demise. The jury declared a verdict of guilty 'but recommended him to mercy'. The judge, Lord Lyndhurst, sentenced Webb to six months imprisonment in the city gaol. The citizens of York considered this sentence to be a gross miscarriage of justice and petitioned the king for the royal prerogative of mercy. The final paragraph of the petition declared:

> 'Your Majesty's Petitioners, therefore, beg to express their confident hope, that by your Majesty's gracious exercise of the Royal prerogative of mercy in behalf of the said Joseph Webb, the justice of this country may be rescued from the reproach of subjecting to severe punishment a Man, against whom no fact appears to have been established, except that of administering to another a Medicine, of the efficacy of which his own experience did not permit him to doubt.
>
> *Patients cured of the Small Pox, are requested to signify the same opposite their respective Names'.*
>
> (*Yorkshire Gazette*, Saturday, 6th September 1834.)

The appeal was widely advertised in many provincial newspapers and soon it had attracted a large number of signatories. Morison also instigated a penny subscription to purchase a piece of plate to be presented to Mr Webb on his release. Unfortunately, Joseph Webb had to serve out the full sentence as announced in the press by the manufacturers of the Pills, Morison, Moat & Co.:

> 'Gentlemen, — His Grace the Duke of Wellington, in conjunction with the late Judge, Lord Lyndhurst, now Lord Chancellor, having decided that he sees "no sufficient ground to justify his Grace, consistently with his public duty, in advising his Majesty to grant the prayer of the petition (signed by 32,492 individuals) for the remission of Joseph Webb's sentence".'
>
> (*Bristol Mercury*, 20th December 1834.)

Joseph Webb was eventually released from York prison on the 12th of January 1835 to be presented with a magnificent 'Epergne and Salver' in silver weighing four hundred ounces. The silver salver was to certify the 'disapprobation of upwards of 48,000 individuals from all parts of Britain and the United States of America at the verdict and sentence passed against him' and their ' detestation and abhorrence of the absurd and barbarous laws which still stain the Statute Book'. (*Bath Chronicle*, 22nd January 1835.)

In 1835 John Day was again listed in Pigot's trade directory, under 'Chymists & Druggists' and also in 'Grocers & Drapers'. By this time there were three 'chemists and druggists' trading in the High Street and the directory informed the enquirer that John Day was still the Post Master:

> **POST OFFICE**, High street, John Day, *Post Master*. -- letters from LONDON arrive every forenoon at eleven, and are despatched every afternoon at three. -- Letters from the NORTH AND WEST OF ENGLAND and WORCESTER arrive every day at twelve and are despatched every afternoon at two.

The year 1837 brought celebrations with the accession of Queen Victoria to the throne and tragedy for the Day family. Their only son, John, died at Holly Green just twenty years of age. At about this time, sometime between 1835 and 1841, John Day vacated the High Street premises and relocated his business to Old Street. He was listed in Old Street in the 1841 census, occupation 'Postmaster', and living with his wife Sarah, his elderly mother, three daughters and employing two servants (although Pigot's 1842 directory still listed him under 'Grocer and Drapers' in the High Street). After the death of John Day in 1847 his widow, Sarah, continued in business, relocating to other retail premises in the High Street where she was listed in the 1851 directory as 'stationer, grocer and post office'.

> **Post Office, High Street – Mrs. Sarah Day postmistress**. *Delivery, 8 a.m. and 6 p.m. Letters must be posted before 9½ a.m., and 5¼ p.m. Money Order business attended to from 9 a.m. to 5¼ p.m.*
>
> (*Lascelles & Co's Directory & Gazetteer of the City of Worcester & Neighbourhood*, 1851.)

Mrs Day continued as the postmistress in the High Street for at least another ten years, certainly until after the 1861 census.

William Alfred Bradley – Baker and Corn Merchant

It is difficult to be precise as to when John Day's tenure ceased and when William Alfred Bradley, a baker, followed him as tenant (Bradley had been established as a baker in Old Street sometime before 1841). The High Street building appeared to be unoccupied in 1841 as it was not enumerated in the census of that year and in the Tithe apportionment, which covered the period 1836-50, the premises were described as 'void'. It is possible that this is the period during which further building works took place. The most significant alteration to the building was the Victorian shop front which replaced the earlier Georgian windows and at this time a wash-house was constructed to the rear of the building. Bradley must have been in occupation by 1850 for Slater's trade directory of that year listed him in the High Street premises under three headings: 'baker and flour dealer', 'corn merchant' and 'maltster', (the number of maltsters in the town had by then risen to ten). In the 1851 census he was listed as living above the shop together with his wife and three children and employing Charles Taylor, a journeyman baker, and a female servant. Alfred Bradley had vacated the High Street premises before the time of the 1861 census and at first continued his business in Church Street before finally relocating back to Old Street.

Charles Cowley, the owner of the building, died in 1852 and the benefit of the rental income from the property passed to his wife. A few years later, in 1856, it was necessary to break the entail resulting from the earlier marriage settlement and a 'Disentailing Deed' was prepared. The various parties named in the deed were Cowley's three children (Alfred Hudson Cowley of Saint Joseph's Retreat Middlesex, Catholic Priest, Charles John Cowley of Upton, coal merchant and Susan Sophia Cowley of Upton, Spinster), his widow, Susannah Cowley, and Robert David Williams of Upton, a butcher. Alfred Hudson Cowley later relinquished his interest in the property to his brother and sister.

George Barnard – Painter and Dealer in Glass and China

The next tenant was George Barnard who was born in Tewkesbury in 1804. He had married Harriett Panting of Upton-upon-Severn and had moved to Upton before 1841. He set up in business in Old Street, first as a grocer and dealer and later, by 1851, he was a glazier and painter. In Billing's Directory of 1855 he was listed as a stationer at the Berlin Warehouse in Old Street. At some date prior to 1861 George was established in the High Street building, living with his wife and family; he was listed as a painter, his wife, Harriett a china dealer and his daughter, Ellen, a stationer. Also in the household were his widowed daughter, Mary Ann Willetts and her eight year old daughter, Mary Elizabeth, who had been born in Cincinatti, Ohio. Little else is known about George who died on the 21st July 1861, but before he was barely settled in his grave his fifty-year-old widow, Harriett, had found a new husband. On the 7th of December 1861 in Saint Michael's church, Bedwardine, Worcester she married sixty-nine year old Elisha Wright Oldham, a railway engineer by profession, who moved into the building to live with his new wife.

Elisha Wright Oldham – Railway contractor and China dealer

Elisha Oldham had had an interesting career. He was born in 1792 in Stretton, Warwickshire, into a family of builders and railway engineers. His elder brother,

Thomas, was one of the contractors on the Great Western Railway which had been granted its enabling Act of Parliament in 1835. Elisha, with his eldest son, Thomas Oldham, established the firm of railway contractors, E & T Oldham, who in 1838 had been awarded three contracts for the construction of the Cheltenham and Great Western Union Railway (CGW). There were three other sons, also railway contractors, Henry, John and Elisha Oldham junior. Elisha senior moved from Warwickshire to Bisley in Gloucestershire, not far from the proposed railway line. The CGW was authorised by an Act of Parliament in 1836 to connect Cheltenham with the Great Western Railway at Swindon. The route of the Cheltenham line had been surveyed by Isambard Kingdom Brunel and construction began in 1838. Messrs Oldham were shareholders in this undertaking and were among the earliest railway contractors in this country. In 1839 Elisha Wright Oldham was the cause of considerable excitement in Cheltenham High Street:

> 'UNFASHIONABLE ARRIVAL! – On Tuesday last, at noon, the first Locomotive Railway Engine, ever seen in Cheltenham, made its appearance in the High Street, exciting considerable attention as it passed along, drawn by twelve horses, on a carriage apparently prepared for that especial purpose. The lustrous stranger was conveyed along the Promenade and through the new opening near the Queen's Hotel, into the Old Well lane, and thence to the railway of the Cheltenham and Great Western Union, at the end of Lansdown Place. This engine has been provided by the contractor, Mr Oldham, for the purpose of more rapidly and effectually proceeding with the works along the line, upon which it is expected to be in full operation on Monday, commencing its leviathan labours about two miles from the proposed depôt. We observed it was very appropriately named "The Excavator," and have been informed its weight is between eleven and twelve tons'.
>
> (*The Cheltenham Looker-On,* 13th July 1839.)

After the birth of the seventh of his nine children Elisha Wright Oldham embraced the Calvanistic Baptist church, and during the construction of the CGW railway a wooden church was provided in Cheltenham for the benefit of the railway navvies in his employ:

> 'PREACHING TO RAILWAY LABOURERS – On Sunday last, the Reverend F. Close preached in a neat wooden temple, near the Birmingham depot, at the extreme end of the Queen's-road, Cheltenham, adjoining the Gloucester-road, the object of which was to induce the men employed on these railway lines to attend and hear the word of God on Sunday afternoon. On this occasion, several hundred persons were present, chiefly of the class for the benefit of whom the building was designed. The reverend gentlemen having read the normal

service of the church, preached from Acts xvi 29, and two following verses, and was listened to with most marked attention. The reverend gentleman, in conclusion, stated that it was his intention to preach every Sunday afternoon in this little building now dedicated to God, and he devoutly hoped that some good would result from the service. Mr Oldham, the contractor, then stated that as the building did not seem large enough, he would be most happy to make it double the size by the following Sunday. We need not add that the offer was most readily accepted.'

(*Bristol Journal* from *The Railway Times*, 14th December 1839)

The railways were still very much in their infancy and construction of the CGW line was fraught with difficulties. In 1841 the Oldhams took over a fourth contract that another firm had failed to complete, but by 1842 the firm of E & T Oldham was in severe financial difficulties and in April of that year the proprietors were declared bankrupt – it took until 1846 for their affairs to be settled. Two of their locomotives, the 'Excavator' and the 'Volcano' were purchased for £500 by Dowlais ironworks near Merthyr Tydfil to run on the plateway serving the works. Elisha Wright Oldham, together with three of his sons, Thomas, Elisha and John, subsequently moved their activities up to Scotland (their credit rating presumably not having reached over the border). The firm of E. & T. Oldham, Railway Contractors, was re-established at Bridge of Earn in Perthshire. This time the principals were his sons, Thomas and Elisha junior. The firm was awarded at least two contracts, one on the Stirling and Dunfermline Railway and another on the Dundee and Perth Railway which opened in 1847.

The Oldhams eventually ran into complications with their Scottish contracts and once again were in financial difficulties; the company was sequestrated in August 1849 ('sequestration' is the Scottish procedure for bankruptcy). Elisha Wright Oldham was obliged to provide security for the payment of the dividend to the creditors of his two bankrupt sons. Having impoverished their Scottish creditors, who seem to have received a dividend of only nine shillings and six pence in the pound, the Oldhams then set off down the Great North Road for Nottinghamshire where, most remarkably, they were soon in business once again as railway contractors near Retford.

Elisha Wright Oldham was granted two contracts on a section of the Great Northern Railway – Hougham to Newark and Newark to Retford, the contracts were for £39,000 and £73,000 respectively (a total of over £10 million pounds today). The Great Northern eventually ran from London to York and the section between London and Doncaster (via Newark) was open by 1852. By this time Elisha was living in some style in Newark together with his wife and family, a groom and two female servants. Once the two Great Northern contracts had been completed all the engines, machinery and sixty horses were put up for auction in Newark and

Elisha moved away from Nottinghamshire. In 1855 his wife, Jane, died in Southam, Warwickshire and by 1861 Elisha had moved to Worcestershire and was living with his son, John, in a lodging house in Wyche near Malvern; he then married Harriett Barnard at Saint Michael's in Bedwardine. The following year (1862) the Midland Railway Company was granted powers to construct a new line connecting Tewkesbury with Malvern. This line was to run through Upton-upon-Severn where a small station would be constructed. One of the contracts for this new railway line was awarded to Oldham and Sons, 'well-known' railway contractors.

Apart from his long career in railway construction Elisha Wright Oldham was a self proclaimed 'expert' on the disposal of sewage. (In 1845 the firm of Oldham had unsuccessfully tendered for a contract for sewerage works for the Aberdeen Harbour Board.) The increasing population and lack of adequate sewers in Victorian England resulted in the appalling pollution of rivers. The hot summer of 1858 caused the infamous 'Great Stink' when the odour of untreated human waste in the river Thames caused members of parliament to consider re-locating to Hampton Court. The lamentable state of Victorian sewers seems to have been a particular obsession with Elisha and he wrote numerous letters on this subject to various newspapers putting forward his own proposals for sewerage works. In 1858 he penned a rather rambling letter to the Editor of the Coventry Times which claimed that sewage could be the salvation of the nation:

Correspondence
To the Editor of the Coventry Times
Sir,-- You will oblige by inserting the following letter in your valuable paper:--
To the Board of Health and Ratepayers of Coventry

Gentlemen, -- Some twelve months ago I begged your board not to make deodorizing works, as your drainage scheme was all delusion. I was sorry to see in the report of the Board meeting reported in the *Coventry Times* of the 15th instant, you now find your river never was so foul, or in so bad a condition, and that after some ten or twelve weeks deodorizing how much it is like the river Thames.

Gentlemen, in the *Builder* of the 11th instant, you have the highest engineering authority stating the metropolitan plans will entail great expense annually and not give the relief expected; and in the same paper you will perceive that gentlemen at Greenwich and all down the river complain and say that they will not have their outfalls so near them, but will seek relief in chancery. Yet, the Metropolitan Board appear determined to go there forthwith, and set at defiance (as they have done all along) all suggestions which do not agree with the opinions of their own engineer. I have told you all is a mistake, and an attempt to borrow, or rather steal the Oldham scheme of 1845, which point I beg to explain.

Gentlemen, it will not have escaped your attention that your late General Board of Health is dead, and the Government say if you and your Board don't go more reasonably about this common sense work, they will take it in hand themselves. Pray let me say that in that case you will lose to your City the opportunity of making a large sum of money of the manure. Lord Palmerston says it is to become the source of great national wealth. Gentlemen, three years ago he saw my plan, where I make the manure, arising in a town of 50,000 population, to amount to the sum of £210,000 in 20 years, or £10,000 annually; and you will see this is more than borne out by Government investigation. Gentlemen, let my plan be carried out, and I promise England a run of trade she has never yet known. If you favour me with inserting this I hope it will go the wide world over.

I am, for self and sons,

ELISHA WRIGHT OLDHAM.

Brandon, near Coventry, Sept. 18th, 1858.

(*The Coventry Times*, 22nd September 1858.)

The engineer of the Metropolitan Board of Works was Joseph Bazalgette (later Sir Joseph) who was responsible for constructing London's sewerage network. These works relieved the River Thames of the influx of sewage and reduced the scourge of cholera.

The untimely death of Prince Albert from typhus in 1861 stimulated further literary output and in 1862 Elisha published a pamphlet on the subject of sewage disposal: '*A Letter Addressed To Both Houses Of Parliament*' with the heading '*His Royal Highness has fallen a sacrifice to the deleterious effects of bad drainage*'. Here he described his 'awful' experiences of metropolitan sewers: 'Where I was living in London for many months, I have seen a drain blocked up at the outlet into the main drain, yet our pumps at the upper end of the street kept us clear of all surface water: thus, the water in the well came from the pump to the tea kettle, thence to the closet, the drain and back again to the pump, --- until we drank one day the excrements or sewerage of the preceeding, and dry weather quickened the operation until the filth of the water was awful in its effects'.

Elisha Oldham was well named, for he adopted an evangelical approach to the problems of the disposal of human waste. Another, wonderfully entitled, pamphlet came off the press in 1864: '*Great Britain at War with the Great Creator's own Laws and Ordinances in all Sewerage Works*', this was subtitled '*The great Creator ordained the body for the food, and the Earth was ordained to give it. Do this, says the Creator, and you shall have abundance, long life, and health*'. He enlarged on his subject in the style of a rector addressing his flock at Sunday service: "… the ordinances of God who, wisely, in generosity and beneficially, ordained the sewerage manure of one year should be reproductive of food for the next".

Generally Elisha Oldham's proposals for sewerage works were sound in principle but the practicality of some of his ideas was questionable. His principle objection to proposed methods of sewage disposal was that the drains were not water-tight and sewage could diffuse into the gravel beds in which they were laid, thereby allowing foul water to enter the wells and contaminate drinking water. Whilst this was a reasonable point to raise, his own suggestions for solving the problems were extreme. To quote from Elisha Oldham's scheme for disposal of London's effluent: 'if put into Oldham's air-tight and water-tight drains, and a powerful steam pump behind it, it is fifty miles out of town in a few minutes, not a breath of foul air can escape; and there it is, a greater good, a greater blessing to the poor land, than it is now a death-producing curse'. [235] If his figures are to be believed then the evacuations of the bowels of London would have arrived in the nether regions of Essex at about six hundred miles per hour. An awesome prospect! In 1866 Elisha attended a Sewage Conference in Leamington Spa where his paper on the subject was read to the gathering of Victorian sewerage experts. This scheme promoted his steam pump and use of a 'Pneumatic Railway' to dispose of the manure (the 'pneumatic railway' was possibly a similar arrangement to one that was briefly in existence at Crystal Palace at that time).

Lamentably, Elisha had not completely mastered the art of fine handwriting and on one occasion the editor of the Royal Leamington Spa Courier was obliged to insert a notice to his fertile correspondent:

> E.W. Oldham (Southam). – We literally cannot read
> your letter. It may contain profound truths; but if so,
> they are vested in a calligraphy that defies the practised
> eye of a printing office.
> (*Royal Leamington Spa Courier*, 31st August 1867.)

(Elisha Oldham was seventy five years old at this point – perhaps we should not be too judgmental about his poor handwriting.)

Elisha Oldham and his wife traded in the High Street premises until they were obliged to relocate their business to New Street in Upton where they continued for a few more years, certainly until 1865 when the New Street shop was advertised to be let. He was still listed in Kelly's 1868 Post Office Directory for Birmingham, Staffordshire, Warwickshire and Worcestershire – 'Elisha Wright OLDHAM, china &c, dealer and stationer, New Street'. It seems that by 1871 Elisha and Harriett had parted company, Harriett had moved to Bridgenorth where she continued as a shopkeeper and Elisha was living in lodgings in Southam, Warwickshire where he died in 1879 at the age of eighty-eight.

---

235 *Worcestershire Chronicle*, February 5th 1862.

UPTON-ON-SEVERN.

TO BE SOLD BY AUCTION, BY

WEAVER & MOORE,

ON THURSDAY, THE 19TH DAY OF JUNE, 1862,

AT THE STAR HOTEL,

AT FIVE O'CLOCK IN THE AFTERNOON;

ALL THAT FREEHOLD FRONT

DWELLING HOUSE,

MOST DESIRABLY SITUATE FOR BUSINESS,

IN THE CENTRE OF HIGH STREET,

IN THE OCCUPATION OF MR. ELISHA WRIGHT OLDHAM;

TOGETHER WITH THE EXTENSIVE

MALTHOUSE, GRANARIES, BAKEHOUSE, STABLE,

And other well-arranged Premises lying behind the same, to which there is a back approach.

THE DWELLING HOUSE

Comprises dry underground Cellaring, Shop, Counting House, Parlour, Kitchen, Back Kitchen, Front Sitting Room, and 7 Chambers.

The premises are very extensive, & admirably adapted for the **MALTING & BAKING** Trades, both of which have been successfully carried on for many years.

Further particulars may be obtained of Mr. T. W. WALKER, Solicitor, Upton-on-Severn; or of WEAVER and MOORE, Auctioneers, Tewkesbury.

W. E. COOPER, PRINTER AND STATIONER, UPTON-ON-SEVERN.

On the 19th June 1862 the building, which was still in the joint ownership of Charles John Cowley and his sister Susan Cowley, was put up for auction at the Star Hotel in Upton.

The successful bidder was Doctor Tyers Wilkes who paid three hundred pounds for the premises as described in the auction notice shown above. The two parts of the other half of the original building were occupied by Thomas Taylor, a broker, and Charles Wilkes, a grocer. The latter was almost certainly brother to Doctor Tyers Wilkes.

Doctor Tyers Wilkes – Chemist and Druggist

Wilkes' parents must have had great ambitions for their infant son for the word 'Doctor' did not indicate his profession, it was his forename. He was born in the nearby village of Bredon in 1818, the son of a farmer, William Wilkes, and his wife, Sarah. Lascelles & Co's 1851 directory listed Doctor Wilkes trading in the High Street as 'chemist and druggist dealing in British wines and seedsman' (although this would have been in a different building in the High Street). The census of that year shows him to be unmarried and employing a female servant. Later that year he married Caroline Handy of Upton-upon-Severn. This census also listed his father, seventy year old William Wilkes, still living in Bredon and gave his occupation as 'Druggist and Occupier of 7 acres'.

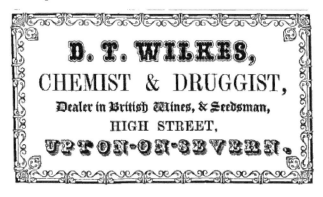

By the 1861 census Doctor Tyers Wilkes was a widower (his wife having died in 1854), still trading in the High Street, living with his two young children and employing an assistant chemist, Benjamin Johnson from Staffordshire. On the 4th November 1862 he married Louisa Edwards, the third daughter of the late Mr J. Edwards of 'The Farm' near Bromyard. After Elisha Oldham had vacated the premises Wilkes relocated his chemist business to the building he had recently purchased; the census returns recorded him working and living with his family in the property for the next twenty years. At least two of Doctor Wilkes' brothers also became 'chemists and druggists'. His eldest brother, William, was the proprietor of a chemist's shop in the Market Place in Bromyard and a younger brother, Seth, was in business in Tewkesbury High Street at No. 150. In 1864 Seth Wilkes married the delightfully named Esthralice Francis, daughter of the late Reverend E. J. Francis, in Tewkesbury Abbey. His brother, William Wilkes, at the age of sixty-one, fell on hard times in Bromyard and, as reported in the Worcester Journal, many of the inhabitants of the town came to his rescue:

BROMYARD

NEIGHBOURLY CONDUCT – A subscription has been raised to the amount of £126, for the benefit of Mr Wilkes, chemist and druggist, an old and much respected inhabitant, who having had a long and severe illness has not been able to attend to his business and support his family. Among the subscribers who took an active part in setting the subscription afoot, were the Rev. N. Stevenson (vicar), the Rev. Mr. Ricketts, Mr. Joseph Corbett, of the Noakes, Mr. Welch, of Bromyard, and Mr. T. Purser of Lower Hill.

(*Berrow's Worcester Journal*, 7th November, 1868.)

At this period in Victorian England the pharmaceutical profession was very much in its emergent stages. The Pharmaceutical Society of Great Britain had been created in 1841, and in 1852 a register of chemists and druggists was established. The society was also granted powers to examine persons for registration. The need for professional regulation and control of the sale of poisons continued to be promoted in the Pharmaceutical Journal and elsewhere. In 1848 the President of the Pharmaceutical Society, addressing the society's annual meeting, had commented:

> When, gentlemen, I think how important a position is held by the Chemist, of how useful a member of society he is designed to be, I turn with sorrow to look upon those with whom the name is in many parts of the country associated. At present, as the law stands, any man, however ignorant – an individual unable even to sign his own name – half of whose shop is stored with butter, bacon, cheese, or tape, shall from the other half have the power of dispensing, to any person applying, preparations of mercury, arsenic, opium etc.
> (*Pharmaceutical Journal*, 1848, vii: p.561.)

It was to be another three years before the Arsenic Act of 1851, which had been promoted by the Pharmaceutical Society and the Provincial Medical and Surgical Association, was passed by parliament. Despite new legislation many poisonings, accidental and otherwise, still occurred. One of the most infamous incidents was in 1858, when peppermint lozenges, sold in Bradford Market, led to twenty deaths, mostly children, with ten times that number falling ill. A druggist selling a cheap sugar substitute had mistakenly supplied arsenic oxide to a local sweet-maker. It was not until the Pharmacy Act of 1868 that further control of the sale of poisons was introduced. The schedule to this Act listed fifteen poisons that could only be sold by pharmacists and included opium, strychnine, belladonna and the fateful mercuric chloride.

The 1871 census listed Doctor Wilkes living at 12 High Street with his second wife, Louisa, his daughter, Sarah Ann, a servant and a pharmacy assistant, George Blount, from Dudley. Another member of the household was Harriett Phillips a

Upton-upon-Severn High Street about the turn of the century.

general nurse. His younger brother, Seth, had died on 16th January 1871 aged just forty-four years (a most imposing memorial to Seth Martin Wilkes is to be found in Bredon churchyard). Doctor Wilkes' wife, Louisa, also died in 1871 at the age of forty-three. Six years later construction of the new parish church was commenced in Upton-upon-Severn and the 'memorial stone' was laid by Mrs Martin of Ham Court. An executive committee, formed for overseeing the construction of the new church, was chaired by Mr Martin; two of the committee members were William Ecklee Cooper, churchwarden and chemist, and Doctor T. Wilkes. The cost of the new church was £13,000 of which £6,000 was contributed by the Martin family and £1,050 came from the Edward Hall Charity (the manor of Upton-upon-Severn had come into the hands of the Martin family of Overbury in the eighteenth century). Doctor Wilkes was listed as a widower in the 1881 census, living with two unmarried daughters, another pharmacy assistant George Barlow from Congleton, Cheshire and a servant (his two youngest daughters had been sent to a school for young ladies in Gloucester). In 1881 Wilkes sold his pharmaceutical business to John Gibbs whose name still appears on the glass panel above the front entrance to the shop. (The freehold was retained by Wilkes.) By 1901 the eighty-two year old Doctor Tyers Wilkes was living in retirement in Lower Westmancote near Bredon with three of his daughters, Amy aged 37, Edith aged 35, and Winifred aged 32, all unmarried. Sarah Ann Wilkes had married his assistant, George Barlow, seven years her junior, who became 'a well known Tewkesbury chemist'. Doctor Wilkes died in 1910 aged ninety-two years.

John Gibbs – Pharmaceutical Chemist

John Gibbs was born in 1855 in St Peter's, Worcester and apprenticed before the age of sixteen years to Edwin Timms, a chemist and druggist of St John's, Worcester. His apprenticeship continued for at least five years until 1877 when he qualified as a pharmacist and registered with the Pharmaceutical Society in that year. (In the nineteenth century the training for a pharmaceutical chemist was totally different from today and apprentices were expected to undergo a long period of instruction as a chemist's assistant before attaining their professional qualifications from the Pharmaceutical Society.) The census return of 1891 listed Gibbs living above the

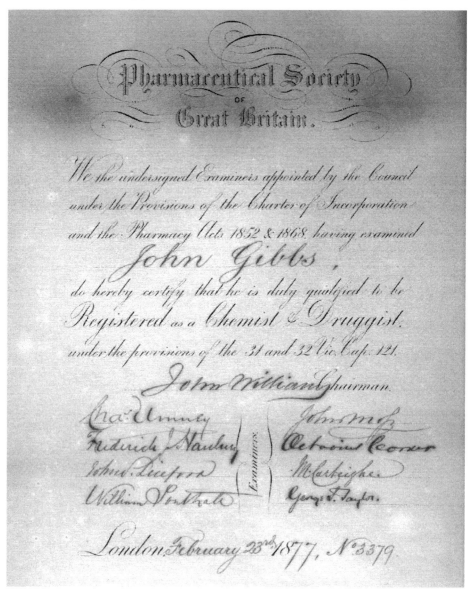

shop with his wife, Harriet, and three young children together with a female servant and Edward Wethers, a chemist's assistant from Kings Lynn, Norfolk. John Gibbs' youngest son, George, died in 1892 aged just one year. By the 1901 census the family had expanded to five children, the eldest son, John, was a pharmaceutical student at this time. Four of John Gibbs' children were destined to follow him into the pharmaceutical profession. In 1901 his wife, Harriet, purchased the freehold of the shop, living accommodation and the malt-house from Doctor T. Wilkes.

The most famous customer whose name appeared in John Gibbs' prescription books was His Highness Prince Victor Duleep Singh, son of the Maharaja of Lahore who was King of the Sikh Empire. In 1898 Prince Victor had married Lady Anne Coventry, the daughter of the 9th Earl of Coventry of Croome Court. This marriage was quite controversial, being the first time that an Indian prince had married into the English nobility. Queen Victoria commissioned portraits of Prince Victor Duleep Singh and his father and these now hang in Osborne House on the Isle of Wight. His Highness provides the conclusion for the subject of debt; Victor Duleep Singh was made bankrupt on 4th December 1902 with liabilities of over £100,000.

It has been suggested that John Gibbs was the source of 'Buck-U-Uppo' which featured in P.G. Wodehouse's book *Meet Mr Mulliner*. This was a miraculous and potent tonic which 'acts directly on the red corpuscles' and was supposed to have been given to the Reverend Edward Isaac, the vicar of Hanley Swan, by a chemist in Upton-upon-Severn (P.G. Wodehouse's aunt, Lucy Apollonia, was married to the vicar). 'When a bishop who came to stay complained of not feeling well, Isaac recommended his tonic and had some to keep the bishop company. Apparently the service that evening had to be cancelled due to the inability of either the vicar or the bishop to do more than totter and smile vaguely'.[236] Regrettably John Gibbs cannot lay claim to Buck-U-Uppo. The Reverend Isaac would, without doubt, have made his purchase from the other pharmaceutical chemist then trading in the High Street, William Ecklee Cooper, with whom he had an account and where he made regular purchases of medicaments.[237] Bennett's 1914 Trade Directory listed John Gibbs who by this time had diversified his trade to include fishing tackle, seeds and the new medium of photography:

> **GIBBS JOHN**, M.P,S., dispensing, agricultural.
> & photographic chemist, seedsman and fishing
> tackle dealer, High st.   Also at Tewkesbury

---

236 http://hanleyswan.net/ *The Hanleys, The website for the villages of Hanley Castle and Hanley Swan.*

237 An account book belonging to William Ecklee Cooper seems to have been acquired by John Gibbs, presumably after William Ecklee Cooper had retired. Gibbs apparently took over his account customers; this account book which covers the period 1884 to 1928 came into the possession of the author and has since been donated to Worcestershire Archives.

After the retirement of John Gibbs in 1920 the business was taken over by his eldest son, also John Gibbs. The pharmacy was acquired by Harry Talbot Cooper in 1931 and following his early demise in 1944 the pharmacy was managed for many years by Helen Gibbs (younger daughter of the elder John Gibbs) until his son, John Talbot Cooper, qualified as a pharmacist and was able to take over the business. John Cooper subsequently continued in business until 1993. The pharmacy is now a branch of a large multiple chemist with the living accommodation above comprising several flats. The other portion of the original premises, once divided into two properties, is now a Spar Supermarket.

Epilogue

All the world's a stage,
And all the men and women merely players:
They have their exits and their entrances;
And one man in his time plays many parts.
(William Shakespeare. *As You Like It*, II. vii.139.)

THIS building has been the backcloth for the lives of many people for nearly five hundred years. It has witnessed many changes over this period. Life in earlier years was not one with which we are familiar today; it was a life lived on 'the edge' without the safety nets of modern society; there were no state benefits, no pensions, insurance or health service. For those people with a little disposable income, the purchase of land and property, to be leased to their friends, neighbours and relatives, provided an income or jointure for wives in the event of the decease of a spouse, annuities for their children and marriage portions for any daughters. They raised money from family and acquaintances by mortgaging their land; for the mortgagee this was a source of income. Litigation over property was commonplace; debt, bankruptcy and insolvency were constant companions; these people lived and died according to their own fortunes or misfortunes. Those who fell into poverty only had the parish to fall back on, and those insolvents who were not able to extricate themselves from their financial difficulties had to endure the rigours of debtors' prison.

It has been a privilege to have been able to follow the lives of so many of the occupants of this building, their families, neighbours and acquaintances. It is remarkable that the title deeds have passed through so many hands over the past centuries and survived intact; they could so easily have been destroyed, this book would never have been conceived and the tales of these people could have remained untold. Perhaps one day the benefactor of the Edward Hall Charity will be discovered, or the missing 'black box' of title deeds pawned to Captain Hopkins will be found and then another chapter in this story can be written.

I trust that I have drawn the correct conclusions from the mass of material that has come to light. As far as possible I have tried to tell the stories by quoting the words of these people from wills, chancery cases, newspapers and letters to evoke a flavour of the times and convey a better understanding of the circumstances in which they lived.

I hope that this book, apart from making fascinating reading, will provide inspiration for others to research the history of an old building. It has brought to life many characters whose stories might otherwise have been lost, and preserved the history of this one particular building.

Appendices

A. John Durston 1640:

     i. Copy of inventory.

     ii. Transcription.

B. John Best 1645:

     i. Copy of inventory.

     ii. Transcription.

C. John Day 1813:

     i. Transcription of Inventory.

Appendix A: John Durston, Inventory 1640.

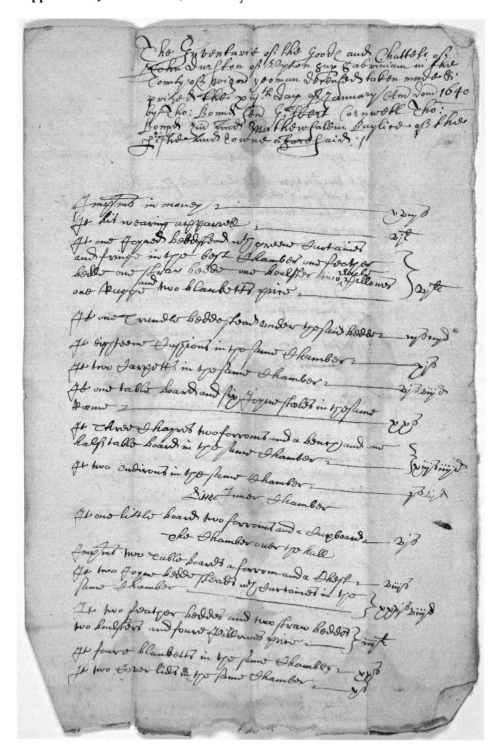

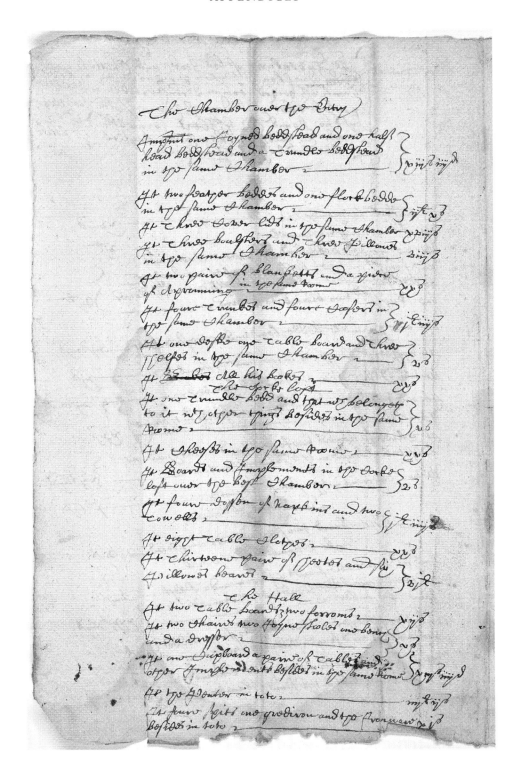

The Chamber over the Entry

Imprimis one Joyned bedstead and one half
head bedstead and a Trundle bedstead
in the same Chamber   xiij viijd

It two feather beddes and one flock bedde
in the same Chamber   iij x

It three bolster bolsters in the same Chamber   xviijd

It three boulsters and three pillowes
in the same Chamber   iiijs

It two pair of Blanckettes and a quilt
of Aprunning in the same Roome   xxd

It four Curtins and four Testert in
the same Chamber   iij iiijs

It one deske one table board and three
stooles in the same Chamber   xd

It ~~stooles~~ all his bookes   xvd
              the forke cort

It one Trundle bedd and that wt belongeth
to it wt other things besides in the same
Roome   xvid

It stooles in the same Roome   xxd

It Boardes and Impliments in the worke
loft over the best Chamber   xxd

It four dossen of napkins and two
towelles   vij iiijd

It eight table Clothes   xxd

It thirteene pair of sheetes and six
pillowe beares   xxvj viijd

              The Hall
It two table boardes two forromes   viijs
It two Chaires two Joyne stooles one benche
and a dresser   xvd

It one Cupboard a pair of tables and
other Implimentes besides in the same Roome   xxvj viijd

It the glenter in tote   iij viijd

It four spitts one grediron and two Iron...
besides in tote   vjs

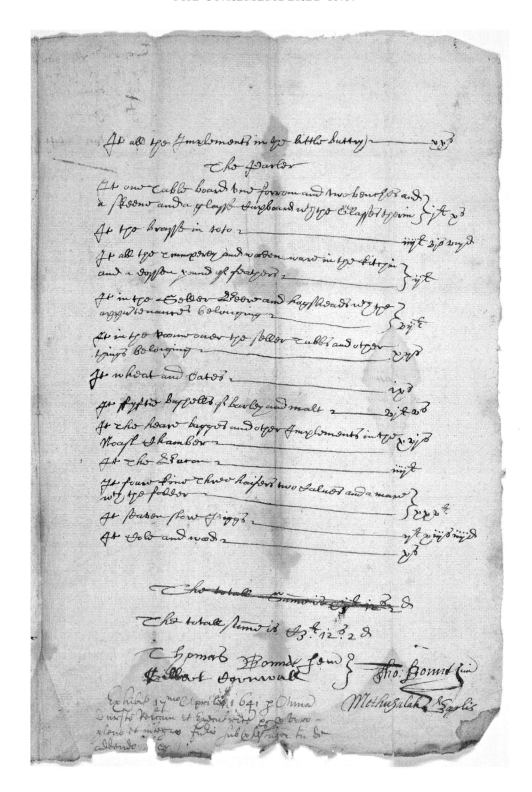

Transcription of the Inventory of the Goods and Chattels of John Durston, 1641.

The Inventory of the goods and Chattels of
John Durston of Upton sup*er* Sabrinam in the
County of Wigorn.[*Worcestershire*] yeoman deceased taken made &
prized the xiij th day of January Ann*o* Do*m*ini 1640
by Tho*mas* Bound S*enior*, Gilbert Cornwell, Tho*mas*
Bound J*unior* and Methewsal*er* Baylice of the
p*a*rishe and Towne aforesaid:

Impr*i*mis in money		xviij^s
It*em* his wearing apparell		vj^li
It*em* one Joyned beddestead w*ith* greene Curtaines	}	
and fringe in the best Chamber one feather	}	vj^li
bedde, one straw bedde one boulster, two ---- pillowes	}	
one Rugge and two blanketts price	}	
It*em* one Trundle beddestead under the said bedde		iij^s iiij^d
It*em* eighteen Cushions in the same Chamber		xj^s
It*em* two Carpetts in the same Chamber		vj^s viij^d
It*em* one table board and six Joyne stooles in the same		
Roome		xx^s
It*em* Three Chayres two forroms and a bench and one half	}	
table board in the same Chamber	}	xiij^s iiij^d
It*em* two andirons in the same Chamber		j^s vj^d

Little Inner Chamber

It*em* one little board, two forromes and a Cupboard	vj^s

The Chamber over the hall

Impr*i*mis two Table boards a forrom and a Chest		viij^s
It*em* two Joyne beddesteads w*ith* Curtaines in the	}	
same Chamber	}	xxvj^s viij^d
It*em* two feather beddes and two straw beddes	}	
two boulsters and foure pillowes price	}	iiij^li
It*em* foure blanketts in the same Chamber		xx^s
It*em* two Coverlids in the same Chamber		x^s

The Chamber over the Entry

Impr*i*mis one Joyned beddestead and one half	}	
head bedstead a Trundle beddestead	}	xiij^s iiij^d
in the same Chamber	}	
It*em* two feather beddes and one flock bedde	}	ij^li x^s
in the same Chamber	}	

Item Three Coverlids in the same Chamber		xviij^s
Item Three boulsters and Three Pillowes	}	
in the same Chamber	}	viij^s
Item two paire of blanketts and a piece of	}	
Apronning in the same Roome	}	xx^s
Item foure Trunkes and foure Coafers in	}	
in the same Chamber	}	j^li iiij^s
Item one deske[238] one Table board and Three	}	
shelfes in the same Chamber	}	v^s
Item All his bookes		xx^s

The Cocke Loft

Item one Trundle bedd and that which belongeth	}	
to it with other things besides in the same	}	x^s
Roome	}	
Item Cheeses in the same Roome		xx^s
Item Boards and Implements in the Cocke	}	
loft over the best Chamber	}	v^s
Item foure dossen of Napkins and two	}	
Towells	}	j^li iiij^s
Item eight Table Clothes		xx^s
Item Thirteene paire of sheetes and six	}	
Pillowes beares	}	vj^li

The Hall

Item two Table boards & two forroms		xij^s
Item two Chaires two Joyne stooles one bench	}	
and a dresser.	}	x^s
Item one Cupboard a paire of Table and	}	
other Implements besides in the same Roome	}	xiij^s iiij^d
Item the Pewter in toto		iiij^li ij^s
Item foure spits one grediron and the Ironware		
besides in toto		xj^s
Item all the Implements in the little buttry		xx^s

The Parler

Item one Table board & one forrom and two benches and	}	
a skeene and a glass Cupboard with the Glasses therin	}	j^li x^s
Item the brasse in toto		iiij^li vj^s viij^d
Item all the Trumperey and wooden ware in the kitchin	}	
and dossen pound of feathers	}	ij^li
Item in the Seller Beere and hogsheads with the	}	
appurtenances belonging	}	vij^li

---

238 The 'deske' in this instance refers to a case or press for standing the books upon.

Item in the Roome over the seller Tubbs and other
things belonging .... vij^li
Item wheat and Oates .... ix^s
Item Fyftie bushells of barley and malt .... vj^li v^s
Item the heaie [hay?] bagges and other Implements in the }
Noast Chamber   } xvj^s
Item the bacon .... iiij^li
Item foure kine three heifers two calves and a mare }
with the fodder   } xxxv^li
Item seaven store Piggs .... ij^li xiij^s iiij^d
Item cole and wood .... x^s

    The totall sum*me* is C3 ^li 12^s 2 ^d (£103 12s 2d)

Thomas Bound sen*ior*
Gilbert Cornwall   Tho*mas* Bound Jun*ior*
                          Methusalah Baylis

Exhibit 17mo Aprilis 1641 p*er* Anna
durston Rel*ict*iam et Executrice &c &c vero
pleno et integro Julio sub p*re*lesta tu de
addendo &c

Appendix B: John Best, Inventory 1645.

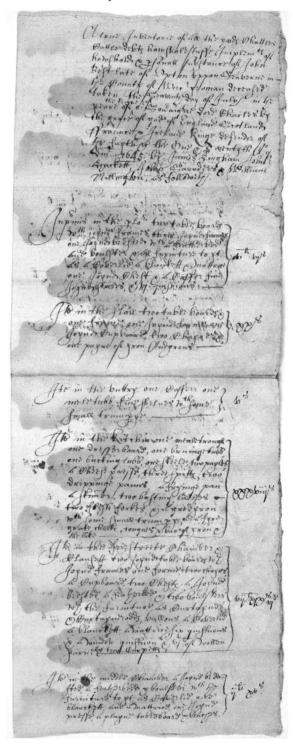

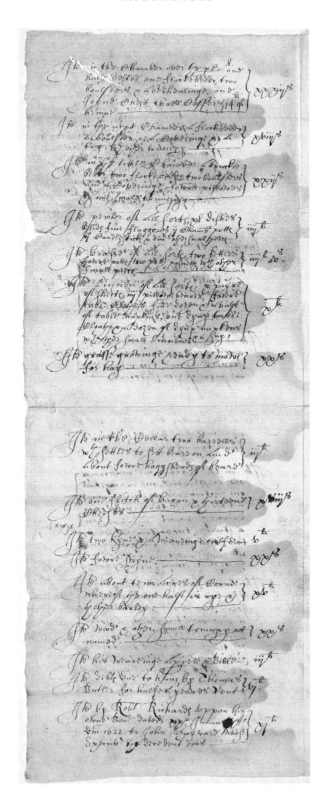

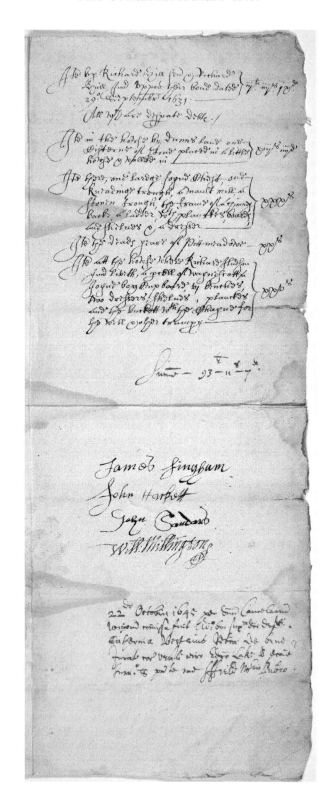

Transcription of John Best's Inventory, 1645.

A true Inventory of all the goods Chattles
Cattle Debts howshold stuffe Implements of
Howshold & personall substance of John
Best late of Upton uppon Seavern in
the County of Worcester yeoman deceased
taken the Seaventh day of July in the
yeare of the reign of our Soveraign Lord Charles by
the grace of God of England Scotland
France & Ireland Kinge defender of
the fayth &c the One & Twentyth Annoque
Domini 1645 by James Lingham, John
Hackett, John Saunders & William
Millington as followeth

Inprimis in the parlor two table boards }
with joynd frames three Joyned fourms }
one Joyned bedstead with a fetherbed }
and boulster & all furniture to yt } v^li vi^s
and a Coverlid a blankett & mattress }
one Joyned chest and a Coffer five }
Joyned stooles & vj quishions }

Item in the Hall two table boards & }
one frame one joynd form one }
Joyned Cupboard, two Chayres } xx^s
one payre of iron Andyrons }

Item in the buttery one Coffer one }
mele tubb five shelves with some } v^s
Small trumpery }

Item in the Kitchin one meale trough }
one dresser board, one bruinge tubb }
one bucking tubb, one skeele, two payles }
a Cheese presse three Spitts, two }
drippinge panns, a frying pan }
a skimmer, two basting ladles } xxxviij^s
two flish forkes a gridyron }
with some small trumpery and a fyre }
grate cheek, tongues & bar of iron & }
the like_____ }

Item in the forestreet Chamber & }
Clausett two Joynd table boards with }
Joyned frames one forme two chayrs }
a Cupboard, two Chests, a Joynd }

bedsted, a featherbed & two boulsters } vij^{li} xjx^s vj^d
with the furniture and Curtaynes }
& Curtaynerodds, hallons, a Coverlid }
a blanckett a mattrice Six quishions }
& a window quishion & vj^{li} of wollen }
yarne & two Carpitts }

Item in the middle Chamber a joynd bedd- }
sted a featherbedd & boulster with the }
furniture to yt and a Coverlid and } ij^{li} xv^s
blankett, and a mattrice, one Joynd }
presse, a playne tableboard & benches }

Item in the Chamber over the parlour one }
halfe bedsted, one flockbedd, two }
boulsters & a bedhealinge, one } xxxij^s
Joynd Chest three Coffers, j4^{li} of }
hempe. }

Item in the next Chamber a flockbed }
a boulster & a Coveringe & a } xxiij^s
tray? with other trumpery }

Item in the little Chamber a truckle }
bedd two flock bedds two boulsters } xxij^s
and a Coveringe fower pillowes }
& some small trumpery }

Item pewter of all sorts xl dishes }
besides five flaggons ij chamber potts } iiij^{li}
ij Candlesticks & divers? other small peece }

Item brasse of all sorts, two kettles }
fowre potts two pott posnetts with other } iiij^{li} x^s
small peece_____ }

Item linnen of all Sorts x payres }
of sheets iiij pillow beares fowre }
table Clothes, five dozen & a half } x^{li}
of table napkins, one dyap table }
Cloath & a dozen of dyap napkens }
with other Small Linnens & a jug }
Item grasse growinge ready to mow for }
hay_____ } xx^s

Item in the Cellar two barrells }
with settles to sitt beare on and } iij^{li}
about fowre hoggsheads of beare }

240

Item one flitch of bacon & thirteene Cheeses	} }	xviij^s
Item two Kyne & a weaning calfe		v^{li}
Item fowre swyne		xx^s
Item about tenn acres of Corne whereof the one half is rye & the other barley	} } }	xv^{li}
Item wood & other small trumpery not named	} }	xx^s
Item his wearing apparell & Bible		iij^{li}
Item debts due to him by Thomas Butler for half a yeares Rent	} }	vi^{li}
Item by Robt Richards uppon his owne Bond dated xx° January Anno Domini 1622 to John Hayward whose executor the decedent was	} } } }	xj^{li}
Item by Richard Hill senior & Richard Hill Jnr.uppon their bond dated 29th September 1631	} } }	iij^{li} iiij^s vji^d
All which are desperate debts		
Item in the house by Dunns lane one Cisterne of stone? placed in a little house & walled in	} } }	xiii^s iiii^d
Item there, one lardge Joyned Chest, one kneading trough, a mault mill, a stonen trough, the frame of a chimney backe, a ladder with planckes, boards and shelves & a dresser	} } } } }	xxx^s
Item the deads yeare of Pitt meadowe		xx^s
Item att the howse where Richard Hudson Junior liveth, a parcell of Waynescott a Joyned box Cupboard vj benches two dressers, shelves, planckes and the buckett with the Chayne for the well & other trumpery	} } } } } }	xxv^s

Summa 93^{li} 11^s 7^d (£93 – 11s – 7d)

Appendix C: Inventory and Appraisement of Stock of Furniture on the premises of Mr John Day at Upton 10th & 12th July 1813.[239]

[The auctioneer has used an alphabetical code for the valuation of John Day's household effects, whilst his shop goods are priced in £ s d.]

Attic Story No. 1

Bar Grate and Chimney board	- r e
Night Candlestick	- o c
Painted Upton Arm Chair	- b -
Pair bedside carpets	- r -
Oak stained post Bedstead and furniture	e - -
Flock Mattress	o - -
Goose feather bed bedstead 2 pillows	u - -
Cotton counterpane	- le -
One Blankett	- m -
pair of Sheets	- lo -
Dressing table dimity Cover	- lo -
Dressing glass & Drawers	- u -
2 Chamber Chairs hair seat	- u e
Mah[ogany] washstand Ewer basin bottle and glass	1 b -
Window curtains rolling window blind	- u -

Maid's Room

Font Bedstead and furniture	1 u -
Feather bed and bolster	d d -
Counterpane	- u e
Pair blankets	- m e
Pair sheets	- lo -
One under blanket	- d -
Chair	- b -
Hair trunk	- lo -
Swing glass	- u -

Store Room

Set Shelves	- 1 -
Wire fender	1 lb -
2 tea trays	1 1 -

---

239 GA D2080-134.

Double tea Caddee	1 - -
4 pewter measures	- e -
Tea Urn	1 lb -
Linen Chest	- lb -
Double dozen of Octagon handle knives and forks Sabre blades	o u -
2 Gravy spoons	o lo -
4 Table Do	o u -
6 Dessert Do	o ld -
12 tea spoons	o y -
4 Salts	- lo -
2 Caddy spoons	- u -
Desert knife	- e e
Pair sugar tongs	- u -

Linen

2 pair of Sheets	o - -
4 table Cloths	o - lo e
2 Breakfast Do	- ly -
12 hand towels 6 Do	- lb -
6 Calico pillow Cases	- lo -
6 Knife clothes	- e -

Drawing Room

Set Cumberland Dining table and card table	y y -
6 fancy Chairs rush seats and 2 Arm Do	1 lo -
Bellpulls Cranks etc	- m e
Rolling window blind	- y -
Cloaks pins rails etc Sable cover	- b -

Landing place

2 Clothes baskets	- d -
Pair glass Sconces	- b -
Rolling blind	- o e
Fishing Stool	- v e
6 prints framed and glazed Tom Jones	o u -
4 small pictures	- d -

Best Bedchamber

~~Masters Room~~

Font Bedstead Cotton furniture	r u -
Cotton Counterpane	- ly -

Item	
2 pair blankets	l d -
Feather bed bolster and pillows	g - -
Straw Mattress	11 -
Wash hand Stand Ewer basin }	- lb-
bottle and glass }	
Dressing table Dimity cover	- lo -
Swing dressing glass	- m -
Rolling blind	- e e
Malvern? night table	- lb -
Malvern? Chest of Drawers	r - -
Upton Arm Chair	- e -
Night bolt lock and key	- e e

Kitchen

Item	
Kitchen range and fender	d - -
Set fire irons	- lb -
Parlour Dᵒ	- o -
2 Chopping knives	- l e
Skimmer	- - e
Ladle	- - e
Fire plate	- l -
Sugar nippers	l e -
Sway[240] and links	- u-
Copper fountain	l - -
Smoke jack and chain	r - -
Purgatory	- u -
Warming pan	- u e
Salt box	- r e
2 pair brass candlestick	- lo -
One pair iron Dᵒ	- o e
One pair bed Candlesticks	- r -
Pair bellows	- r -
Candlibri	- l e
Pair snuffers and tray	- o -
Scotch bonnet	- l -
Colander	- o -
Pair tin Scollop shells	- o -
Dudgeon	- - e
toasting fork	- l -
pepper box and egg Slice	- l e
Pair nutcrackers & 2 nutmeg }	
Graters }	- o -
8 Day Clock	b - -
Dresser and Shelves	11 -
Coffee Mill and pepper Dᵒ	- e-

Item	
Set of table mats & jugs }	
and 4 half pints }	- d -
Ironing board	- u e
Window blind	- e -
4 chairs	- lo -
Round table	- b -
2 pairs flat irons and Stands }	
4 Shelves in pantry }	- m e
One Drawer	- o e
4 cup boards	- u e
2 oyster knives and 6 Common }	
knives & forks }	- m e
Knife tray	- o e
Fire hastener	l - -

Pantry

Item	
Pewter Quart	- o -
7 pickling jars	- r -
Japana bread basket	- o -
3 brass cocks	- r -
Bread marker	- l -
Dripping pan and Stand ladle	- d -
Gridiron	- o -
2 tin Oil Cans and Cocks	- u -
2 wood Bowls	- o -
pair wood Scales	- o e
Currant Sieve	- l e
Sugar Cover breaker & shell	- r -
Set shelves	- b -

Yard

Item	
2 Wash tubs & 2 pigs troughs	l o -
Water tub and brass cock	- lb e
6 Oak posts	- e -
Wheelbarrow }	
Spade and 2 Sheafpikes }	- lo -

Brewhouse

Item	
Copper furnace }	
Iron Dᵒ }	b - -
2 tubs }	
pail bucket and washing bench	- b e
Frying pan and spitting boxes	- m e
Clothes horse 3 kettles & }	
3 Saucepans }	- u e

240 Sway: an iron bar suspended in the chimney
for hanging pans or kettles.

Cellar

4 half hogsheads }	
2 smaller Casks }	d r e
3 trams benche & 2 brass cocks }	

Parlour

4 chairs satin hair seats	l d -
2 Upton Chairs	- u -
3 Rolling blinds	l d -
3 Green blinds	- e -
Mah[ogany] Dining table Green }	
Cloth }	r - -
Dimity Window Curtains	l m -
Bath Stove Grate	- lo -
Round Mah[ogany] pillar & Claw }	
table and green Cloth }	l d -
Bell pull Lock bolt etc	- u e
Writing Desk	l b -
Plated Ink stand	- b -
Glass	
Pair Wine Decanters	- u -
12 Wine glasses	- u -
12 Beer D°	- lo -
4 Goblets	- e -
6 Rummers	- m -
6 pattypans	- r -
4 salts	- lo-
Set Castors & 1 muffinier	o - -
China &c	
Set tea China	r r -
6 breakfast Cups and Saucers	- d -
5 Coffee D° Slop Basin sugar }	- b -
D° black tea pot & coffee D° }	
Plate rack Mahogany tea }	- u -
Tray and Canister }	

Plated ware

6 tea spoons and 2 table D° }	- d -
2 pair Candlesticks }	

Shop

Oak Counter }	
Nest of shelves 12 Drawers }	
Set shelves }	
Nest with 128 Drawers }	
Shelves top and bottom }	u - -
7 corner Shelves }	

2 Window Shelves }	
2 Other shelves }	
Bell Mortar & Stand	- lo -
One Marble D° and pestal	- u e
Glass D° and D°	- d -
Small brass D° and D°	- r
-	
Patent lamp	- lb -
2 Marble Slabs	- b -
2 Iron melting Ladles	- o -
3 knives and Hammer	- o -
2 phial racks	- r -
Iron spreader	- l -
5 pair small scales W^{ts} etc	- lb -
1 large D° & D°	- m -
Glass Measure	- l e
Ink stand and 2 Slates	- l -
2oz Tincture bottles	l g -
2oz Earthen jars brass covers	l e -
2oz Syrrup pots	- l -
2oz Extract glass brass Covers	l - -
8 Gum boxes	- d -
37 powder bottles brass }	l m -
stoppers }	
50 Medicine D°	l b -
57 pint bottles brass stoppers	l e -
7 large Shop Window glasses	l l -
9 large bottles glass stoppers	- g -
6 jars	- e -
36 glass bottles	- g -
2 shop sieves	- d -
4 shelves	- d -
4 Oil Cans Measures }	- o -
Tundishes etc }	
8 tea and Coffee cans	l lo -
Additional Shelves in Shop }	
And Grocery Counter }	- lo -
2 Stools	- d -
2 thread rollers	- o -
2 Scale hangers	- r -
Pair hand Scales & weights	- y -
Sets of Earthenware }	l u -
Large Beaufet }	

Warehouse

Part of an Alembic	- o -

[**Valuation now changes to £ s d which have been added to the numerals to aid readability**]

One Gallon Syr Buckthorn Juice	- 2s -
Jar Dº	- 4s -
2 Jars Conserv Hips	- 4s -
Abt ¼ Cwt of Quassia	- 4s-
3lb Guaicum Shavings	- 1s -
2lb Pomegranate	- 1s 4d
Quantity Ivrry black	- 1s
Large Quantity phial bottles	}
Quantity of pint & ½ pint Dº jars &c	} £3 - -
7lb Cocullus indicus	£1 1s -
2¼lb Magnesia	- 4s -
One Gallon rose water	- 3s -
12lb Turmeric	- 7s-
20lb Sasafras	- 12s
7lb Bayberries	- 5s 6d
40lb Glue	£1 - -
7lb Bale Ammoniac	- 4s -
6lb Grains Paradise	- 6s -
9lb Lamp black	- 6s 6d
8oz Spts Sal ammonia	- 1s 6d
12oz oil Vitriol and bottles	- 1s -
2lb Herb tobacco	- 5s -
3lb Coriander Seeds	- 2s-
100 poppy heads	- 1s 6d
12lb Cinnamon seed	- 9s -
4lb Lyon Blue	- 7s -
4lb Juniper berries	- 2s -
4lb powdered bay leaves	- 2s -
3lb powdered Senna	- 1s 6d
6lb Jamaica pepper	- 7s 6d
7lb Liquorice powder	- 4s 8d
12lb Carraways	- 10s -
3lb Gumarabic	- 6s -
7lb Pimento	- 10s 6d
7lb Horse Spice	- 4s 8d
3lb French Verdigris	}
and 3lb English Dº	} - 1s 10d
4lb Gallinghall [Galangal] root	- 6s -
14lb Crown blue	- 18s -
1lb Gentian	- 1s 4d
14lb H. P. D.[241]	- 3s 6d
3lb Sac Saturnii [Sugar of lead]	- 5s -

2lb Alkanet root	- 3s -
12lb Ground Ginger	- 8s -
12lb Jamaica ground pepper	- 9s -
8lb Blue	- 6s 6d
7lb black Lead	- 2s 6d
60lb Race Ginger	£3 10s
About 5 reams Shop papers	£3 5s -
13 Incres of writing paper	- 13s -
7 packs waste paper	- 14s
Jar bottles etc	- 2s
3 parlour brushes	- 6s -
6 Dº	- 9s -
6 hair brushes	- 12s -
Hair and Nail bucolic	£1 8s 3d
Tooth nail brushes plate	}
brushes etc	} £1 - -
16 packet herb tobacco	- 1s -
Tooth powder Sealing wax	£1 - -
2lb Sealing wax	- 10s -
8 boxes Salts Lemon	- 4s -
Abt 60 cases of Court plaister	- 10s -
Quantity cotton wicks	- 7s-
18 bottles Ess Anchovies	£1 2s -
Quantity Tincture Senna	- 7s -
Pint & ½ Tinct Myrrh	- 6s -
Pint Tinct Columba	- 4s -
Pint Tinct Gentian	- 4s -
Pint Paregoric	- 8s -
Pint Tinct Balsam	- 8s -
Pint Tinc Bark	- 8s -
Pint Tinc Asafoetida	- 4s -
Quart Tinc Rhubarb	- 8s -
Quart Tinc Valerian	- 8s -
Pint Tinc Guaicum	- 4s -
D Tinct Jalap	- 4s -
Sal Tartar 8oz	- - 6d
Sal Soda 12oz	- 1s -
Extract Lead 2lb	- 1s -
Kali Tartaric 8oz	- 1s -
Tinct Lytta [Spanish fly] 1 pint	- 4s -
Spt Voe Foetida 4oz	- 2s -
Vin Opium 4oz	- 2s -
Tinct Ginger 1 pint	- 4s -
Tinct Squill 4oz	- 2s -
3oz Flower Benzoin	- - 6d
½lb Magnesia	- 1s 8d
½lb Powdered Bark	- 3s -

241 HPD is most probably Hordeum Periatum Decorticartum or Pearl Barley.

8oz Tincture Opium	-4s -
1lb Kali Sulphur	- 1s -
2oz Oil Aniseed	- 2s -
2lb powdered bitter Alloes	- 10s -
½ pint Tinct Aloes	- 3s -
4oz Ol juniper	- 2s -
½lb Smelling salts	- - 6d
1lb Ess Burgamot	- 10s -
1lb Camphor	- 8s -
Quantity Gum Arsenic [242] etc	- 10s 6d
1½lb Extract Lead	- 1s -
3oz Balsam Copaiva [Coaiva]	- - 9d
6oz Opodeldoc	- 1s -
Pint Spirits Hartshorn	- 1s 6d
12oz Paregoric	- 2s 6d
12oz Tincture Rheubarb	- 2s 6d
8oz Tincture Bark	- 2s -
Tinct Myrrh 12oz	- 3s -
Ol Auriganum [Origanum] 1lb	- 12s -
Spt sal Volatile 8oz	- 1s -
Aqua Ammonia - 4oz	- - 6d
Spt Lavender - 6oz	- 1s -
Nitric Acid Vitrolic Acid etc	- 6s -
Spts Wine and Camphor 12 oz	- 7s -
Tinct Valerian orange of Benzoin	- 7s -
Tinct Senna. Tinct Asafoetida and } Snake Root abt 1 Quart each }	£1 4s -
Tinct Jalap 1lb	- 4s -
Tinct Gentian 12oz	- 3s -
Ditto Helebore. 4oz	- 1s -
Volatile Tinct Guiacum 1lb	- 4s -
Tincture Calumba 1lb	- 4s -
Tincture Aloes 8oz	- 2s -
Do Styptic 2oz	- 1s -
Powder in Bottles	£2 - -
Extracts Essential oil etc	£2 - -
Conserves etc	- 5s -
Basillicon Ointment etc } Glaubers Salts }	- 7s -
Oils Oxymel Squill etc	- 5s -
Phiall bottles	- 8s -
Opium	- 4s -

½lb Turkey Rhubarb and } ¼lb India Dᵒ } Gum tragacanth }	£1 - -
Verdigris	- 4s -
1lb Gum Benzoin of Eluru	- 6s -
Sundry Gums	- 16s -
2lb Isingglass	£2 - -
Plaisters Quack Medicines etc } Horse powders }	£3 4s -
12lb Coffee	£1 - -
12lb Lump Sugar	- 13s -
1 : 0 : 0 Glaubers Salts	£2 16s -
¾ Cwt Flour Sulphur	£1 10s -
½ Cwt roll Dᵒ	£1 - -
40lb Saltpetre	£1 12s -
128lb Lump Sugar	£6 18s 8d
¼ Cwt Brown Sugar	£5 7s 6d
¾ Cwt Dᵒ	£3 7s 6d
20lb Currants	- 15s -
2 Cwt whiting	- 19s -
6 Cwt Alum	£8 8s -
6 Cwt Copporas	£3 - -
6 Cwt Tobacco	£17 7s -
Cask Black Lead 1 . 0 . 22	£2 2s -
18lb Soft Soap	- 12s -
14 gall Olive Oil	£5 12s -
12 Dᵒ Linseed Oil	£3 12s -
4lb Starch	- 8s -
Twine and Shop thread	£2 - -
22lb rice	- 11s
2lb Starch	- 3s
2lb Blue	- 2s 6d
6lb Hyson tea	£3 6s -
7lb black Dᵒ	£2 9s -
5lb Green Dᵒ	£1 16s 3d
4lb Coffee	- 8s -
6lb Common Dᵒ	- 9s -
4lb Snuff	- 18s -
2 Gallˢ pale Oil	- 13s -
9 bottles Soda Water	- 3s 9d
3lb Windsor soap	- 4s -
4lb Castilli Soap	- 6s -
½lb Saffron	- 5s -
2lb Leaf tobacco	- 8s -
14 lb Rag tobacco	£2 19s 6d
Total £336 : 12 : 6	

242 This should most certainly read
'Gum Arabic' – there is little wonder
that these people regularly poisoned
themselves with quantities of arsenic!

Addendum

Lieutenant Thomas Goddard

Lieutenant Thomas Goddard, father-in-law to Thomas Jelf Sandilands, appears to be the same Thomas Goddard of HMS Victory who was injured during the defence of Fort Mulgrave on the 17th December 1793. This action occurred during the French Revolution when the city of Toulon was taken by the royalist forces who called for aid from an Anglo-Spanish fleet. On 28th August 1793, Admiral Sir Samuel Hood of the Royal Navy together with Admiral Juan de Lángara of the Spanish Navy, arrived in Toulon with a force of 13,000 British, Spanish, Neapolitan and Piedmontese troops to support the French royalists' cause. At this time HMS Victory was the flagship of the Mediterranean fleet under Admiral Hood. The city of Toulon fell to the revolutionaries on the 19th December. Many of the royalists were slaughtered.

Goddard was mentioned in a despatch from Admiral Hood to Henry Dundas, Secretary of State for War, on 20th December 1793: 'I am sorry to add that Lieut. Goddard, of the *Victory*, who commanded the seamen on the heights of Grasse was wounded but I hope and trust not dangerously'.

Sources:
The naval history of Great Britain, from the declaration of war by France in 1793, to the accession of George IV. William James, Frederick Chamier. p.79.

Lord Hood and the Defence of Toulon. John Holland Rose. p.160.

Battles of the British Navy: From A.D. 1000 to 1840. Joseph Allen. p.339.

Naval Chronology, Or an Historical Summary of Naval and Maritime Events from the Time of the Romans, to the Treaty of Peace 1802: Vol. 2. Isaac Schomberg. p.249.

Select Glossary

Note: The definitions given below refer to the meanings within the context found in the inventories and wills in this book, some words do of course have alternative meanings.

andirons (andyrons): a pair of horizontal bars made of iron, supported by a short foot to the rear and an upright, often ornamental, pillar with two feet to the front. They were placed on either side of the hearth to support burning wood. The upright pillar could have hooks to support a spit for cooking meat.

appie ware: nappery ware – see below.

apronning: most probably a length of cloth for fabricating aprons. The word also occurs in two other Worcestershire inventories: Adam Wilson, draper, 1595/6 'On ell of aporning – 1s 0d' and Thomas Porter, butcher, 1570/1 'a pece of apernynge of 8 els – 4s 0d'. (An ell was an obsolete measure of length, in England, usually 45 inches). [See Alan D. Dyer, *Probate Inventories of Worcester Tradesmen*, 1545-1614.]

arras: a fine quality tapestry fabric originating from Arras in northern France in the fourteenth century.

bands: several possible meanings, but in this account it is probably neck-band or collar. Subsequently developed into the more ornamental ruff worn in 16th and 17th centuries.

bedhealinge (bed hilling): a coverlet or quilt for a bed.

bedstead: the frame supporting the flock bed or feather bed.

bed stocks: that part of a bed consisting of a wooden frame, the sides and ends having a series of holes through which strong cords were drawn to form a tight mesh. This provided a support for a woven rush mat and the other bedding i.e. the feather bed or flock bed. Hence the term 'matted and corded'.

Also an earlier name for a bedstead.

bouge = budge: a fur lining, often lamb's skin, usually dark, with the wool dressed outwards.

brandiron: probably same as a gridiron q.v.

broche = broach: in this context a spit or skewer for roasting meat on, supported by 'andirons' in front of the fire.

bucking tub: a washing tub for clothes.

bucking: the process of steeping, or boiling, cloth or yarn in an alkaline solution of wood ashes. Used as a cheaper alternative to soap which was then an expensive commodity.

buckler: in this context possibly some kind of implement for pressing. Chambers Cyclopaedia Supp. (1753) gives: BUCKLER *of a cask*, denotes a moveable head, whereby to compress the contents of it.

buffyne = buffin: a coarse cloth in use for the gowns of the middle classes in Tudor England.

bushel: a measure of volume, consequently the weight would vary with the commodity, in the case of cereals it would be approximately 60lbs.

buttery: a storeroom used for food and drink or a room for brewing and keeping ale or beer.

carpett: in the sixteenth and seventeenth centuries a fabric for covering for tables, benches etc.

cards: probably, in this context, refers to wire combs used in the preparation of wool for spinning.

cassock: in the sixteenth century a kind of long loose coat or gown worn by either sex.

cawtherne: a cauldron.

chaffing dish: a dish containing food to be placed on a chafer. *q.v.*

chaffern, chaforne, chafer: a small brazier with a lid used for containing hot coals, ashes or charcoal for heating food and drink. (Some sources do not make a distinction between the above two items, yet there is obviously a difference for they are appraised separately.)

chamlett = camlet: originally referred to expensive eastern fabrics and afterwards to imitations. Variously made from silk, wool, linen, hair etc. During the sixteenth and seventeenth centuries it was made of the hair of the Angora goat.

cheeks: the side pieces of a grate or hearth.

civer: possibly = kiver, hence a cover. (see Jesse Salisbury, *A Glossary of S.E. Worcestershire Words* p.56)

clausett: a closet, a small room.

cobberd: in this context probably a cupboard.

cobberns = cobirons: in pairs, a simpler version of the andiron but with a series of hooks for supporting the spit or broach in front of the fire.

cockloft: small upper room under the ridge of the roof, usually reached by a ladder.

corn: a generic term for cereal crops (barley, rye or wheat).

counterfeit dishes: Milward states there is uncertainty as to what these exactly were. But possibly another name for porringers.

cousings = cushions.

coverlid = coverlet: cover for a bed (from French *couvre-lit*).

cratch: a rack or a cradle.

curtaynerodds = curtain rods: rods for hanging fabrics around beds (window curtains were not in use until the eighteenth century).

desperate debt: a 'bad' debt.

diaper: linen or cotton fabric woven in a simple diamond pattern, the surface produces different reflexions of light. Since the fifteenth century, used for napkins, towels and tablecloths. The weave originated in Ypres hence the cloth 'd'Ypres' became corrupted to 'diaper'.

doblett = doublet: a close-fitting garment worn by men from the fourteenth to the eighteenth centuries.

durance: a stout durable cloth made from wool or worsted.

dyap: appears to be an abbreviation of **dyaper = diaper.**

elming = elmen: of or pertaining to the wood of the elm tree.

engin(e): in this context a device for cutting tobacco.

fallayes = fally: a variant of the word **felloe:** the curved pieces of wood which when joined together constitute the rim of a wheel.

faggots: in this instance bundles of sticks or wood as fuel for fires.

feather bed: a mattress stuffed with feathers.

fitches: vetch (the plant *Vicia sativa*), or, probably, in this instance its seed or beans used as cattle fodder.

flaxen sheets: sheets made from the fibres of the flax plant, *Linun usitatissimum*.

flish fork = flesh fork: a fork for removing meat from the pot.

flitchen = flitch: a side of bacon or other animal, salted and cured.

flock: waste wool or cloth used as a stuffing for cushions or mattresses etc.

flock bed: a mattress stuffed with flock or wool.

form: a long seat without a back, a bench.

forrom = form: probably spelt as it was pronounced in south Worcestershire dialect.

foynes: trimmings for, or a garment made from, the fur of a polecat or a weasel.

furnis = furnace: The Oxford English Dictionary has an interesting definition under 'Furnace': '**4.** A boiler, cauldron, crucible. See.... **1884** *Upton on Severn Gloss.*, *Furnace*, a large boiler set in brickwork, for brewing, making soup, &c'.

geve: a variant spelling of 'give'.

grediron = gridiron: a platform of iron bars, supported by **andirons** *q.v.* or with short feet, with a long handle, for roasting meat over a fire.

hallon: the OED gives this as a partition (northern dialect) which is unlikely in this instance. It is more likely a to be a variant of 'hallyng' (see Bristow): a piece of tapestry, painted or stained cloth etc., used as a wall hanging. (John Best – Inventory 1645.)

hempen sheets: a better quality sheet made from the finer fibres of hemp.

hogshead (hodgshead): usually a measure for liquids, containing 63 old wine-gallons (equivalent to 52½ imperial gallons). Also a cask for other commodities, the capacity varied according to the locality and the contents. A hogshead of tobacco was approximately 1000lb (453kg) by weight.

horsebread: a cheap bread prepared from beans or dry split peas, bran etc for feeding horses (also used for human consumption for the poor in medieval Europe).

horse-meat: feed for horses, often of oats and mixed corn.

hurden sheet: a coarser linen sheet made from hurds or hards, the coarser part of flax or hemp. The cloth was also used for sacking.

inkle: a type of linen tape.

joyned = joined: description of furniture made by a 'joiner' and jointed using mortice and tenon joints. The joints were often secured using small wooden pegs.

kneading trough: a wooden vessel with four sides for kneading dough.

kuler = cooler: an oval tub used in brewing to cool the wort or to cool warm milk in the dairy.

kyne = kine: archaic plural of the word cow.

limbeck = alembic: a still for producing spirits.

links: probably chains.

male: this could refer to a 'male pillion' or a 'male saddle' both for carrying luggage, or to a 'travelling bag',

matress (mattrice) = mattress: a case of canvas or other coarse fabric stuffed with straw, hair or flock etc. used as a bed.

medley (cloth): a cloth woven with wool of different colours. **medley gown:** a gown made of such cloth.

mele tub = meal tub: a container for meal (grain or pulses ground to a powder, as opposed to flour ground from wheat).

metheglin: a spiced or medicated variety of mead, originally peculiar to Wales.

mockado: kind of cloth, usually made of wool. Originally made in Flanders and much used for clothing in the sixteenth and seventeenth centuries.

moncorn = mongcorn: a mixed corn – a mixture of two kinds of grain, usually wheat and rye, often sown together.

murrey: a cloth with a colour like that of the mulberry – purple-red or blood colour.

nappery: household linen, often table linen.

painted clothes: sheets of canvas or cloth with pictures painted on them, sometimes depicting religious scenes, often used to keep out the draughts or hung on walls as decoration. These were a cheap substitute for expensive tapestry.

pillow beeres: pillow cases.

platter: a flat dish or plate for food, made of earthenware, wood or pewter. (This appears to be larger than a trencher.)

possenott (posnet, postnot, postenet): a small metal cooking pot with a handle and three feet.

pottenger = porringer: a vessel or small basin made of wood, metal or earthenware for holding broth or soup etc.

potthook: an iron hook suspended over a fireplace for hanging a kettle or cooking pot on.

presse: a large cupboard, usually with shelves, or a hanging press, like a wardrobe.

quirn = quern: either a small hand mill for grinding malt etc., or two circular stones superimposed for grinding wheat or corn.

quishions: cushions.

rosen: resin.

readle probably meaning **reddle** or **raddle:** red ochre often used for marking sheep.

scimber = see skymer.

showle = shawle: a wooden shovel without a handle.

skeele: a wooden bucket, trough or tub for containing milk or water etc. A butter-skeel was a tub for washing butter and a dough-skeel a trough in which bread was made.

skymers (skimmer) = scummer: a utensil with a long handle and a shallow perforated bowl, often of brass, used to remove scum from the cooking pot. It could also be a similar implement made of iron used for removing ash from the hearth.

stone blew (blue): a compound of indigo with whitening or starch used in the laundry.

strick = strike: A variable quantity of dry measure used until the sixteenth century in various parts of England. Some sources say equal to one bushel, but others give a half-bushel or even two or four bushels.

tagged: here referring to the marking of cattle – having the tail tipped with white or any other distinctive colour.

table board: used like a table, with boards supported by trestles.

testerne = tester: a canopy over a bed, supported on the posts of the bedstead or suspended from the ceiling.

thave: the word occurs in Nicholas Deckles' Inventory: 'vj thaves and throkes' , A similar reference occurs in another Worcestershire will (Humfrey White, 1581): '.... ij axeltrees ij plowbeames vj throakes & shethes, ij payles & two crowbreads.'

The 'throke' (or throck) is the lower part of a wooden plough on to which the ploughshare is fixed. The word *'thave'* is difficult to interpret but possibly is local dialect for part of the wooden plough (possibly derived from the verb 'thave' which can mean to give, bear or sustain).

throke, throake = plough-throck: the share beam of a plough.

trencher: a plate or platter of wood.

trestles: the timber supports for table boards.

trindle: either a small wooden wheel used in a truckle bed, a small wheel for a wheelbarrow or that part of the wheel called the 'felloe'.

trucklebed (trukellbed): a low bed running on castors or truckles, it could be stored under a standing bed.

trumpery: items of little or no value; trifling, paltry, insignificant or worthless.

trundlebed: = trucklebed q.v.

tonn = tun: either a cask of definite capacity or a measure of volume for wine and other liquids. Usually equivalent to two pipes or four hogsheads. A volume of 252 old wine-gallons.

twist: a thread or cord composed of two or more fibres or filaments of hemp, silk, wool, cotton, etc.

wain: a large cart drawn by oxen or horses usually with four wheels but some sources state two wheels.

wainscot: here referring to furniture (bedsteads, etc.) made from a superior quality of oak imported from various countries including Russia, Germany and Holland.

weye = wey: a measure of dry goods varying according to commodity; in the case of barley or malt it was, in some areas, equivalent to six quarters or forty eight bushels.

wheel stocks: the nave or hub of a wheel into which the spokes are inserted.

wickyarne: yarn for candle wicks.

Sources:

1. Oxford English Dictionary.

2. Glossary of Household, Farming and trade terms from Probate Inventories – R. Milward (1986).

3. The Local Historian's Glossary of Words and Terms, J. Bristow (2001).

4. Probate Inventories of Worcester Tradesmen, 1545-1614 – A. D. Dyer (1967).

5. Class Act Fabrics ... glossary of fabric terms ... from about 1600 to mid-1900s (http://www.classactfabrics.com/index.html).

6. A Glossary of West Worcestershire Words, E.L. Chamberlain, (1882).

7. A Glossary of Words and Phrases used in S. E. Worcestershire, Jesse Salisbury, (1893).

8. A Dictionary of Archaic Provincial Words, Vol. II, James Orchard Halliwell (1847).

Original Documents Consulted

1. Title Deeds relating to 12, High Street, Upton-upon-Severn.

Copy of the Deed of Purchase, 2nd October 1636: John Flook & Edward Flook to John Best.

Purchase Deed, 17th August 1710: Mary & John Towns to Samuel Gatfield.

Feoffment, 20th September 1710: Mrs Towne & Son to Mr Samuel Gatfield.

Deed to declare the Uses of a fine, 27 March 1718: Mrs Towne to Samuel Gatfield.

Bond to perform Covenants, 12th March 1739: Mr Samuel Gatfield to Mr Edward Nicholls.

Assignment of Mortgage, 25th March 1741: Mr Edward Nicholls and Mr Gatfield to Mr Willoughby.

Deed Poll, 26th March 1744: Mr Gatfield to Mr Willoughby.

Lease and Release, 1st & 2nd February 1749: Mr Samuel Gatfield to Mr John Willoughby.

Fine 1749: John Willoughby and Samuel Gatfield.

Mortgage for £100, 20th March 1750: Mr John Willoughby to Mr Obadiah Arrowsmith.

Assignment of Mortgage for £100, 11th December 1752: Obadiah Arrowsmith John Willoughby James Brooke.

Lease for a Year – 26th March 1759: Mr John Willoughby to Mr John Cottrell.

Release and Confirmation 27th March 1759: Mr James Brooke by the direction of Mr John Willoughby to Mr John Cottrell.

Bond for £100, 9th October 1759: Mr John Cottrell to Mr John Wells.

Lease for a year, 9th October 1759: Mr John Cottrell to Mr John Wells.

Mortgage in Fee, 10th October 1759: Mr John Cottrell to Mr John Wells.

Lease for a year, 20th November 1769: Mr John Wells and Mr John Cottrell to Mr Samuel Sandelands.

Release of a house and premises in Upton, 21st November 1769: Mr John Cottrell to Mr Samuel Sandelands.

Articles of Agreement, 13th November 1772: Mr Sandelands and Mr Webb.

Copy Probate of Will and Codicils, 1st August 1806 & 3rd October 1806: Mr Samuel Sandelands deceased.

Lease & Release of a Messuage and premises, 18th & 19th May 1809: Mr James Skey and another to Messrs Matthews & Thacker.

Mortgage for £500 and Interest, 7th September 1809: Messrs Matthews and Thacker to Mr Samuel Beale.

Assignment of Mortgage for securing £600 and Interest 7th April 1810: Mr Samuel Beale by the direction of Messrs Matthews and Thacker to Mr John Ireland.

Lease and Release 29th & 30th June 1814: Messrs Matthews and Thacker to Mr Samuel Thacker.

Copy Chyrograph of Fine, Trinity Term 59th Geo 3rd: Callow Plt and Thacker Deft.

Lease for a year, 16th June 1819: Mr Thomas Thacker and others to Mr John Callow (Attested Copy).

Conveyance of the real Estates of the late Mr Samuel Thacker upon trusts for Sale 17th June 1819: Mr Thomas Thacker and others to Mr John Callow (Attested Copy).

Lease for a year 22nd July 1822: Mr Thomas Thacker to Mr Chas Cowley.

Release and Surrender 23rd July 1822: The Mortgage Trustees and Devisees of the late Mr Samuel Thacker to Mr Charles Cowley.

Disentailing deed, 7th April 1856: Mr Charles John Cowley Mr Alfred Hudson Cowley and Miss Susan Sophia Cowley.

Appointment and Grant, 26th April 1856: Mr Alfred H Cowley to Mr Charles John Cowley and Miss Susan Sophia Cowley.

Auction Notice 19th June 1862 and Conditions of Sale, 19th June 1862.

Sale receipt, 19th June 1862, Doctor Tyers Wilkes.

2. Chancery and Exchequer Records
Chancery Records
C 2/JAS/H5/44: *Hall alias Oliver v. Griffiths,* Bill and Answer.

C 2/CHAS1/B15/40: *Baker alias Williams v. Best,* Bill and Answer.

C 22/10/16: *Baker v. Best,* Depositions.

C 22/599/38: *Baker alias Williams v. Best,* Depositions.

C 6/211/9: *Bound v Bound,* Bill and Answer.

C 6/234/13: *Ellery v Symes.*

C 22/245/35: *Ellery v Symes,* Depositions.

C 5/511/6: *King v Bound.*

C 5/511/7: *King v Bound.*

C 22/956/38: *Bound v. King.*

(These three cases came to light just before publication and only C 5/511/7 was examined – this was a Bill of Revivor presumably instigated after the death of Thomas Bound in 1677; the original case was probably C 5/511/6. The interrogatories and answers may be in C 22/956/38.)

C 11/1168/17: *Smith v Gatfield,* Bill and three Answers.

C 11/993/18: *Smith v. Town,* Two Answers.

C 12/2149/16: *Cozens v. Green,* Bill, Answers and Schedule.

C 12/2426/16: *Cozens v Sanderson,* Answers and Depositions.

C 105/29: *West v Greene, Correspondence,* Calcutta.

C 12/1391/39: *West v Greene,* Bill of Complaint.

C 13/189/68: *Sandilands v Cuming,* Bill of Complaint.

C 13/186/5: *Sandilands v Gaisford et al.,* Two bills, three Answers.

C 13/336/19: *Sandilands v Greene,* Bill and four Answers.

Exchequer Records
E 176/7/20 Vintner: John Hall, Upton upon Severn. Sept. 28, 13 Eliz.

E 176/13/22 Vintner: John Halle, Upton upon Severn. Sept. 28, 13 Eliz.

3. Probate Records
National Archives

Bound, Thomas. Upton-upon-Severn.	07 May 1657	PROB 11/264/209.
Bownd, Thomas. Upton-upon-Severn.	23 Nov 1667	PROB 11/325/441.
Clarrow, Thomas. Upton-upon-Severn.	07 July 1716	PROB 11/553/62.
Flowke, John. Deerhurst, Glos.	06 May 1594	PROB 11/253/60.
Greene-Goddard, Eliza Maria. Stody, Norfolk	30 July 1810	PROB 11/1513/186.
Green, John. Calcutta. Exhibit: 1781/526.	1781	PROB 31/697/526.

Halle, John. Ripple.	15 Mar 1548	PROB 11/32/382.
Hopkenes, John. Bristol, Gloucestershire.	29 Jan 1616	PROB 11/127/20.
Husband, Thomas. Upton-upon-Severn.	30 June 1808	PROB 11/1481/313.
Pynnock, John. Longborough, Gloucestershire.	26 April 1557	PROB 11/39/139.
Pynnock, William. Hanley, Worcestershire.	18 May 1555	PROB 11/37/336.
Sandelands, Samuel. Severn Stoke.	27 Oct 1807	PROB 11/1469/153.
Wyett, Gabryel. Worcester.	19 June 1550	PROB 11/33/209.

Gloucester Archives

Fluck, Edward. Whitfield, Deerhurst, Glos.	GA 1662/ 31.
Portman, John. Twyning, Glos.	GA 1642/42.

Worcestershire Archives

A – Letters of Administration, I – Inventory, W – Will.

Baylis, John	Upton-upon-Severn	1647	WI
Best, John	Upton-upon-Severn	1645	AI
Bound, Katherine	Upton-upon-Severn	1704	WI
Bound, Thomas	Upton-upon-Severn	1677	W
Childe, William	Upton-upon-Severn	1605	I
Cornwell, Gilbert	Upton-upon-Severn	1647	AI
Deckles, Nicholas	Worcester	1590	WI
Dunn, Richard	Upton-upon-Severn	1614	WI
Durston, John	Upton-upon-Severn	1641	WI
Fell, William	Upton-upon-Severn	1641	WI
Gatfield, Samuel	Upton-upon-Severn	1670	WI
Gyles, John	Worcester	1612	AI
Goodyeare, Thomas	Upton-upon-Severn	1641	WI
Hall alias Oliver, Anne.	Upton-upon-Severn,	1622	WI
Hall, Edward	Upton-upon-Severn	1588	I
Hall alias Oliver, Francis	Upton-upon-Severn	1621	AI
Hall, Jane	Upton-upon-Severn	1588	WI
Hall, John	Upton-upon-Severn	1591	WI
Hall alias Oliver, Nicholas	Upton-upon-Severn	1600	WI
Hall alias Oliver, Richard	Upton-upon-Severn	1587	WI
Hall alias Oliver, Richard	Upton-upon-Severn	1624	WI
Hall, Thomas	Upton-upon-Severn	1571	WI
Hall alias Oliver, Thomas	Upton-upon-Severn	1623	A
Hall, William	Upton-upon-Severn	1561	WI
Jarrett, Alice	Warwick	1608	WI
Jelf, James	Queenhill	1772	I
Jelf, Thomas	Queenhill	1774	A
Oliver alias Hall, Edward	Upton-upon-Severn	1587	W
Portman, Thomas	Upton-upon-Severn	1648	WI
Thacker, Samuel	Upton-upon-Severn	1810	W
Towne, John	Upton-upon-Severn	1718	WI
Towne, Thomas	Upton-upon-Severn	1707	AI
Turner, John	Upton-upon-Severn	1690	I
Warberton, George	Worcester	1585	I
White, Humphrey	[*No place*]	1581	WI
Willoughby, John	Baughton	1762	W
Wilson, Thomas	Upton-upon-Severn	1669/70	AI

(Many other probate records were examined, mainly for Upton-upon-Severn.)

Bibliography

Alcock, N.W., *Old Title Deeds* (Phillimore, 1986).

Arkell, T., Evans, N., & Goose, N., *When Death Do Us Part* (Leopards Head Press, 2004).

Ashworth, W.J., *Customs and excise: trade, production, and consumption in England, 1640-1845.* (OUP Oxford, 2003).

Barnard, E. A. B., *The Sheldons: being some account of the Sheldon family of Worcestershire and Warwickshire* (Cambridge England: The University Press, 1936).

Barty-King, H., *The Worst Poverty – A History of Debt and Debtors* (Budding Books, 1997).

Beale, J. H., *The Law of Innkeeping and Hotels including other Public Houses, Theatres, Sleeping Cars* (Nagel, 1906).

Blackstone, W., *Commentaries on the Laws of England* (1765-1769).

Bristow, J., *The Local Historians Glossary or Words and Terms* (Countryside Books, 2001).

Caulfield, R., *The Council Book of the Corporation of Kinsale from 1652 to 1800.* (1879).

Chamberlain, E.L., *A Glossary of West Worcestershire Words.*

Clark, P., *The English Alehouse – A Social History 1200-1830* (Longman, 1983).

Cope, S.R., *WALTER BOYD – A Merchant Banker in the Age of Napoleon* (Alan Sutton, 1983).

Cornwall, J., *Reading Old Title Deeds* (FFHS, 1993).

Coysh, A.W., *Historic English Inns.* (David & Charles, 1972).

Crawford, A., *Bristol and the Wine Trade.* (Bristol Branch of the Historical Association, 1984).

Dyed, W., *The History and Antiquities of Tewkesbury* (1790).

Dyer, A.D., *Probate Inventories of Worcester Tradesmen, 1545-1614* (Worcestershire Historical Society, 1967).

Dyer, A.D., *The City of Worcester in the Sixteenth Century* (Leicester University Press, 1973).

Dyer, C., *Making a Living in the Middle Ages, The People of Britain 850-1520* (Yale University Press, 2002).

Everitt, A., *Landscape and Community in England – The English Urban Inn, 1560-1760* (The Hambledon Press, 1985).

Flenley, Ralph, *The Register of the Council in the Marches of Wales 1569-1591* (Society of Cymmrodorion, 1916).

Francis, A.D., *The Wine Trade* (A. & C. Black Ltd., 1972).

Gerhold, D., *Carriers & Coachmasters – Trade and Travel before the Turnpikes* (Phillimore, 2005).

Gerhold, D., *Courts of Equity – A Guide to Chancery and other Legal Records* (Pinhorns, 1994).

Goodenough, R., *Researching the History of a Country House* (Phillimore, 2010).

Green, C., *Severn Traders* (Black Dwarf Publications, 1999).

Grier, J., *A History of Pharmacy* (The Pharmaceutical Press, 1937).

Habib, I.H. *Black Lives in the English Archives, 1500-1677: Imprints of the Invisible* (Ashgate Publishing Ltd., 2008).

Harrison, D., *The Bridges of Medieval England Transport and Society 400-1800* (Oxford University Press, 2009).

Harrison, W., *The Description of England* (1877).

Hillaby, J., *Ledbury: A Medieval Borough* (Ledbury and District Society Trust Ltd., 1997).

Hindle, P., *Roads & Tracks for Historians* (Phillimore, 2001).

Hogue, A.R., *Origins of the Common Law* (Libert Fund Inc., 1986).

Horwitz, H., *Chancery Equity Records and Proceedings 1600-1800* (PRO Handbook No.27, 1998).

Hurle, P., *Upton: Portrait of a Severnside Town*. (Phillimore, 1988).

Jessop, W., *Privateering in Elizabethan Bristol: A Case Study on John Hopkins* (MA Thesis, Bristol University, 2004).

Jones, A., *Tewkesbury* (Phillimore, 2003).

Jusserand, J.J., *English Wayfaring Life in the Middle Ages* (Cedric Chivers Ltd., 1970).

Larwood, J. and Hotten, J.C., *English Inn Signs* (Blakedon Hall 1985).

Lawson, E.M., *The Nation in the Parish, or Records of Upton-upon-Severn* (1884).

Leadbetter, C., *The Royal Gauger or, Gauging made Perfectly Easy* 3rd ed (1750).

Leland, J., *Itinerary* (ed. Hearne, 1711 & 1744).

Marcombe, D., *English Small Town Life: Retford 1520 – 1642* (Department of Adult Education University of Nottingham, 1993).

Milward, R., *A Glossary of Household, Farming and Trade terms from Probate Inventories* (Derbyshire Record Society, 1993).

Moore, S.T., *Family Feuds – An Introduction to Chancery Proceedings* (FFHS Publications, 2003).

Munby, L.M., *Dates and Time – a handbook for local historians* (British Association for Local History, 1997).

Nash, T., *Collections for the history of Worcestershire* (1799).

Oldham, E.W., *A Letter Addressed To Both Houses Of Parliament* (Worcester, 1862).

Oldham, E.W., *Great Britain at War with the Great Creator's own Laws and Ordinances in all Sewerage Works* (Worcester 1864).

Oliver, V.L., *Caribbeana being Miscellaneous Papers relating to the History, Genealogy, Topography and Antiquities of the British West Indies* (London, 1912).

Pevsner, N., *The Buildings of England – Worcestershire* (Penguin Books, 1992).

Pinches, S., *Ledbury – people and parish before the Reformation* (Phillimore, 2010).

Richardson, A .E., *The Old Inns of England* (B.T. Batsford, 1942).

Salisbury, J., *A Glossary of Words and Phrases used in S.E. Worcestershire* (1893).

Schurer, K. and Arkell, T., *Surveying the People* (Leopard's Head Press, 1992).

Smith, G., *Something to Declare – 1000 Years of Customs and Excise* (Harrap, 1980).

Stone, L., *Road to Divorce – England 1530-1987* (Oxford University Press, 1990).

Stuart, D., *Manorial Records* (Phillimore, 1992).

Tarver, A., *Church Court Records* (Phillimore, 1995).

Tate, W.E., *The Parish Chest* (Phillimore, 1983).

Thirsk, J., *The Rural Economy of England – Collected Essays* (The Hambledon Press, 1984).

Trevelyan, G.M., *An Autobiography & Other Essays* (Longmans, Green and Co., 1949).

Trevelyan, G.M., *English Social History* (Longmans, 1946).

Vanes, J. ed., *Documents illustrating The Overseas Trade of Bristol in the Sixteenth Century,* (Bristol Record Society, 1979).

West, J.W., *Town Records* (Phillimore, 1983).

West, J.W., *Village Records* (Phillimore, 1997).

Wilkinson, S. *Soley's Orchard: The Bounds and Humphrey Soley* (Upton News, December 2008, see also http://www.upton.uk.net/history/soley/soleyindex.html).

Willis Bund, J.W., *Calendar of the Quarter Sessions Papers, 1591-1643* (Baylis and son, 1900).

Wright, L., *Warm & Snug, The History of the Bed* (Sutton Publishing, 2004).

Index